THE YEARS
THAT WERE FAT

The Last of Old China

THE YEARS
THAT WERE FAT

The Last of Old China

by George N. Kates

WITH AN INTRODUCTION BY
John K. Fairbank

PHOTOGRAPHS BY
Hedda Hammer Morrison

THE M.I.T. PRESS
Massachusetts Institute of Technology
Cambridge, Massachusetts, and London, England

Foreword

THE special charm of George Kates's description of his days in Peking in the 1930's is its cultural awareness. To a greater degree than most of the American students who were there at the time, he had been a part of the Atlantic community. He had grown up in various countries of Europe and Latin America, learning French and German and Spanish, and then had studied at Harvard and Oxford. His years at Oxford alternated with periods in Hollywood, of all places, where he served as specialist in the material culture of the European past as re-created in movie sets. Surely here was a product of the West, not simply the American West — that homeland of businessmen and missionaries — but the European West with its diverse cultural background.

When George Kates came to Peking in 1933, he was close to forty and knew what he wanted. He immediately distinguished himself from the other Americans who were studying Chinese there by concentrating on the traditional way of life. Old China hands of the age of Victoria would have said that he "went native." The young Americans in Peking in the 1930's did not see themselves as "old China hands" and were fascinated by the China around them, whenever they could spare the time, but they were intent on becoming Sinologists — and Sinologists tend to be purposeful creatures, determined to master a language and professional technique that they hope will unlock the secrets of a civilization, so determined, in fact, that they sometimes disregard the civilization immediately available to them. George Kates did not disregard it. With a strong antiquarian interest, he elected to study the traditional society still at hand in the byways and hutungs of the ancient capital. Few observers from abroad have moved further into the Chinese scene in the time allowed. Already versed in the material culture of European civilization, he set out to master the Chinese art of living and sought to capture the aesthetic and human experiences of everyday, upper-class life in the old China.

The result is a book that gives one, in a remarkably flexible and telling style, the quality and feeling of a way of life, that of the Chinese scholar-aesthete, that has now disappeared. Since 1949, the civilization of Confucius has been quite submerged. The face of Peking has been remade. Chinese society has been revolutionized in every sense of the word.

The greatest American disability in dealing with the new China of today is our lack of perspective. So few Americans became acquainted with the traditional China that survived down to the 1940's that we have in this country very little image of the background behind Chairman Mao's screaming teenagers with their Red Guard arm bands. Thought reform, mammoth processions, student ditch digging, and other raw phenomena of today can bewilder and even terrify the Western newspaper reader. We need to enlarge our picture of China's future alternatives by being better acquainted with the different ages in her past. No country has ever succeeded in remaining permanently revolutionary in a state of constant disharmony, flux, and upset. Even while Chairman Mao is struggling to persuade his masses of doubting followers that permanent revolution is here and is somehow pleasant or at least desirable, we should keep in mind a picture of the old China which believed in harmony, peace, and quiet.

Marco Polo was the first Westerner to describe the old capital of China in its grand design, and the early Jesuits were the first to appraise its architectural values. George Kates is one of the last Westerners to take its measure. After his seven years in Peking, by the end of which the Japanese had come in to occupy it, the old China finally disintegrated under the blows of warfare and social revolution. What Kates describes cannot be found today. The people have changed, the scene has changed, and so has the way of life. To some degree, no doubt, this is simply a result of the world-wide modernization that has us all by the throat. But Peking had retained the special qualities of a civilization built on the sense of balance and decorum. In the 1930's it was still true that a solitary female could walk at any time of night through the streets and alleys of Peking all across the city without danger of robbery or molestation. (I don't know how many tried it, but we all believed it possible and I think we were correct.) If this is still true today, it may be for a different, more modern reason — the presence of police. I suppose every student of Chinese culture would like to get back to the Peking that used to be and so gain a perspective on how life was lived there. In the absence of a time machine and travel opportunities, this book can be a substitute.

George Kates tells how he found and furnished his Chinese house and established his routine as a student of the community around him. He describes his Chinese teachers and the spoken and written languages which provided the key with which to enter the Chinese world. He devotes a chapter to his servants and their style of living, their problems with him and his problems with them, and their life together. All this is done with sharply etched illustration that will evoke quick memories in foreigners who once lived in China's capital.

Mr. Kates describes the city with a special competence because he made it a particular object of scholarly research. In his chapters the activity of the shops and of the streets is balanced by his first-person account of the Forbidden City, of the archives where he read the old documents, and of the history of many buildings through which tourists of modern times have generally passed uncomprehendingly. He made it a hobby to study the origin of the buildings and the layout of the city. He studied with particular attention the three lakes to the west of the Forbidden City, the old Summer Palace to the northwest of Peking that was destroyed in 1860, and the new Summer Palace still west of there that was subsequently built up and today forms a great public park. He also records another of the many happy features of existence in Peking: access to the Western Hills and their temples and footpaths.

Finally, as all foreigners felt the need to do after living in old China, he appraises the traditional culture, especially the character and outlook of the Confucian gentleman, that "superior man" who was truly civilized and disciplined in all his human relationships. Offsetting this he records some of the traits of the common or "mean" people who are thoroughly engrossed in material concerns. Of course, in all foreigners' writings about China these topics are recurrent. The distinctive point about George Kates's book is the immediacy of his discussion. This is not a product of library research but of experience in Peking, day by day, with a sophisticated and yet enthusiastic concern for the precise details and forms of human intercourse and enjoyment — an eyewitness account.

In this way the book is a monograph of a special kind. Catching the ancient ways at the last possible moment before their extinction, it bypasses the revolutionary struggles of the modern age, the student movement and the stirrings of rural reconstruction and rebellion. One would not guess that in these same years Edgar Snow was writing in Peking and went from there to interview Mao Tse-tung in his cave at Yenan. A red star was indeed rising over China even as George Kates was exploring the ancient palaces of the vanished Sons of Heaven. Many people nowadays wonder where Chairman Mao and his violent revolution came from. On this Kates gives us an insight by refraction. His book recounts his experience as a foreign participant-observer of the way of life of the ancient scholar-gentry ruling class. In the 1930's this vestige of the great tradition was all too plainly vulnerable to modern change and now it is far to seek. But no historian will deny its contribution to China's present and future.

March 1, 1967

JOHN K. FAIRBANK

TABLE OF CONTENTS

*Eight pages of photographs by Hedda Hammer Morrison
will be found following page 118.*

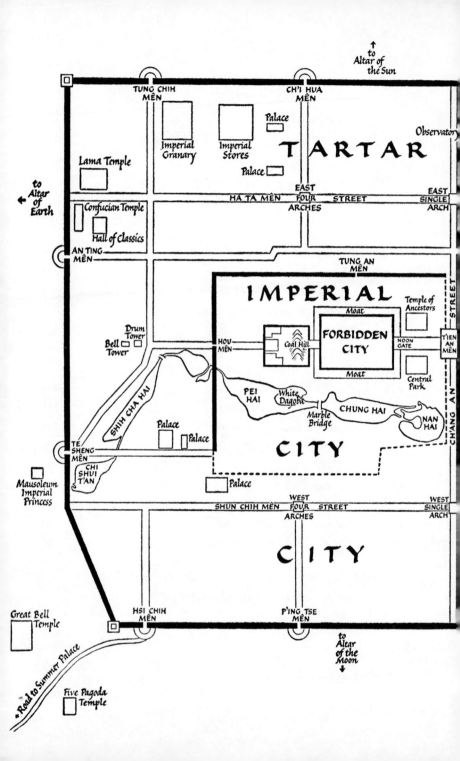

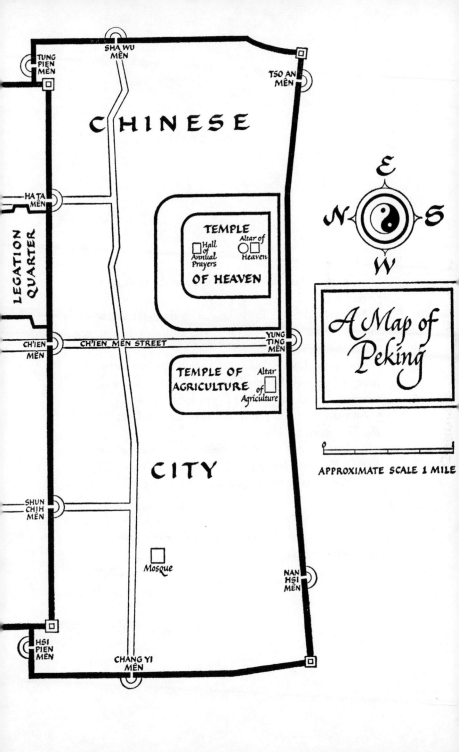

... In my dream, behold, I stood upon the bank of a river:

And, behold, there came up out of the river seven kine, fatfleshed and well favoured; and they fed in a meadow:

And, behold, seven other kine came up after them, poor and very ill favoured and leanfleshed, such as I never saw in all the land of Egypt for badness:

And the lean and the ill favoured kine did eat up the first seven fat kine:

And when they had eaten them up, it could not be known that they had eaten them; but they were still ill favoured, as at the beginning. So I awoke.

GENESIS, 41:17-21

And in the seven plenteous years the earth brought forth by·handfuls.

GENESIS, 41:47

CHAPTER 1 *I Look over the Wall*

IT SEEMED an unusually warm month of June, in the year 1933. The Shanghai Express, a very slow train, had labored for several days over the broad stretch of this earth's surface extending from the Yangtze River in the South to the great plains of North China. It behaved like a cruising tramp, stopping in mid-country, spending leisurely half hours at local stations. Now the chuffing engine was moving sedately, drawing up under the walls of Peking. I was in one of the compartments of a third-class railway carriage, eager and exultant. It was a moment I had longed for.

Having pierced the outer walls, the train pulled slowly beside the Water Gate platform of the main station, leading to a broad avenue within the city itself. I stepped out, to tread for the first time the earth of Peking. Here were to be spent, as in the biblical parable, the seven "fat" years of my life; after which thin cattle also came out of the river of time. Here I was to enjoy riches of life surpassing anything I had elsewhere known.

How was it that I, an American in my early middle years, should find myself here for no practical reason whatever; launched by my own will to pursue what turned out to be, beyond question, the single most rewarding adventure of my life? To explain, I must go backward for some distance.

My family's general habit of living had been international. I had grown up familiar with many countries of Europe, and with Central

1

and South America as well. An English governess, and later a succession of fräuleins and mademoiselles, had taught me some of my languages. I had gone to school in Mexico City and in New York; to college both at Columbia and Harvard and further at Oxford. I had traveled thoroughly in the Old World; I had once cruised—on a fully-rigged sailing vessel—as far as Australia and South Africa. Except for Scandinavia and Russia, Greece, the eastern shores of the Mediterranean, and Egypt, I had covered the accepted rounds.

Perhaps I could not altogether be blamed for feeling minor enthusiasm only, regarding conventional life in my own country. I had lived out of it for such long stretches during the formation of my habits and character. Perhaps the pattern of American urban winters and summer migrations, of light-minded parties among those of my own age only, affording rather slim resources for conversation; or animated life in summer cottages, with daily bathing and sailing, picnicking and dancing—pleasurable as these might be for a group who had grown up as intimates together—were not what by training I now was fitted for. So that when an opportunity came for a big change, to take a step of consequence, to go to the Far East and thus also fill out the largest missing area in the atlas of my wanderings, from long habit of travel I almost automatically grasped it.

I could not then know that the civilization of China—unlike all those familiar to me borne along on the streams of Greco-Roman or of Christian living—would appear as of such stamp and consequence, of such depth as well as charm and novelty, that its impact would change my life. Once a beginning to this venture had been made, all went as easily as water flowing downhill. In the midst of my Chinese years, in an intermediate stage, I may have felt that the new allegiance might eventually compel me to make at least a partial surrender of the old. Yet I outgrew this, a common disease of every intellectual childhood, and thenceforth a definitive integration of all that was precious to me, West or East, became my goal.

So, with no more explanation, and above all with nothing in this book to prove any total superiority of East over West, or the reverse, I shall begin this simple enough tale. It is composed of hours that were tranquil rather than agitated, made of peaceful enrichment rather than the excitement of adventure. This is no book for those in search of any melodrama of the "inscrutable East," of intrigue or treachery plotted in an exotic setting. That was the only China—when I got there—which I did not find. In these pages, rather, I hope the reader will discover China's bright skies and fair hills, the beauty and charm of another world, and the variety of the men and women who peopled it, the China that in days of quiet labor and hopeful progress granted to me the very meaning of my life.

Yet "Why China?" At the time my decision was made, most of the stay-at-homes promptly asked the same question, from censorious uncles, bristling with family responsibility, to the most vapid woman beside whom I might find myself at an uninteresting party. The chapters to come will—I hope among matters of greater interest—attempt to answer that question, to which I never was able to return a civil answer in kind. The best reply might really have been that of Byron, when he was once questioned about why he had left his wife. "The answer," he retorted, "is so simple that I cannot tell you!"

The sequence of events, however, was logical enough. I was in my late thirties when I left Hollywood, where away from my normal base of university life, I had spent five swiftly moving and diverting years surrounded by all the trappings of its fabricated "glamour." That, though, is another story. By education and by long discipline I had been trained to be a scholar and Hollywood was a venture made on surmise only.

The Chinese have a proverb to the effect that if one rides a tiger, all may go well for a precarious while, but it becomes increasingly difficult to dismount. For a while my odd pendulum-swing had been from Oxford to Hollywood and back again. It was a curious combination, but it proved stimulating. At one end was my English college, medieval Queen's, conservative and unhurried. Here I was engaged in the tediously slow business of procuring the last of my academic degrees, an English doctorate. In Oxford, amid endless conversation, teas and dinners, with games and sport and long walks about the countryside, I continued to "read" in European History and the Fine Arts. I spent the frequent vacations of the English university year on the Continent, in one charming place after another.

At the other end of the swing, I had been lucky and invented for myself what was then a new job, plucking various absurdities, in the interest of Paramount's foreign market, from all the films with foreign settings then being made in that company's Hollywood studios, or on nearby "locations." During the day there was varied and even challenging work. In the evenings, on the tops of rimming hills or in beach houses, or else in the palm-surrounded big hotels, there would be parties. The stars and executives all became familiar. This was my American side.

Balancing the two had certainly proved diverting enough; and it also amused me to observe how my prestige in either of these so disparate places was helped by even slight further success in the other. The dons of Oxford, I discovered, secretly yearned for money (and I was making money, lightly and readily); while in the villas of Santa Monica the producers' wives, considerably ahead of their busy husbands in adjusting themselves to their new wealth, were much less secretively wooing culture (and surely, it always and inevitably appeared to them, I had that!).

Moreover, after two years in the California studios, the producers themselves granted me leave for the whole of the year following—except for minor "foreign market" errands in Paris and Rome—to return to England and there finally to acquire the coveted Oxford "D. Phil." I left Hollywood with a crisp new contract in my pocket, drawn up at a considerably increased salary, and plans already fixed for the time when I should eventually return to bland California again. The routine luxuries of American life were already mine.

Something, nevertheless, was wrong about all this, subtly yet increasingly wrong. The feeling grew that here was a problem I should eventually have to face and solve; since overtly I was having successes that others ranked highly, without even maintaining self-respect. Further, it became disquieting to observe how with each pair of advances along my double line, I continued to grow less and not more content. Finally the hollow sense of an ever-diminishing return became too great any longer to be ignored.

Certainly, in France, to visit a duchess on a leisurely provincial journey might seem one variety of ambition gratified; and in the studios I could still enjoy watching my salary checks roll in, embossed with always larger numbers of so many dollars "exactly." Yet exultation from such causes was a matter for secret shame. The perils of capitulation to snobbery, on the one hand, or else to vulgarity and greed on the other, were imminent realities: integrity itself was in danger.

There began growing a now quite conscious need to discover some further, a new and deeper, direction in which to move. More and more crucial questions impended. Meanwhile my days in Oxford were over; my "welcome while" in those enchanted scenes for youth had passed. And a prefiguring of myself as a middle-aged, no doubt overworked and neurotic Hollywood magnate, flabby, bald and myopic —perhaps with a penthouse overlooking metropolitan New York that I should never have leisure to occupy, filled with refined furniture and other magpie gleanings, became insistent and was quite too horrible to be borne.

In Hollywood, at this time, we were making "French versions" that were my special responsibility. They were of Maurice Chevalier's current pictures; and, as chief prize of an international stable, he was mated as at stud to various American actresses in turn. We contrived to have him talk or sing every sequence possible over in French, or both stars used French for their musical numbers together. Chevalier, glad to be able to present himself more vividly to his own best public, took willingly to the scheme; the actresses brushed up schoolday French. Then we spliced these improvisings with silent film, "backing" the latter with scraps of music to cover obvious deficiencies. In those early days of the transition from silent to sound pictures, such patched reels were a salable product.

The first of these odd ventures had bubbled with amusement. It also was a puzzle demanding ingenuity. Yet even here, the sliding, diminishing return began setting in without delay. "Production difficulties" kept growing, moreover, as did our budgets. A point was finally reached where the hybrid scheme, competing with a much more suitable product meanwhile created in France, seemed no longer practical. For the first time in my five years in Hollywood, the pace slackened.

In the spring of 1932 I leapt rapidly from my tiger, at this one brief moment when descent was easy; and straightway found myself—a little surprised—alone, whole, and unbitten, walking rapidly in the opposite direction. From lush Hollywood, again on secure paths, first I traveled back to familiar and conservative New England. In Rhode Island I saw and bought a small Noah's ark of a yellow clapboard house, built in the mid-eighteenth century, round the corner on a winding back road from an old snuff mill that had been the birthplace of Gilbert Stuart. This became my unpretentious base, in pleasant, unspoiled country. Some months were absorbed in improving it and setting it in order; and I first enjoyed a season of domestic pleasure. Then the autumn passed and I remained alone there to spend a winter in the country.

A time came on of sweet solitude and reflection. There kept growing in me, steadily, an insistent urge to break out from the whole world in which I had hitherto moved, to live at last my "true" life altogether as I wished it. From this pure height Oxford and Hollywood, with their conventional pleasures and stereotyped distractions, seemed really not too far apart. From this dispassionate remoteness I could discern how much both stressed objective success, how unswervingly both worshiped—however differently—at the shrine of the familiar "bitch goddess."

My days were my own, of course, to do with what I would; and I had ample leisure for desultory reading. Yet I still cannot fathom how chance led me gently down the lane of excellent translations from Chinese poetry. I can remember, though, the sense of an impending discovery of the first magnitude, the glowing wonder of a pure new joy. Again and again I found in these brief poems something that relieved me, gratefully returned to a better self, from impalement upon the horns of my recent dilemma. So the books multiplied, as did musings about them in quiet hours; and finally there came the need for a new decision. Should I perhaps seriously undertake to learn the difficult language that would bring me nearer to this mystery?

I consulted, and found that it would be possible to return to Harvard once more, there to re-enroll myself prosaically, to sit in some dull college building, with fire escapes at the windows, in the familiar college yard, with students much younger than myself, young men with other ambitions and other destinies; there to do—what? The scheme was unpalatable.

So I drove back to my little house, now lost in the drifts of the snowy countryside, with a small stack of grammars and textbooks from the college library; and beside my own hearth I set about to explore the beginnings alone. The solitude, the white silence, were ideal for the experiment. Rapidly I verified my first surmise that here indeed was a completely new way of looking at the world, wholly unsuspected during all my formal education, one that consistently refreshed and expanded my deeper self, with power and ease such as I had never guessed before. This was really to be lifted to heights, with splendid prospects. The familiar pleasures of Europe shriveled in the comparison. Glimpses of a quite other scheme of life, distant and heroic, inherent in the very formation of the ancient picture writing underlying Chinese characters, promised more insight into the mysteries of historical time than any discovery I ever had made. My new occupation absorbed me.

Early in the following year, now well-launched upon a course that might seem to others, I knew, sheer folly, I decided to take passage in a ship, and go to China itself. The reader should know at this point that I had very little money with which to do this. A margin account with a large brokerage firm that had gone into bankruptcy had transformed nearly all my Hollywood earnings into pure fool's gold. In time, I came to see that this final transmutation, this reversion of the intrinsically base and unstable back to itself once more, did fittingly end my California adventure.

So I went to the Boston Common, one tender spring afternoon, when thoughts floated naturally away toward other horizons, to do business at Cook's. With a ticket in my pocket for a berth in a ship going through the Panama Canal, and thence to Victoria, in British Columbia (where I was to transfer to the Canadian Pacific's white

Empress of Asia), I felt confident that I had veered not away from, but comfortingly nearer to my true, if still little revealed course.

There came a morning, after several weeks of travel, when looking through the ring of my brass porthole, low in the ship, I gazed for the first time down upon muddy and swirling, yellow-brown and summer-warm waters, the estuary of the Yangtze. Later, after a long day, Shanghai finally loomed ahead, the smoke-filled air of its curving Bund reminiscent of mighty London. Here, halfway across the world, I had reached a metropolis again—yet one with components utterly different from those already familiar.

Here I disembarked, each minute filled with new sensation. Half-stripped coolies in multitudes, turbaned Sikhs, White Russian water police; occasional curving Chinese roofs between newer buildings, rickshas, giant advertisements in characters: actors and scenery, all were different. Passing through customs I made my way without haste, through dead urban air, to an international hotel. I well knew that this was not China, although there were native elements in the amalgam.

In Shanghai, therefore, I remained for but one night, dining amid the babble of the hotel restaurant; and departing on that following for Nanking. I wished to be on my way. Nanking, then the capital, became another torrid day, spent largely from breakfast onward in the darkened and shady house of our Consul General. That evening at Pukow, the broad Yangtze crossed by ferry in late rosy light, voluble Chinese in fluttering silk gowns fanning themselves beside me, I entered the Shanghai Express, that very slow train, which crawled haltingly toward the tawny northern plains, to my destination from the beginning, Peking.

Somewhere on that journey, as the wind blew the golden dust of North China over the earth's gentle slopes, amid low mud-walled farmhouses and everywhere grave mounds made of the soil itself, I arrived in the country that for the next seven years of abundance was to become intimately my own.

CHAPTER II *A Scholar's Household*

THE Shanghai Express deposited me on a platform just below the surprisingly medieval thick walls enclosing that part of Peking known as the Tartar City. When the European fire chariots were first run upon their iron roads, as the Chinese phrase it, it had become necessary to coin words for everything connected with them. So a railway platform was oddly dubbed a moon-viewing verandah; nothing nearer to it, in the Chinese world, could be thought of.

Upon this moon-viewing verandah, then, I descended. Porters shouldered my luggage, and I found my way through the archway of the lofty Water Gate. Here a broad canal once had pierced the great walls; and the paved boulevard that now covered it ran first through the modern Legation Quarter and then into more native parts of the city.

Once beyond the barrier, my bags were hoisted into one ricksha, I mounted another, and off the vehicles sped to the Peking Language School. Here missionary care had made for newcomers a sizable group of rectangular buildings, cemented, clean, and as much as possible reminiscent of the West, with grass-plats, tennis courts, and even mild shower baths and other "foreign style" comforts. It was not China; yet I was grateful for the comparative ease with which I could here immediately take the preliminary steps toward mastering a proud and uncommunicative tongue, as well as a way of living thoroughly different from any familiar in the West.

If I had one conviction about the technique of opening up any new country, it was that with fluency in speech all the rest would follow easily and naturally. If one must shift from one foot to another in owl-like silences, the very tinkle of the amused laughter that eventually one cannot but rouse, chills the blood. One then has no heart; and timidity in crossing these frontiers, difficult at best, is a poor habit to develop. So I determined to pay the piper generously first; and then trust him to play good music for me. In this I was not disappointed.

Fortunately my small room on an upper story of the Language School, had a side window that gave out not toward missionary families on leave, apparently content to chat endlessly as they sat about on the neat lawn, but instead intimately to a back alley. This was literally my first window on the Orient. Here in midsummer, flushed with the pleasure of some first purchase of a trinket at the neighboring fair, the bright evening light made lyric by the perfume floating in the still air of recently bought "evening fragrant jade," a wax-colored flower of deeply sensuous scent, I looked and listened as shifting scenes of Chinese life came indolently past beyond the missionary wall.

My scheme of attack on the language began conventionally enough, although I started without delay, feeling strongly that it must under-lie all other plans. Together with earnest missionaries in summer clothes I spent the first warm season in Peking, going over the be-ginners' course with beginners' teachers, in no way deviating from the system considered proper for these first steps. Of course, I wanted to see the city promptly, too. So I often slipped away for the fun of a great fair, held three days out of every ten at Lung Fo Ssŭ, a temple by happy chance only a brief walk from the ordered lawns of the school.

Outside the decent missionary gates, another and pleasantly tur-bulent world was waiting. Under the sails of the cloth awnings of the fair, the babble, the milling crowds, the great game of bargaining, buying and selling, made a grateful relief from institutional tameness. Here I made my first two purchases, a small yellow glazed dish and also a blue and white porcelain-covered jar. I can still remember the excitement of these earliest biddings in Chinese, at one-third the asking price—which was what the missionary "old hands" had told me to try—and how the objects were promptly thrust into my inexperienced hands! I have them still.

When this summer session ended, taking a teacher with me, and only light luggage, I went by ricksha (a long ride) to the Language School hostel in the Western Hills. Except for a single elderly couple, two dignified White Russians living in retirement there, its few brick houses were that year deserted. The accommodation was crude, the Chinese food obviously adulterated to agree with supposed foreign tastes. My Chinese teacher, middle-aged, rotund, and easy going, was a cheerful man for daily society; and the roomy screened porch of the separate house set apart for our combined use was perched high upon the slope of an unusually steep and rocky hill, with a broad view of tawny fields of already ripening grain lying far below. In the shade, we thus looked down upon a serene and peaceful world.

Here I spent the long midsummer days, writing, practicing brush strokes, pronouncing the new and difficult syllables. Early or late, I could be off at will for a scramble up to the peaks or down to the plain; and a mere moment after my decision, the screen door banging behind me, I was in the countryside of China, alone.

How completely the vastness of this Asiatic land enfolded me! In the heat, the distant hills were the deep color of mountain bluebells. The peasants kept out of the glare when the sun was high, so that often the roads I traversed in my khaki shorts and Western leather-soled shoes were deserted. Yet walking digested the discoveries of the past hours; and the high and airy small brick house was good to come back to.

Upon returning to Peking, after one more short course I ceased to be a day pupil in the Language School; although for years I had first a native teacher from our American Legation, and then one whom I requested from the staff of the school again, specially permitted to come out to me. Happily, of course, I had already made my first beginning in now distant Rhode Island. For if language is always a barrier, that of China cannot inaptly be called her other Great Wall, so superbly difficult of assault is it, and seemingly also so endless.

Almost upon my arrival in Peking, I began to be told of the fabulous difficulty of this study. I heard of eccentric consuls who had spent long and barren years investigating complex dialects, which nobody really understood; and of the local British scholar who went about with a box of dark glass forever shielding his eyes: he had used them up, it was said, reading too many Chinese characters. During my first days in the Language School I was solemnly warned by the unenlightened that too much work would affect my brain here, especially if it were attempted in summer. Or else I was informed that reading vertically—as Chinese is written—would be hard on the sight.

Besides the tellers of such tales, there were also the professional Sinologues, although many of these I had now left behind me in the Western world. Such specialists were convinced that Chinese history (at least as history to their taste) had ended long ago; and certain pedants even maintained that the contemporary daily speech, although the living property of some four to five hundred million souls, was beneath the dignity of higher learning. So, usually from a distance, these specialists became wiser and wiser about matters ever more remote; although they were often helpless—I came to learn—when they arrived in Peking, the fountainhead of all their studies, and wanted perhaps to have a pair of shoes cobbled, or (as was not unusual) had an altercation with the cook. When I began to understand what the advocates of this orthodox school could not see, like owls blinking in the sunlight, I was less impressed. After only a modest few months, I could comprehend matters, not unimportant, that they elaborately missed.

The feeling of what I must do gradually crystallized itself into a formula. I would treat Peking as Paris. There, in time gone by, I had once lived very simply, much nearer to the heart of Gallic France than my friends of passage, perched during their short journeys in more fashionable parts of the city. Peking as Paris it would be for me, for speech and daily communication, for food and shelter as well, and even—if self-consciousness did not interpose—for dress and other matters of local custom.

Wiseacres of long residence, generally established foreign style in the Legation Quarter, and the diplomatic corps generally, called this "going native." The words were supposed of themselves to be sufficient admonition to deter one from such an awful course. Further, the occasional "flitterati," as I have since heard them called, who really had gone native, did bear out the dread prediction. Other ruddy-faced Europeans, complacently defying Western hygiene in no secret way, declared that they seriously feared for my health if I actually planned to live in a completely unimproved Chinese house.

Yet my scheme was different from those they disparaged in that it in no way aimed at picturesqueness for its own sake; and also because I had early resolved not to waste energies by seesawing between two worlds contradictory in the local pattern. As soon as I was no longer bound to places considered "civilized," constrained to the routine that inevitably went with them, I felt sure that I could readily begin to plow deep into what was so simply about me. And so indeed it turned out.

Of all the joys of those bygone days the best and most intimate —except for relations to persons and continuing advance in the discovery of the world that was China—centered about the establishment of my own household. To run it well and economically led me down wholly unsuspected paths, into local and native situations which the tourist or the guest can never know. Here I myself came by adoption to be considered almost Chinese, custom prescribing unsuspected limits yet probity achieving unhoped-for rewards. My little kingdom was eventually administered according to strict local propriety—*kuei-chü*, it was called, "rule and compass"—by two servants who became part of my own life. They were so truly sons of their own land that they had never learned the devious language of any foreigner—and with it ways to circumvent him. Indeed so little had they mastered the non-Chinese world that neither of them could even mount a self-propelling chariot, in other words a bicycle.

When one of the two went on an errand or to market by ricksha, this might come a little higher, in fractional coppers. (Today, alas, so terrible has been the loss in value of China's currency that the complete living of several years for all three of us no longer buys a single postage stamp, for letters that come occasionally as from another world.) Cleaving to the required and only proper way of doing what was necessary if a Chinese household were to be set up correctly and well run, we breasted one by one every conceivable problem through the rolling seasons. And as the seasons turned to years I too grew in confident mastery of the operation. At that time the comparatively brief span of my sojourn was of course not revealed to me. I was building for permanence, ever enlarging my original foothold. Yet I must first go back to beginnings; all this developed only gradually, with the passage of time.

The Language School held no disappointments but only help for me during my first months in Peking. Without speech, I was by no means yet ready to grapple with the difficulties of setting up native housekeeping. I was aware of this, and therefore grateful and *pro tempore* content. I had from the beginning, further, that precious window from my missionary bedroom which gave on to the back alley that was really China. In retrospect, most of those first summer evenings as I sat preparing lessons at a bare little desk, I was really observing an enormous play—in which the characters were all real—held out-of-doors amid what still seemed to me quite improbable scenery: "Act I. Midsummer. A maze of house walls, to the west of an old Manchu palace, Peking."

The stage was perpetually animated, the action timed as by an impresario. I learned then for the first time how everything in China at some time or other comes bounding along on a carrying pole. The peculiar rhythm with which the springy wood rises and falls to the almost trotting pace of a coolie carrying a heavy load, or the quiet stalking of long-robed figures when the baskets are empty, these are the norms of Chinese energies. Only one must multiply them over the breadth of the land by myriads upon myriads. For man is the beast of burden in that land, his muscles are his intimate and often his only capital, the very guarantee of his survival. Since other laws of physics apparently are valid there, perhaps he is right when he assures us that when a flexible stout pole rises high, almost twanging the taut basket strings as it leaps, half the time the load is carrying itself! The carrying pole is a primary Chinese invention.

On those long evenings, as the rosy dusk faded, I could listen to the

brisk babble, finally diminishing to a murmur, of al
buying and selling, through house doors, of such thi
peddlers as curious foods to eat and drink: the fresh c._,
ing beans, the iced bitter-prune soup, or almond tea. After bargaining,
they finally went within, to give someone unseen beyond the walls
the satisfactions of taste, and to the vendor at the doorway a little
lighter burden and a few more coppers. Bitter toil this was, yet its
rewards were sweet; and for all the scheming to cadge an extra copper
wherever possible, it was a deeply human proceeding, in which neither
party could attack the personal dignity of the other without himself,
in public estimation, losing face.

For an informal open court, the inevitable "cloud of witnesses" is
ever ready in China to pronounce judgment on such matters. In time
I saw many an unthinking Westerner, or later perhaps some Japanese
officer punch-drunk with recent conquest, put into his place so in-
escapably that he could only recognize and publicly accept the subtle
moral defeat. This was achieved simply by the slow action of the bystanders, always free to look and never abashed at using their privilege;
free to comment on what was happening upon the public stage, the
open street. I too learned to gaze upon the onlookers, with a new
composure.

In my room, then, dreaming of how I should enlarge my foothold
upon this new strand (for the curious quality of Chinese life to ex-
pand itself physically by all available means, to acquire property and
prosper with it, had already taken deep hold of me), I would lie down
on my crunching bed. Then through the night, half through my sleep
I could hear the strange sounds of the clappers and cymbals of the
night watchmen. I think they must always have gone in pairs, those
gentle Peking watchmen, characteristically attempting to frighten
away marauders rather than to run any risk of encountering them. The
sonorous wood of their clappers echoed rhythmically, so that its repeated *tic, tic, toc-toc* gave the slumbering burgher, hearing it even
through his dreams, an accurate sense of the progress of the night
watches. As the double hours—each twice as long as our own—went
by, the signals on the clapper lengthened. Following its staccato an-
nouncements came the muffled, vast, percussion of a pair of gigantic

~ymbals. I still recall how this hushed metallic sound voyaged through the deep night air, making me, too, now reposing safe within the great walls, secure to plan what I should do, and possess, on the morrow.

Months passed filled with other adventures. Even before I rented my own first little house, there were three other places where I was to live. Two were in the courtyards of friends; one was an inn. In the first I had a pair of narrow and elongated rooms facing a pleasant although shallow court. European glass windows gave on to its quite operatic scenery, complete with fronds of overhanging foliage and a small tile-roofed projecting kitchen. These rooms were against the street, and behind their uneven plaster walls was a Peking lane or *hu-t'ung*. The life of the street was now becoming familiar enough to me so that if at dawn I heard the rumble of heavy wooden cart wheels just beyond the head of my bed, I knew that this was an early load of sacks of freshly ground flour coming into the city, flour from which the North Chinese made the *ping* or unleavened wheaten cakes, which they ate instead of the Southerners' rice.

In this house was a paved square inner courtyard planted with four lilacs so tall as to be really trees. The dusty northwest winds were usually blowing when they came to blossom in the spring, to remind us that Peking was not so far from the high deserts of Central Asia. Yet there were usually one or two evenings when a silver moon hung tranquil over the roofs and we were drawn by the spectacle to a small colonnade on the north side of this court. There we sat facing due south as all proper orientation in China requires. Repose was in the air, and we were usually half-mesmerized from the fatigues of a spring day. The scent of the lilacs made us drowsy with a sense of infinite life going along its renewed way, beyond the walls and mysteriously in the lanes.

Moonlight seemed to have drained the perfume from the feathery flowers, and their color was pale in contrast to the cracked rose lacquer columns or the shadowy gold and blue-green bracketing of the cornices above. We sat quietly on, observing it all—obliquely, almost as from a box at the opera. Only when the moon rose high in the sky, and its light became colder, did we break the spell.

He who possesses a Chinese courtyard, possesses both by day and night a well of light, which the seasons endlessly fill with incalculable riches. One winter's day, in the house where I lived subsequently, a small tree that grew in its courtyard was at its wintry barest, when of a sudden there was the celestial rush of wings, and a large flock of bluejays in graceful movement peopled its branches as if to substitute their own lovely plumage for the leaves now withered and gone. The effect was astonishing, but once created the birds promptly flew away again, as if they knew quite surely what they had done.

The owner of this second house was an artist who had temporarily deserted Peking and North China to examine the more lush charms of Siam. I fell heir to his larger quarters, which provisionally I had completely to myself, with only the main room of the largest court, his studio, unheated and therefore closed for the winter. To the east I had my private dwelling; and from my bed all was silver (the artist had so papered his walls) and rich color. High polished blond hardwood wardrobes, with lofty "hat cupboards" set on top, simple furniture of excellent design with gleaming brasses, partitioned this room into study and alcove. One low little door, its soft wood fancifully carved and painted in chalky blues and pinks, led to a small bathing chamber like a secret hive. Here in semi-darkness and in warmed damp air, a bath seemed conventionally Oriental.

Across from these quarters, symmetrically and to the west, was a combination of living and dining room; and attached to it, matching my bathing chamber, was a small kitchen. On the wall in the center of the main room was suspended a large scroll, an ancestor portrait of an old crone in faded scarlet robes, her phoenix headdress dripping with strands of heavy pearls. Often she alone presided at my solitary meals, to which I was summoned each evening by a white-gowned and slippered servant. Full as I was of the excitements and lessons of the day, this at the moment was company enough for dinner.

It was this servant who taught me my first Chinese song. With only moderate success, I fear, I tried to imitate the curious intonation necessary. Yet as I gradually began to master it a change came over me: I could feel how it would be were I Chinese, singing of what was my own.

Thus ran the song:

> Beneath the trees, one asked the young apprentice.
> He answered saying: "The Master's gone to gather herbs.
> He remains indeed in these very mountains;
> Yet the clouds are so thick, one cannot know where."

As my delivery grew to approximate correctness, I could picture myself within the misty hills of Chinese landscape, also seeking a master who had disappeared into the billowing clouds, searching for herbs that brought the body purity, and finally immortality.

A fire would be crackling in the Western cast-iron stove, a sweet would be followed by fruit, with a finger bowl of amber Peking glass; and I would be sitting alone, absorbed in some new revealing detail, probably learned only within the last hours, of the great scheme of living so long ago fashioned in the Chinese world, its precepts unconcerned with our own. Mysteries were being revealed, dignities conferred, which even that morning I had probably never even suspected.

When the tenant of these courts eventually returned to Peking, I decided to venture somewhat further into the native pattern, this time moving to a local inn, one lane away. It had once been quite a large palace, in this good old quarter of the city; and although I had here only a single room, opening onto a so-called "mixed" courtyard, there were many other better courts along ramified passageways within its walls. There was also a withdrawn arbor, painted a vibrant deep green and covered with wisteria, in a small paved garden down an internal lane at the back.

Arrangements at the inn were most convenient. I could have Chinese food, such as, for example, steamed dumplings stuffed with savory chopped vegetables, served with hot tea, brought to me at any hour of the twenty-four that fancy might dictate. I also now had an excellent opportunity to see completely Chinese life at close quarters. Fathers and mothers lolled with their children lying upon their beds, the doors wide open to our common court now that spring had come. Gentle animal caressings, completely unabashed, went on in almost puppy fashion for hours on end. This was—for me—a new variety of fondling. However hard life may later become, most Chinese children are certainly well loved.

Old men would order broad tubs of scalding water, and sit at their doorsteps in the court, slowly soaking their feet in public after a long day, meanwhile chatting contentedly with their neighbors. Civility and good humor made up the pattern of this communal living; here was the way an old people got along together when privacy was not possible.

There was also a single Japanese student, my neighbor, who had come to Peking to study, and was meeting with quite apparent difficulty in mastering the rudiments of Chinese. His ancient teacher shouted at him daily; but a typical Japanese trouble in the control of his breath made imitation unsuccessful. So the shouting continued. Through sheer repetition I reaped a part of the benefit. Once a month, regularly, this young man would disappear for an officially granted "night off," since he was a student sent from Japan by his government. For the next twenty-four hours his small room would be closed and silent; then the following day the tense reading and monotonous repetition would be resumed.

To have lived thus naturally, with such neighbors, in a completely Chinese *tsa yüan* or "mixed court," later always gave me an assurance of knowing, rather than of merely guessing, how life went on in humble dwellings. For not many Chinese can afford to spread out as could, in Peking, even the most unpretentious Westerner; and in that inn I learned how much ordinary Chinese manners were based upon the virtual impossibility of ever achieving solitude except by the hazard of circumstance. Twenty-five centuries ago Confucius was already counseling his countrymen to avoid crowds and noise, to cultivate quietness; and the rich definitely did appreciate these amenities. Yet Chinese families were seldom as small as in the modern West; and almost never in the old order, of course, could a young husband and wife possibly live together apart from their elders.

The time came eventually, after several months of this life, and after a last interlude as the guest of another absentee owner, when

I felt ready to move into my own house. After diligent search I discovered a suitable small court, isolated and near to the east city wall—which I could thus climb on early morning walks—at a rental so low that even with the two Chinese servants whom I now hired, I still was spending only the smallest sum every month. Financially I knew that the experiment would prove no strain.

I determined from the outset that my new establishment should be completely Chinese, to such an extent that the first winter I heated my rooms only with coal-balls (coal dust mixed with clay), kept flaming in an old-fashioned and shining pot-bellied Chinese brass stove, without a stove pipe. Further, I slept on a *k'ang*, the raised brick platform found in every North Chinese house, similarly heated from below by a small portable brazier, and so arranged with flues that a minuscule fire would gently warm the whole of its felt-covered brick surface. In the dark night all was Orientally cozy, my high beamed ceilings ruddy with flickering light from the stove.

To the south, there was a small house for my servants, opposite the main one for myself, a combined kitchen and storeroom to the east, and no building but a high white-plastered wall enclosing the court to the west. My own dwelling, facing south of course, was thus bathed in afternoon sunlight. The whole formed a single cell, small and compact, yet making a paved space under the open sky, all in complete privacy.

Here were learned my first lessons in housekeeping. Yet in retrospect this house occupies only a little place in memory, since before even a year had gone by it was supplanted by what was to become, and remains for me, "my house in China."

This was a larger and a much more dignified dwelling. It had no less than three communicating courts; all its roofs sloped harmoniously. Within the first court grew a gigantic linden tree so ramified that it spread its benison over a large part of the property. This treasure my servants discovered for me only after methodical search, and much reading of small handwritten notices pasted at entrances to lanes in all parts of the town I had thought well of. It lay within the Imperial City, on the site of the former Wax Storehouse, still the name of its lane, where once eunuchs had been in charge of the candles supplied to the palace. It was also delightfully near both the Forbidden City and the pleasure grounds of the imperial lakes, as well as the Chinese university, where by this time I had begun to attend lectures.

Never had foreigners lived in the place before, and this was one of the grounds for my choice. Its old-fashioned rooms were innocent of improvement. The place still belonged to an old palace eunuch, bobbing and rotund, who formerly had been, I was told, in the personal service of the Emperor, from whom this property had come as a gift. He possessed, honorifically and somewhat unusually, the doubtful luxury of a harridan of a wife, whose bad temper and scolding tongue promptly became a source of grinning amusement to my servants, who felt that their origin was only too baldly obvious. This strange couple continued to live at one side of my new domain, in a second and smaller house which they also owned, over the wall. On a still day we could overhear quite a little of their outdoor conversation. Since they had never made any changes, my courts fortunately still had all their traceried windows intact, and so retained their proper appearance.

We negotiated and negotiated, through intermediaries; finally a suitable sum for rental was determined. The conservative owners were apprehensive, but on my part I was happy to agree to alter as little as possible. When with internal excitement I had first walked through the long empty rooms, dust lying thick on the floors, there was a *k'ang* in almost each of them. I wished to preserve only one of these—for my own bedroom—since they did take up much space. Yet I agreed to save the brick from those we dismantled, and I ordered it placed in an internal alley behind one of the side-houses, lest when my days should be over the eunuch or his wife were ever to wish for their many platforms back again.

No electric light, no wooden floors (brick covered with matting sufficed), no heating apparatus except several cast-iron stoves, and no plumbing did I ever install. During all my years there, kerosene lamps were brought in to shed their soft light at nightfall; and as for running water, long ago in Oxford I had learned how unnecessary this was, with willing servants, if one were unhurried. I did not rip out the pretty geometric window tracery, to install more glass than the little I found; there were no unsightly wires, no clumsy digging for ill-concealed pipes or ducts. Nothing marred the excellent lines of the large well-proportioned inner court, my private one; and so my house, while extremely comfortable, remained more authentically Chinese than any that I can recall belonging to Western friends.

From the beginning, the place fitted the three of us perfectly. The servants, indeed, made their plans with particular satisfaction: this was a kind of installation they knew how to manage. In keeping house, a bachelor is always faced with a dilemma. Either he does things too well, and his setting becomes elaborate; or else he is a solitary, living gracelessly in rooms devoid of amenity, unable to offer proper hospitality. Together, the three of us might avoid these extremes. From the first we sensed that the whole was ours, slowly to be perfected perhaps, but permanent and not a makeshift.

From the lane one entered by a *cha-lan mên*, or "barrier gate," plain and of solid construction. Its red color had now turned to faded rose; its double doors were broad enough to allow one leaf only to be opened for visiting rickshas. By a gentle incline the gray brick paving sloped downward into my first court, where across from the entrance was a deep and roomy, flat-roofed, kitchen. My great tree grew here, outside the kitchen door, its rugged branches sparkling with snow in winter, under the pure blue sky of North China, and a palace of foliage to keep the earth shady and fresh when the summer sun burned overhead.

To the north of this outer court was a very small intermediate one, where my servants lived, within easy call from within. My second, and formal, entrance gate gave on to this. It was quite elaborate, as custom prescribed, with much carved gray brick decoration under its ornamented ridge, and red lozenges bearing auspicious characters painted upon its green door panels. Set squarely opposite it was a "screen of respect," also of carved brick, forming part of the wall shielding my third and last court, for dwelling. To this one entered by a further gate, also with double doors; but for privacy it had been set obliquely across from the first. Both entrances had the high wooden thresholds that make a foreigner, for his first few months in any

Chinese city, feel as if he were on shipboard. Within, finally, was my own dwelling space—three houses, a main one and at right angles two slightly lower side-houses facing each other—the most comfortable and tranquil habitation that I have ever known.

From the first we arranged the flowering plants in this inner court, and the lotus that we kept in a shallow tank there, completely in Chinese fashion. From this place open to the heavens, we watched the seasons in their turning majesty, always surrounded by some token of what grew to its best in each.

Oleanders and pomegranates, in earthen pots, alternated on a low stone step running the full length of my main house. This, facing south, is always the largest and best building in the traditional system; and whatever was placed to grow there always received the best sunlight. In front of both my east and west side-houses, opposite each other across the court, I set out fig trees, in broad earthenware tubs. I never ceased to marvel how quickly their leaves grew each spring, when the dumpy tubs were rolled out from their winter storage in a small "ear room" attached to the main house. (I had two of these ear rooms, so-called because they were projections added to the sides of the deeper main building.) The figs gave further pleasure when the fruit turned from bottle-green to inky-purple, becoming so ripe that it would split open of itself in the sun. While walking about in comfort at home, I could then stop at one of the small trees, pluck one at will, and eat.

In the autumn we set out many potted chrysanthemums, never so grand of course as in the palace, where the last young Empress had had little silver bells fastened to her own plants, which then tinkled in the wind as the year grew cold. Nevertheless they were fine in color, rusty reds or pale yellows, and according to Chinese superstition their clean scent prolonged life. Everyone knew that the chrysanthemum was thus the flower of immortality; and one often heard that it was also admired because at the end it knew how to die with dignity and grace. In China one takes the allegory of flowers seriously.

I did not experiment with goldfish because to breed them properly required more apparatus of shallow buckets and flat wooden tanks—topped with wire mesh to keep off curious birds—than I wished to install in this place. Yet my rose lotus, on center in its deep tub of gray earthenware, directly opposite my traceried main double doors, reflected the sky in the water under its leaves; and the allegories of its growth, its fleeting hours of marvelous beauty, and then its decay, were the grandest of all.

From my first little house I moved over enough furniture to start housekeeping quite decently in these roomier quarters. Soon, however, I was enthusiastically making plans for expansion, and even downright luxury. In a grandly decaying capital, temptation was constantly spread before me. Everywhere the old order was crumbling; its once fine possessions no longer usable by many now lacking even the necessities of life. Had one wished to do on a large scale what I was doing on a small one, the opportunities would have been magnificent. Proud palaces were being dismantled or demolished. Every petty merchant, too, practiced the fine art of conjuring up new desires, which his eloquence sought to turn to urgent needs in just such heads as mine.

Yet for the objects of daily use that I wished to buy, if one were known not to be rich and also spoke the language readily, one need never have the uneasy fear of being cheated, or the disgust of finding that imitation had been foisted upon one. Further, I bargained for nothing ruthlessly taken from its setting, nor shorn of its roots. My unpretentious good furniture, the simple pewter or porcelain dishes for my table, were bought unhurriedly as they caught my fancy. Also they were not merchandise with which one could easily be swindled.

Sometimes, of course, my purse could not bear the drain of some latest enthusiasm; yet there was in Peking a typical *pan fa* or "working plan" even for this. The sympathetic owner of a good curio shop outside the Great Front Gate, in the Chinese City, who was a quiet sensitive man, saw me one wintry day thus smitten with desire, unable to extricate myself between a sudden longing and the inability to gratify it. As we sat in his back room, quietly drinking steaming tea at a table covered with a stretch of fine Chinese carpet, he deftly helped me to help myself.

"Take this home with you, now," he said, referring to the quite unnecessary object that at the moment completely held my fancy—

it was an old, plain, deep-yellow ivory, scepter—"and then, when you have loved it sufficiently, bring it back to me again!" We smiled at each other; in China ample leisure made this a solution altogether acceptable to both parties (although I did keep the object, as one retaining pleasant associations).

So through the years, the local porters who earned their living bearing heavy objects upon their heads, carried through my barrier gate, one after another, pieces of the most excellent simple furniture, of hardwood so dense that it was said to sink in water, so beautiful in grain and surface that it was often like the back of a fine old violin. Even at a time as late as this, nothing like it in design or quality had yet appeared in American museums; their random and fussily carved late "teak" pieces, like the heavy cloisonné ornaments that often accompanied them, were curios rather than household furniture.

I also hunted out every kind of fabric, from old brocade to stenciled peasant blue cotton, every kind of metalwork, gleaming brass or copper, satiny pewter, a little ivory, much red leather, rugs of fine color from western China, whole categories of scrolls and inscriptions, small objects of dark lacquer, of brass-rimmed burl or other curiously grained and unknown woods. It remained a student bachelor's house, of course; for although the elaborate always did exist alongside the plain wherever I went searching, I chose only the latter. My sober range of dignified furniture, I found, was one almost unknown to the West, whereas the complicated varieties were only too familiar, in part because of the general level of taste in our stupid nineteenth century, and in part also because of the vested interest of Philistine merchants.

As time went along, and as my teachers and servants made matters clearer, I became aware that I had stumbled upon a discovery. At first unknowingly—following my personal tastes—and then with conscious intent, I was apparently reconstructing the vanished setting of the scholar class, of the old *literati*, with objects for elegant if unpretentious domesticity rather than for display at court. This was the way private houses had looked in days of now vanished prosperity, before the old tradition broke down after its melancholy impact with an aggressive West. The sobriety, the simplicity, and the good taste were the scholar's; and I found that they had long existed, unnoticed by the art historian, as the normal furnishing for the men of taste and intelligence of their time.

No matter in what field I directed this search, I was constantly struck by the infinitely varied ingenuity with which the Chinese fashioned even the simplest objects. It was a skill that never could have led to complex mechanical discovery; it aimed too directly at some simple comfort, at producing some pleasure that refined the art of living. These satisfactions once procured, it stopped.

Yet boxes opened or closed in the most diverting or inconceivable ways; pots poured out two liquids from a single spout—by concealed stops on a hollow handle, contrived by air pressure to hold back the unwanted one, kept separate within. The form of any object, from a lacquer bird cage to a brass foot warmer, was never repeated. Each time the problem was genially conceived, and carried out individually.

Shopping therefore actually became a stimulating exercise in the abstract possibilities of shape and volume, of geometry. One always came back from such an expedition enlightened about a still further way of subdividing a circle, for instance, or of designing a lobed edging—perhaps for a table, or a tray—completely charming and logical, yet one that somehow had never come to mind before. Also, of course, it might never later be seen elsewhere.

So great was the choice offered, that until one was sure one wanted an object it was best not to run the risk of buying upon first inspection; something better might so easily appear later. I learned, nevertheless, that if one were sure, purchase should be unfailingly prompt. How many prudent economies does one regret in this life; and how easily do we apply effective consolation for our minor extravagances!

My house, then, little by little became furnished, not too richly yet no longer sparely; and each new purchase, like musical glasses, would set vibrating again all my pleasure in former ones, from which it drew fresh harmonies. I extended my schemes, too. At the time there were no limits in view. I suspected that the gods might grudge the profundity of my content; that leaner years might of necessity follow those that were fat. Even a little happiness seems more than life can long offer, and of this I was aware. Yet I went along without too much reflection since I had about me so much beauty constantly giving me new enjoyment, and I continued perfecting my installation, learning daily of further objects, large or small, unknown and charming. Always I tried to acquire one excellent example. The process was effortless, specimens would appear as of themselves, and the whole became an absorbing game. In the Wax Storehouse, we were ever prouder of the visible result. Even my eunuch landlord and neighbor, on his rare visits, was properly impressed.

Alas, we built even then upon a shifting foundation. Seven years later the inevitable day came when all was to be put into packing cases. By then I was considered lucky to be able to take any possessions away with me. Like all the other foreigners, in time I became myself a visitor whose days were over, drawn again to join his fellows beyond the sea. The "guest man"—a polite way of referring to foreigners much used in Chinese phrases of courtesy—found that from the first he had been destined finally to go back to his own "external country." Yet I must not get ahead of my story.

CHAPTER III *Wisdom from the Elder Born*

THE first steps were now taken and I was becoming increasingly vocal. China had proved to be in no sense a baffling land of mystery. The day began as in any other land, with its small tasks and cheerful routine. Once I had my own house, I could plan its hours and discuss domestic plans as I ate my breakfast. The simple pleasures merely of walking abroad in the open street, of exploring various quarters of the city, of asking questions, talking and being talked to in easy conversation: all these were also mine.

Yet from the beginning I set myself fixed hours, and laid out the ground to be covered. My pursuit was not to be methodless; nor were leisure and freedom from the need to earn my daily bread—if I could contrive to live with utmost simplicity—to become pretexts for idleness. Although my plans took on their developed and complete form only after I had become well established in my own independent household, I should like here to describe a little the daily routine of my tranquil, long, and leisurely lessons, during which I gathered impressions of the character of successive teachers in such detail that they remain with me as if received in childhood.

How much do I owe to the chief of them, Mr. Wang, of insights into Chinese nature! He had contrived to make his humdrum life, composed of a daily routine of monotonous teaching and domestic privation, symmetrical and reasonable indeed. His face was gentle, yet it was that of a man privately more wearied than pleased by most of the relations he was under the necessity of making. His eyes were kind; and his glance could at times glow when some new thought would catch and hold him. His side-face made you like him. He would so much more have preferred, I am sure, merely to have stayed home than daily to face his current assortment of bounding new missionaries, or else crabbed old ones, in the Language School. Yet he probably had never felt that such a choice could be his.

He wore a soft brown fedora as a concession to modernity, yet not so much to prove that he was advanced as to avoid being considered too definitely conservative. He even owned a pair of longish, light yellow, Western shoes that would appear underneath his dark blue or purplish robes when the lanes were specially damp underfoot. These leather shoes were equally a compromise with the modern world. His Chinese clothes he wore with an unself-conscious air of good breeding. Somehow the very sound of them as he crossed a high threshold, or the way in which he quietly spread his skirts with his fine hands as he took a chair, betokened a man of culture. He was no hack, although his colleagues were hacks; he remained closed and therefore secure, if only because he knew so well by indirection how to turn aside effectively any indiscreet remark or lolloping conduct on the part of some new and immature pupil.

He soon discovered that I sensed all this clearly; and that I also (with no career to make in China) was repelled as he was by the unseemliness with which new arrivals in the school brashly announced that they had come to hawk a salvation they forthwith declared superior to anything evolved long before by his own Confucius. If they were "diplomatic" or more rarely B. A. T.—British American Tobacco —arch-familiar in China, we both knew that the grand debate on morals would affect them not at all. When Mr. Wang became assured that we thus had the same sense of decorum, barriers fell. Yet I remained more unwilling than ever now to press in upon his carefully guarded privacies; and upon this base we built a tranquil relation—partial it is true, but one that lasted us peaceably through many years. He became my formal teacher.

Winter or summer, tea was served endlessly. When I had acquired an establishment of my own I never ceased to marvel at the patience of my servants, to whom this constant coming and going never caused a flurry. For a civilized Chinese becomes almost helpless unless you place beside him a steaming pot, even if it is filled only with scalding water; and everyone soon senses the importance of keeping it continuously filled. Tea is brought to you invariably as you enter any proper shop. Business, any business, is impossible without it. At every hour of the day, oceans of it must be wasted in every province of China; yet it is imperative that hot water always be kept ready to brew it promptly. As it is said that the water buffalo will perish if he is not allowed to immerse himself daily; so too the Chinese find their tea indispensable.

With tea, then, and with our changing books, we installed ourselves beside the stove in winter, and later when I had finally acquired my own courts, fanned ourselves in a shady corner of my innermost one in summer. My "Elder Born" or *Hsien Shêng*—this is the teacher's title of courtesy, since his more mature spirit has preceded yours to birth—and I would converse endlessly, finally about everything in the world!

It was always a dignified proceeding. Our bows of greeting were never too stiffly formal; this would have denoted inferior manners. Yet they were never omitted. The *Hsien Shêng* was daily announced; and a few seconds later he would cross some inner threshold, always neatly dressed in a dignified long gown of stuff appropriate to the season. One could hear its sound before he himself appeared. Three hours later he departed. Never did those hours hang heavy on my hands; and discoveries never ceased from the first day to the last. Even when anticipating other and exciting pleasures, I still looked forward to my regular lessons.

Although their attitude was invariably correct, I seem to remember that one teacher or another, after months of slowly maturing confidence, would occasionally make some slight expression of weariness at his destiny. One surely could not condemn this; his was often a dull task, and surely ill-paid. Dignity, however, was always fully maintained. A teacher remained one's teacher, one's Elder Born, for the whole of life. It was not a light relationship. He was to be given respect, veneration even; and the bond is one that Chinese recognize with a real sense of obligation. Westerners who regard it slightingly cause a deep wound. His standing, unflaggingly maintained, consoled many a poor drudge for the eternal monotony of his labors.

Even a teacher's salary was never called merely salary, but "dried meat money" instead, since this was a historic perquisite of tutors. According to tradition, the actual service was not indeed one that could be bought or sold. In our time, the pay was merely in unimaginative paper money; yet one always had to put it carefully into an envelope so that it would not show, and then at the correct moment politely present this with both hands—one would be so lax as to constitute rudeness—to the Elder Born.

Later, as soon as I had enough both of the spoken and the written language to follow lectures, even though at first sketchily, I sought for and was given the privilege of attending Peking University, Pei-ching Ta-hsüeh, as an auditor. Even at this late date I must have been somewhat of an oddity in this place; although later an American woman and a lone and eccentric Britisher, on a fellowship from Cambridge, also joined some of the classes.

Chinese auditors were not rare. One of my professors told me that they were often his best students. In general these were boys too poor to pay even for enrollment; they thus gave up all hope of a degree, living miserably in nearby inns. They held great disputations among themselves, and were in appearance and by temperament so many Chinese François Villons, leading disorderly lives yet aglow with the pure ardor of learning.

At the university, which was in my own quarter of Peking, no one seemed to think in any way strange the Chinese clothes that I had found it pleasant and sensible to wear. Even in midwinter the classrooms were unheated, and a fur-lined gown was there doubly appreciated. Nor did my presence ever give rise to any self-consciousness —although there was plenty of interest. I began gradually to achieve the solid satisfaction of understanding a demonstration on the blackboard, even when the Chinese characters for it were chalked hastily, which of course made it doubly difficult to follow.

Each month there was less of the unknown to puzzle me; and more of China as seen by and for herself. It was contemporary China, of course, yet so far was this life removed from that of Legation Street and the quarters inhabited by Westerners generally that it dispelled them to complete unreality. Here I was not "The Oyster," as I later learned that I had been nicknamed among the foreigners. Here was openhearted and earnest endeavor and intellectual concentration. There was deep interest in such matters as, for example, the first attempt by a brilliant young professor to interpret certain phases of China's long history economically—by a method "Western" to him, yet still Eastern enough to me.

Or I could listen to wonderful criticism of T'ang poetry, or of the earlier classical Odes, by a scholar who must have known by heart thousands of lines of the most beautiful verses in the language. This teacher would draw on the blackboard the arrangements of palaces vanished a millennium ago, so that in the mind's eye one could see again why a long-dead poet had once mentioned green willows, let us say, as on a hill behind the glittering roof of a certain great hall. Why were these colors or effects selected rather than others? Or why —perhaps about 800 B.C.—was the stitching on the fur robes of young men of fashion, mentioned in a ballad, made thus and not so?

One old professor, whose manner was so mild that I never could determine the precise moment at which he would stop casual conversation with some student on the front bench to broaden his remarks a little and actually begin lecturing, took us tranquilly through the heroic plays of the Yüan dynasty. His gentle digressions from the China of our thirteenth century were long and meandering, yet they never ended without a neat point. About me were young faces aware that the literary splendors of their country were passing in review. It was a high and pure world to have entered; the other one, down in the diplomatic quarter, was by now well lost. Then daily, charged with new enthusiasm, I returned home to my nearby courtyard for a light lunch, frugal but most neatly served; after it a nap, when possible, on my south-facing, felt-covered, brick *k'ang*; and soon the *Hsien Shêng* would be announced and our afternoon-long conversation would begin again.

Gradually in those days of intellectual excitement, which paradoxically were made up of long hours of quiet study, a wholly new region of the mind, unsurmised before, was progressively discovered and explored. These were a scholar's joys, the rewards of his discipline; and my efforts could not have been better expended than in the very fields that praised him long and earnestly: Chinese history and Chinese literature.

First of all, though, had to come the language itself, its structure and form, its tones and characters. And a broad zone strewn with stumbling blocks lies before the beginner in spoken Chinese. There are the four melodic tones of voice with which all sonorous Pekingese is inflected; as well as whole collections of words each with completely different meaning and yet precisely the same sound. To make matters more complicated, these words included many necessary to express the commonest ideas. How was one to make proper distinctions, since they had all been fixed in the language for centuries, and now could not possibly be changed?

Let me first present the reader with a short description of the tones, the preliminary major difficulty. Every syllable can be pronounced in Mandarin, which is the official language, in four distinct ways. At the beginning, these sounded so alike that the first step actually was to hear the quick, slight, differences with one's own ear. Other dialects, spoken across the land by millions, but never used at court or for official business, included as many as eight or more tones. The clear and charming spoken Chinese of Peking, fortunately, had but four. Yet even for these practice was something like learning to play upon a harpsichord, with several banks of keys and also a pedal or two to work at the same time.

One could take a syllable, for instance, and pronounce it sharply, at a somewhat higher pitch than is usual for a Westerner, then stop it abruptly. Or in uttering this same sound, one could raise one's voice, as if to ask a question. Further one could also curl it, first down and then roundly up. Finally, one could begin high to end low; but if the sound had once come down, it must never be allowed to rise again. To make quite sure of this, which was difficult, one of my early teachers advised me to observe camels' pads; and since in Peking these are the beasts of burden commonly used to deliver coals to householders, I amusedly set myself to dog them, watching their curious tread, trying to catch from it the difficult knack of going down, and then staying down.

The first of the tones made one feel disagreeably emasculated; its pitch was too high. To my own ears, even today, it is too shrill to be altogether pleasant. The last was correct, we have seen, only if it descended sharply to remain low, which sheer eagerness often prevented. For the endless drill if my new Chinese were not to become toneless—a common and horrid malady—the Language School had contrived a series of cells on an upper floor, where victims of a singular form of torture met each with a teacher, to school themselves in this one phase of the grand attack, by stern endeavor and maddening repetition.

Even ten minutes or so was exhausting; but then a bell would ring and one changed teachers. This was repeated several times, to permit one to acustom oneself to different voices pronouncing the same so short yet so difficult syllables. Although overtly a simple enough routine, it was, I really believe, one of the most grueling intellectual tasks I ever undertook.

After a number of shifts, we Westerners were allowed to escape, to play volleyball out-of-doors, for a recess. The Chinese teachers must have regarded our all too obvious relief as confirming their worst suspicions about the ever-present light-mindedness of foreigners. Yet even in shorts, shouting in the excitement of a lively game, glad above all to be away from those little rooms, somewhere within my aching cranium still would be blaring some such desperately short sound as "Tzŭ," (first tone), "Tzŭ?" (second tone), "T-z-ŭ" (third tone), and *Tzŭ!*" (fourth tone)—weaving erratically up and down, trying to progress safely, perhaps half the time wrong.

Even after a number of years, in moments of emotion or haste, tones might still fly off incorrectly, uttered by some little slip to mean something ludicrously different from what one had intended. Then one felt perhaps as a bird might feel if, miscalculating simple flight from one branch to another, it unexpectedly found itself in mid-air, having missed its perch, unable to alight correctly anywhere.

The rewards of industry were nevertheless satisfying. Ricksha boys and servants could be addressed intelligibly; and it was encouraging to watch them brighten when they understood simple questions. The toneless speech of the inept foreigner left him permanently outside gates that these goodhearted Chinese made haste to open, if only the knocking were comprehensible. Pride at such minor successes made further plodding much more supportable.

Merely as human speech, when properly spoken, Pekingese is a melodious and delicate tongue. It is capable of the subtlest shadings of civilized thought. All Chinese knew this. I still hear it with the pleasure one might have in hearing a clear and vibrant language spoken in some land of Chinese immortals. It is piquant in metaphor, rich in revealing cross-sections, cut always in another direction from ours, through material nevertheless common to mankind. Its formulae are delicately considerate, truly polite; and it never resembles the singsong guttural intonation, or the flowery abracadabra represented as its facsimile by the ignorant. It furnishes the stimulation, the excitement, of a completely different system of speech.

The homonyms, or characters of identical sound but different meaning, brought still other problems. Reformers always begin by demanding why one cannot simply "write" Chinese with the alphabet, and thus abolish a good part of the difficulty of the language. This one can indeed do; and with fair ease if one will make a code of equivalents and then abide by it. But it gets one nowhere. Every Chinese character is a separate picture, a symbol, or a unique derivative or combination of several, and that character does to the eye always convey an individual meaning. Yet the Chinese have so few distinct sounds for all these many flourishing characters that in reading the literary language not even a Chinese scholar can follow another by ear alone: he must actually see what is being pronounced!

Were this to be everywhere necessary, the nuisance of it would become intolerable. On a lower level, using plain speech for everyday existence, the common people long ago found a way out. The monosyllable *chi,* for example, in my pocket dictionary represents no less than one hundred and sixty-four different characters. The meaning of any one of them by itself fits this one sound, in one or another of its four possible tones. Yet a single one only means, let us say, chicken.

To utter the word "chicken," however, so that out of the whole collection it alone may be understood in the marketplace, one amplifies it a little, and says instead "small-chicken-child," *hsiao-chi-tzŭ*. This is universally understood, exactly like a word of three syllables, since the sounds are run together, and means quite simply the ordinary chicken.

By obvious Eastern logic, the word egg becomes "chicken-child-son," also a combination of three syllables. Thus single sounds are strung together to make longer words sounding quite like our own, "white words" as the Chinese call them, or plain speech. To reproduce these accurately in transcribing spoken sentences, the single characters must still all be written out, in groups of twos or threes, as above. Yet in literary work this is quite unnecessary, since the single root character never presents any ambiguity. Indeed, precisely because of this the documentary language is a marvel of concision.

The system is far from perfect, but the Chinese neither can nor will alter some thirty centuries of linguistic development in an attempt to meet the criticism—to them both irrelevant and impractical—of uninstructed foreigners. Difficulties crop up, of course, even among themselves. One often sees men, especially if from different provinces, in conversation scribbling an imaginary character upon the palms of their own hands, to make sure that a companion understands beyond any doubt just which one they had meant to convey. It is rapidly traced with the forefinger, in imaginary ink, as its sound is repeated. The person addressed looks, usually gives a quick assent of comprehension, and on goes the talk. Sight, again, resolves all doubts.

Tones help greatly, of course, to break up these long parades of like-sounding syllables; and to a Chinese ear they are completely different sounds. The two provinces of Shansi and Shensi—neighboring, as if to make it harder—are intentionally spelled by us differently, to make certain some distinction between them. This was found necessary in our system merely for postal identification. They actually have the same sound; although to the Chinese ear the difference is unmistakable because the tone of the first syllable in Shansi is high, while in the word Shensi the same sound is curled down and up again. Such are a few of the difficulties of tones and identical syllables, vital meaning forever hinging upon almost imperceptible trifles. Truly patience was necessary.

One thing that granted it to me was the wonder of the written language. This springs from premises so completely different from our own, and over long centuries has evolved into such a marvelous instrument—the very existence of which is unsuspected by Westerners generally—that I should here like to enter into at least a cursory explanation of certain elements in its structure. There is no better clue to the workings of the Chinese mind.

In all our familiar world, in Greece and Rome, through all Europe, the alphabetic script, if not the only known, certainly has been considered the most sensible and practical system for writing. Children learn to write by linking sounds together, and then by analogy: "B-A-T is bat." To the Chinese, however, a number of the commonest words in the language are actually simple pictures, in the course of time radically condensed, reduced to the fewest essential strokes, yet pictures none the less. The horse, even today, still keeps his four legs and tail; the cow has lost one horn, but retains the other. Birds—objects of passionate interest to all Chinese—are divided into two categories—those with short tails, like the sparrow, and those with long. All birds, however rare their variety, then invariably have one of these two symbols as a component part of the character used for their names.

A Chinese child, in learning to write, is thus presented as part of his heritage with what is tantamount to a gigantic, celestial box of toys. Stowed away in its ample partitions are images of all visible things, and symbols further for those invisible. To write he must learn to select and combine from them. This is a grave, an almost philosophical process. Small wonder then that when later he comes to study such a language as English, he does not too much prize a system that however effective it may be as a rapid code, leaves out for him great and traditional symbols representing the wonder of the world.

In learning to write Chinese, it is as if the student himself were invited to participate in a grand review of all things tangible and intangible. Certain characters further make it possible for him actually to relive, in moments of surmise, fragments of the ancient history of a

vanished race, as he divines how their formation proceeded from
archaic thinking. Those to whom this is uncongenial, and therefore
"impractical," never seem to sense the pleasures, and groan at the
labor involved.

The Chinese character for the sun, for example, 日, was in its most
ancient form precisely what any child would draw: a round disk, ○,
either filled in, or perhaps marked with the sign "one," ─, since this is
the first of the planets. With a need for more rapid writing, and the
corresponding invention of the quick-moving flexible hair brush, which
replaced the older hollow and wick-filled reed, radical abbreviations
were introduced; and in time the circle came to be drawn as a rectangle, since the supple brush could be flicked down corners in less
time than it took to draw the round figure carefully. Similarly, the
oldest form of the character for the moon is simply the crescent that
any child would draw. In time it was changed to 月, simplified, given
angles, to make it more like the others. Yet even today it still retains
one horn of its crescent.

What, though, it will surely be asked, did the Chinese do when they
wished to invent characters for abstract terms, for things invisible
and therefore not to be put into writing by the mere process of forming
abbreviated pictures? The answer is often simple. When, for example,
a character for the word "brilliance" was needed, the sages apparently
proceeded as follows. They thought carefully of exactly what, in this
world, was brilliant. Surely the sun was, and surely the moon also.
Why not, then, put the two together side by side; and henceforth give
to that combination and to no other, everywhere and always, this
single meaning? Such is apparently what was done: today we read
the character 明, and it signifies this one quality.

Yet one must not oversimplify. The result was not always so readily
obtained nor is our modern reading of it so sure. The Chinese character for thoughts is a combination of a field, 田, with a heart, 心 : 思—for
that is where thoughts come from, or perhaps in an agricultural
society where they go. There are thousands of characters formed
similarly, by deeply revealing combinations. It is also typical of the
system that several interpretations are possible; the inventors, dust for
so many centuries, kept no record of the reasons for their decisions.

Another device, which spawned numberless characters, including many for concrete objects, was the rebus. "Eye sea U"; we have all as children played such games, using pictures instead of spelling, 👁 〰 **U**. The poverty of Chinese sounds made this an especially tempting way to distinguish homonyms in writing. For instance, plum tree, a single syllable in Chinese, has exactly the same sound, although in another tone, as the Chinese word meaning every. How could one write it? On the left of the character one put the sign for a tree, since the plum is a growing thing; with a trunk, 丿 , coming out of the ground, 一, and a taproot and other lesser roots below ground level, thus: 木. One then placed next to this the symbol already evolved for the word "every": 每. As a result there was formed the compound character meaning plum tree alone: 梅.

If the system is congenial to the student, study becomes a continuing invitation to explore reaches of the Chinese mind accessible in no other way. It subsists concise and unchanging, the transmission of a complete view of the world across great stretches of human time. So I sat, summer and winter, all my years in China, ever discovering further combinations and new characters, or understanding the symbolism of old ones better, handling them like jade pellets—beautiful, dense, and of superlative hardness.

The first time one met a new combination, it might be an enigma. Then down some rivulet of thought would suddenly appear the ancients' idea of barbarians, whose campfires were watched by fierce dogs, so that the symbols for both fire and dog were joined to make the character; or perhaps their feeling about snow, "rain with a hand holding a broom." Well, one could sweep it away! Or there was the character for rain itself, shown descending thus, 丨 , from enveloping clouds which were themselves under the vault of heaven, 冂, complete even to four drops that had always carefully to be painted in at the end, 雨. Then all things in the world related with rain, such as the snow already mentioned, 雪, had the topmost part of *their* characters amplified by this so-called "rain radical," only now diminished, drawn broad and flat, 雨, a process not at all unlike the division of a heraldic shield into quarterings.

The excitements of beginning to read were therefore of an order completely unknown in the West. In Peking I could bicycle down a crowded business street, and long before I was able to seize connected meanings, could catch on the large shop signs or hanging banners whole collections of "grass radicals," "metal radicals," "three drops of water" for liquids, or "two drops" only for *ice*; since the third one, my teacher explained, had frozen as it had dripped.

There were "gates," with both leaves brushed in,門, or "horses," 馬, or "carts," the latter two-wheeled as in antiquity, and represented in plan, looked at from above,車; and many others. The ancient Chinese world, seen through Chinese eyes, was about me on every signboard, neatly classified into categories down to the cloth for its shoes or the metal for its canisters and trays. Even after years of familiarity, I do not believe that the original meanings of these components have ever wholly disappeared from consciousness. Gradually one absorbed the logic of the ancients into oneself.

I also noticed that Chinese children, even when very young, learned their first lessons in much this same way. Paper slips, generally the size of playing cards, were cut; education was to begin. On each was traced a character, boldly and properly written—and none was too poor for this. "What is this?" "And now this?" The answers generally came prompt and shrill; with proud, if Lilliputian, literary pleasure, at perhaps the age of three. Nor was the help of grandparents unwelcome. On the contrary, I have seen many of them participating actively, and with obvious pleasure, at the very beginnings of the process. It was a serious business. The script itself was to be revered; so much so that in days only recently past, no paper with any writing on it could later be used for utilitarian purposes. Even as trash, it still had to be collected and burnt properly and separately.

Foreign students also used the above method for learning their first few thousand Chinese characters; although usually with thicker cards, on the reverse of which were translations into their own language, as well as the transcribed sounds and the all-important tones. It was indeed possible for the Westerner to invent varieties of solitaire, or busy himself with a grand review while being pulled through the streets in a ricksha—a practice not uncommon among the serious—or to devise private ways of gaining a minute here and there, if only one kept a small deck in one's pocket. Thus the study of these Chinese puzzles became, typically enough, in itself a diverting new game.

Writing was another. The characters should always be made with a brush, dipped into what is very properly called Chinese ink. Turning corners nicely is a trick, a flick of the wrist that must be learned. Horizontal lines, also, must always rise a little as they go from left to right, at the slight angle natural if one traces them with the right hand away from the body. They should further be drawn, the teachers' say, as if they had been designed to "shed water." There are many similar principles, as well as devices for proper balance, all of which must gradually and carefully be learned.

One of the most important was that in formal writing all characters should occupy the same area, and also be inscribable within an—unseen —rectangle. Thus a good calligrapher first planned upon a sheet of paper an invisible grillwork; if he were not quite so good a calligrapher as that, yet wished to make an inscription carefully, he might even lightly rule in the actual lines, which were later effaced.

Characters vary widely, furthermore, in the number of their brush strokes. The number one, as we have seen, is merely a single stroke, —. Two is 二; three 三. Yet some patience-testing examples have complicated combinations running from twenty- to thirty-odd strokes apiece. In writing, when all are used together, a balance obviously has to be struck. This the good calligrapher never forgets. He is concerned to make his characters with few strokes bold and vigorous, and those which are complex, by contrast fine and delicate. The same radical may also appear fat or thin, and come high or low. It may be used alone, or as one of several components, according to the exigencies of its position.

To plan all this well, to "organize" characters as the Chinese phrase it, thus becomes very early, yet remains through life, a conscious effort. Increasing mastery of calligraphic skill is, like any other, unending. Yet this finally makes every literate Chinese to some degree an artist, and certain ones masters commanding techniques that we sense only dimly in the West, even when we consider certain phases of abstract painting.

To progress from this technique of writing, to paint with the same brush and ink the actual world about one—its trees, its birds and its flowers, or the mist in the mountains—entails for any educated man only a comparatively minor adaptation of abilities acquired in childhood. Every literate Chinese is therefore a potential artist, in our own sense of the word. Yet it may surprise some Westerners to learn that painting is definitely ranked as second, in Chinese estimation, to calligraphy, especially to calligraphy by the hand of a master. For the latter is abstract, and is therefore more evolved and difficult, a much more personal art. It can convey powerful moods and meanings, rhythms and balance, by most subtle means.

To mount the heights of calligraphic skill is therefore to ascend very high mountains indeed. There comes a point beyond which Westerners can understand only imperfectly; where almost without exception they must stand outside the loftier gates, certainly so far as actual practice is concerned. Even after years of effort, their clumsily brushed-in characters seem to Chinese eyes the work of awkward children. When the traditional Chinese thinks about his own culture, I believe that this is one of the chief causes of the disdain, for such it is, visited upon the unenlightened foreigner.

Even the physical materials for this literary venture were altogether different from those that were basic in the West. Beyond the structure of the language, its tones and the characters, there were the actual objects for writing: brush and ink, the stones upon which to grind it, seals, vermilion seal pad (to make impressions), all the proper appurtenances of one's desk—with further, of course, the countless varieties of Chinese books themselves. All these were for use as in another world. They were extremely pleasant objects to buy, and to learn about. One soon came to distinguish coarse from fine, the outstanding from the merely excellent. Among Chinese scholars I found that this was always a congenial subject for conversation.

First of all, naturally, came the Chinese brush. I had to learn to paint my way into my new kingdom. One could of course trace characters with a fountain pen; at lectures the modern students did, proud of possessing such an object. Its clip projecting from the flap of their

Chinese gowns was to them a badge of their own conception of modernity. Yet certain teachers would not touch a pen; its hard point, they declared, ruined the natural sensitiveness of the wrist.

Brushes came in so many varieties that my teachers would talk as if they were investing in skates or skis, questioning the shop assistant about how they would glide, if they turned corners easily, and so on. Customarily we also bought a peaked brass guard with which to cap each slender brush. A new brush had always to be broken in, carefully soaked in lukewarm water, only gradually put through its paces. These were only ordinary brushes. The giant brushes for inscriptions, or for large auspicious characters made to be displayed either singly or in pairs, were completely different both in material and shape. Their stubbier, thicker handles might even be of jade. There were many of these, here and there, on display in the Forbidden City, which in retrospect I perceive to have been a very literary palace.

In various apartments there, or in the palaces of the princes, one often saw suspended, hanging outward from under the ceiling, pairs of red paper lozenges bearing gigantic characters for Happiness and Long Life. These necessarily had been traced standing, with sweeping motions of the arm, perhaps even by the Emperor himself, to be sealed officially with one of his great seals, and then carefully preserved "ever after." No gift in China was more face-making than this.

Good ink sticks, used by men proud of their calligraphy, commanded high prices. Certain varieties dried glossily, or else would grind better. Yet the stationers' shops, among the neatest in the whole city, had simple kinds also, each always in its own small box. In the palace, we could see whole collections of them on display in a number of halls, still in fine presentation cases of brocade. Their black surface was almost always picked out in gilt, imaginatively molded in delicate relief; and the sticks themselves were formed into most novel shapes, miniatures of every possible object under the Chinese sun. At one time or another these palace examples had probably all been very face-conferring presents; they were displayed with ivory-handled brushes, alongside writing paraphernalia of jade.

The ink stone was an even more complicated matter. Hard baked clay that sold for very little might serve for ordinary purposes. A really good one, however, could easily bring a stiff price. They, too, came in every regular and irregular shape conceivable, with unexpected ingenuities of arrangement to provide both the necessary grinding surface and a depression to hold a small quantity of liquid ink already ground. One merely rubbed the dry stick upon the smooth wet stone, carefully adding drops of water until one had what one wanted. The final mixture must be smooth and opaque, yet not too thick. Even trained monkeys, one was told, had in the old days been taught to do this industriously for their masters. Yet it took a while to acquire the knack, and to distinguish stone from stone. There were coarse grains and fine, inscribed stones, stones that had belonged to famous personages; indeed, there was no end. It was only after I had lived in Peking for several years that at last I found one I definitely wanted for myself, quite small and carefully fitted into a plain hardwood box of handsome burnished grain, of good quality yet one that I could afford.

Of paper we bought only the simplest, although the lines and borders, and in particular "invitation stationery," came in many varieties. The latter was to inform others that your rooms had been swept and wine cups washed, as went the standard phrase, and would they lend your humble servant the brilliance of their company—for lunch or dinner? Such cards had shadowy figures generally representing some ancient bronze or elaborate curio so nicely printed in faint color under the wording that purchase was made doubly tempting.

This small pleasure was as nothing, I came to learn, compared with that felt by a good calligrapher, when in the shops that kept such rarities he might finger a fine sheet of three-hundred-year-old paper, simply waiting for his skill to have characters of one style or another traced upon it. Such paper was not for the foreigner, although I did buy varieties richly speckled with gold leaf, in yellow or rose, when for instance I requested a teacher, to inscribe a pair of matched verses —one for each side of the doorway in my study—with these lines that I had stumbled upon. The mood was of dying autumn:

[*Within*] The lamp shines gently in the quiet mountain room.

[*Without*] Rain falls steadily on the cold chrysanthemum flowers.

I also bought the best paper I could afford when I asked to have a fan painted by a friend, one of the last of the Manchu princes, whose calligraphy was noted. This was customary; and if the paper was good enough, one could give pleasure as well as receive it.

All the foregoing, though, yielded to the ramification of knowledge about seals. Here was a major literary continent, by me newly discovered. No stone, no hard metal known to man, crystal, porcelain, or wood, was left unutilized. Shapes were unimaginable in variety. Seals came in sets, or in pairs, or else they were made hollow, box within box like a miniature nest of children's building blocks, each side incised with an inscription. There were also many kinds of characters to be used, from "seal" proper, the most archaic and formal, through scripts special to bygone dynasties, finally even to cursive "grass" writing. There were small symbols, or sets of curious and purposely cryptic mottoes, to be stamped upon the margins of letters as fancy dictated. There were *yang* or male seals, with the characters in red and the background blank; and also *yin* or female, where this arrangement was reversed.

One had to learn what to seal, where to seal, how to press the seal evenly; and above all what seals to use. One had an official seal, utility seals, certainly one for each of one's literary names, and perhaps several further, engraved with devices corresponding to facets of one's character. Men of letters or artists progressed from one to another as their styles developed; and such details were matters of common knowledge to the scholar. One had seals to be used only in certain rooms, in the Study of Breadth Conferred, or the Studio of the Solitary Moon. Connoisseurs, especially imperial ones, conferred prestige by leaving the imprint of some seal on every fine picture they had inspected. Combinations of characters that were obscure had to be interpreted. Although this was interesting, it consumed much time. One early learned the appearance of familiar seals belonging to celebrated men; above all—in and about Peking—those of the eighteenth-century Emperor Ch'ien Lung, who sealed his way imperially and relentlessly through a reign of sixty years. There was simply no end.

Then there was the vermilion ink pad, as it was called, which also came in many qualities, and the purchase of which was never to be undertaken lightly. Also, though seals could be carved for money, such work was always deprecated by the sensitive man as mechanical and inferior. Fine seal-cutting was by tradition a gentleman's pastime; and seals were the scholar's gift. In Hangchow, in the South, there even existed a society founded for their study alone, to preserve their lore.

My own first seal was a modest one of "chicken's blood stone," so-called because of the deep pink-red veining marking its gray ground. It was carved commercially. I stamped it upon hundreds of sheets of letter paper, upon books, even to receipt bills, or to make official any document. I learned to ink it properly, to keep it clean, and when applying it to give the necessary small extra pressure to each of its four corners in turn, never using it upon too hard a surface. I learned how the characters on seals were composed in various groups, how certain formulae were to be chosen for this or that purpose. In Chinese eyes my higher education had begun.

There were other objects besides seals always to be found on a scholar's writing table. The little vessel that held the water for grinding ink, with the delicate curving spoon used to ladle it on to the ink stone, was of importance. One could buy it perhaps in Sung porcelain, or one might have a bronze one. Jade, too, was not infrequently used. Apparently anything was possible, except the chance of ever finding a duplicate. This would have been insufferable in Chinese eyes; and of course machines were undiscovered when the best of these little vessels had been made. A Chinese, morever, takes special pleasure in using his imagination afresh for such purposes, and fancy's only law, we know, is her inconstancy.

Other larger and shallower vessels were to be kept filled with water, to be used for washing brushes. There were also wrist-rests, of bamboo, ivory, porcelain, or other materials, as personal for comfort as pillows. Indeed small hard pillows they were, to raise and steady the hand for fine work. There were metal rulers; there were paper-weights, in pairs, also of metal, some heavy enough to keep a large sheet taut when spread upon the writing table.

There were capacious brush-holders, the finest of which, I thought, were cylindrical and quite uncarved, of the heaviest and handsomest

woods obtainable. There were also stands upon which to place ink
sticks still moist from use, so that they could dry properly. Ingenuity,
in fashioning all these, apparently determined never to make any end;
at least I never found one. This seems an intrinsic property of all
such Chinese objects; the native inventiveness on this scale and for
these purposes, does indeed seem never to exhaust itself.

A similar variety also applied, I found, to books. My first purchases
were humble little affairs, bought for minuscule amounts, perhaps
reproducing some famous anthology of T'ang poetry with artless cuts
to illustrate each poem, line-drawing showing palaces and temples,
bridges and causeways, or chambers of audience with imaginative furnishings. The classics were more sober, printed traditionally with
heavy and broad, very old-fashioned characters; yet they existed in
editions so cheap that almost every school child in the old order of
things once possessed his own Confucian *Analects* or the revered *Book
of the Golden Mean.*
"Learn it by heart, now," they were told, "and if it is properly engraved upon your memory, you will always be able to understand its
true meaning more fully, as you go through life!"
Chinese books are in general made of quite fragile paper, with the
leaves doubled so that the folded edge is turned outward; and the
paper is of course printed on only one side. The binding of each
fascicule, often colored, is also not very durable. Numbers of such comparatively thin volumes, however, are finally housed within a well-
made cloth case called a *t'ao,* which is the true outer cover; and for
this one may use even the finest brocade or silk tapestry. Little clasps
of jade or ivory, or else more humbly of carved bone, keep it secured,
and these are often carved to harmonize with the binding.
After a while, when I had begun to acquire a sense of these things,
it was a pleasure to go to a good bookseller's and to inspect his lofty
shelves. In their various *t'ao* the books were usually arranged not upright but flat, with what would be for us their tops turned outward.
Telltale pendant paper streamers also marked their titles; and the
resulting effect was somehow quite like that of a medieval sorcerer-
apothecary's shop. This or that *t'ao,* more interesting than the general-

ity from some lure of title or elegance of casing, always seemed from its shelf to beckon: "Take me!"

If one did, though, *caveat emptor*. Traditionally there were never distinct editions of books in China as with us in the present-day West, never any regulation to prevent an imitator from cutting for himself a new set of wooden blocks, one for a page, modeled upon the old text, and thus reproducing any book that he could acquire. The comparison of editions consequently became for the scholar almost a sporting event. One might come a cropper in the very last volume of some prize, to find a few pages missing; so one always was told carefully to count them all. This my servants would help me do. Yet if a page or two were imperfect or lacking, when the book had been purchased in a good shop the loss was always most obligingly made good. The bookseller's copyist set cheerfully to work, matching paper, mending torn pages, comparing texts (like as not with a copy borrowed down the lane, from another shop in the same quarter), and then carefully imitated the missing portions by hand. I have seen this done with such painstaking skill that for a moment the eye was deceived.

When all is said and done, however, what did I read in this wonderful tongue? What secrets did I uncover; what of value did I acquire? Here I must confess to a real disappointment. Of course there were the poems. Short verses, occasionally of only four or eight lines apiece, could induce a haunting mood—literally often with the thrust of a few powerful syllables—which often we cannot establish in much longer works. Chinese style then became, as somewhere I have seen it described by Somerset Maugham, "glitteringly compact." Yet the going was definitely harder; even with plenty of time, the final yield was somewhat less than I had anticipated.

Years later I was cheered to hear perhaps the most eminent Chinese scholar of our time remark that he believed his own countrymen, even when well educated, did not really understand more than a certain proportion of any classical text they read. Difficulties are ubiquitous; ambiguities abound; ten problems grow out of one! The language has grown so tangled and involved with age, its myriad allusions raise such complicated questions concerning the long chronicle of the past, and require so much learned interpretation—dealing as they often do with archaic ideas or objects now long gone from this earth—that the ordinary Chinese simply resigns himself to a continuous tendency toward the obscure, and behaves a little like a myopic man who might prefer not to wear glasses at the opera. At least imagination yields him a satisfactory return; and by comparison the reality might be somewhat disillusioning.

This will never do for a Westerner. He must apply his lenses or his calipers; he is not cheerful in ignorance; and he usually is determined to prod until he has received valid enlightenment. There has thus grown up a new and extremely complicated science, that of modern Sinology. It is a fruit of Western learning grafted onto a stem that continues to remain rather alien to it. As a discipline it also tends to make men learned rather than wise.

The Chinese of the old school, by contrast, felt that at any moment they understood as much as they were meant to; and they tranquilly studied on, always learning more. They had prodigious memories, and they also made for completely different ends. It was the refining influence of literature that remained their goal through life; details were details. Never, truly, shall these two meet.

I have only this to say: those few oldest scholars, of the highest learning, of whom I had occasional glimpses in Peking during their sunset years, were so transmuted, had been made so humane and so gentle by their long studies, that a complete justification of their own system spoke majestically from their faces. The visiting Westerner, however well informed, never fared well by comparison. For their own purposes the Chinese methods were supreme; and in communicating a tradition of enlightened living from generation to generation, their literature never failed them. This was the grand style; and it was to conserve this treasure that the art of Chinese writing had first been developed some three millennia back in the mists of the past. Much had meanwhile come and gone; much had failed of transmission, at least with the meaning and clarity that once had made it vital to the early sages; yet the old texts, unaltered, remained.

CHAPTER IV   *The Comforts of Life*

ONE after another, the years continued to go well; and I remained sanguine. My household was now established. In the best of cheer, I settled in gratefully to enjoy its deft and willing service. Let me describe how such a small domain as mine was administered, who ran my pocket-handkerchief kingdom for me, and ran it with charm and wisdom. First, however, one must explain what servants are, and how they function in the Orient generally.

In our twentieth-century West, the new variety of democratic self-service, created by applied science, has temporarily blinded us to the naturalness of older arrangements. For until our own time, only yesterday, servants were a normal part of the order of the world. Indeed until machinery transformed the application of physical force, all domestic tasks had to be performed manually. And there was never a scarcity of willing hands eager to be allowed to do just such simple work—especially in poor or crowded lands where mouths were many.

Before locks and latchkeys were stamped out by thousands, to take one example, there had to be at all the doors of antiquity a "talking lock," in other words a watchman. Who brought in a lamp, at night, before electricity was invented to transfer almost heatless light from great distances merely by pressing a switch? A servant. Who arrived with water before—as it still seems to Chinese eyes—water in complicated piping began to arrive "of itself"? A servant. Even today there is no strangeness to a Chinese about any of this service. Seen from the eyes of ignorance, it is the imported machinery that is surprising.

Further, among the masses of Asia it is taken for granted that there must naturally exist in this world ranges of uncounted wealth and bitter poverty, unfamiliar in their almost measureless contrasts within our own pattern. In China, formerly, the Emperor in theory possessed the whole world, or at least what was to Chinese eyes the central and significant portion of it. The poor, at the other end of the scale, in the East have always had less than is theirs in any Western land. There was no dishonor to this; in Chinese minds it was simple fact, not even material for wonder.

To become a servant in China, to perform manual labor for another, is consequently merely to act in accordance with a common fate, which demands no special attitude. When Chinese take service with foreigners, though, it is in general because they are seeking actively to better their condition, even at the price of changing basic habits, although of this many Westerners are unaware. The power and prestige of the master, in the Chinese system, is also extremely important; it affects the servant at every hour of the day. Relationship to power, moreover, personal relationship, is for him instinctive.

The much talked of "squeeze," also entails no moral shame. It is really only a well-understood commission for handling sums of money or amounts of property. In one form or another every purchase is subject to its application; it can almost be said to be the invisible tip given to an agent in any economic transaction. A porter is an agent, for he carries articles; a doorkeeper is an agent, indeed a formidable one, for at his will he admits them behind gates. One lives thus surrounded. Eyes are sharp, brains are quick; and under the surface minuscule amounts of invisible credit are forever being ladled away, good-naturedly, persistently, and with that hopeful cheer which even the slightest progress toward security seems perpetually to rouse in Chinese breasts.

This may explain some of the aspects of Chinese service at times sharply irritating to the unreflecting Westerner, who may use a similar technique himself, but in operations where the scale is larger. This, however, is a distinction that he generally fails to draw. It may further help to make clear why, if any mutual profit is involved, the Chinese so soon are to be found working together according to dynamic law. Yet if properly administered, the arrangement also works for the master as well as against him.

"Become rich and powerful," the servant seems to say, "and if I have served you well, I too shall become more secure. Prosper exceedingly," he continues, "and with the years my own lesser fortune will have been made also."

In the old days, the linkage to power began at the top with the Prime Minister, often described as "above a myriad men, below a single one." In actual practice it goes down to the very bottom of the scale, to the last tattered ricksha puller dragging irregularly after him a worn-out vehicle. With no public law, as we know it in the West, to enforce abstract and impartial justice, power and above all personal relationship to power, wherever and however they may be found, are the common preoccupation.

Soon after my arrival in China, I realized one day that I was being flattered when I was told by a Language School ricksha puller: "Afterward, in the future, you will use neither self-propelling cart [a bicycle], nor foreign cart [a ricksha]." "At that time," he added, "you will sit a vapor-chariot [an automobile]!" The implication was that if my studies—different from the missionaries—led to this successful issue, everyone should be content; I, assuredly, because my "face" would thus have grown very big indeed, and those who served under me because, obviously, they too would be prospering.

This is one reason why in pleasant quarters there is such willingness, so much alert politeness and so little apathy to ordinary Chinese service. Everyone is playing for some personal stake and even that moment may be perfecting his skill, which keeps him interested and makes matters generally enjoyable. It also lends an air of intrigue to the smallest negotiation. Deftness in both directions on the social scale— up and down—assures good winnings.

Exactly how much squeeze occurred in my own household, I carefully refrained from ever trying seriously to find out. That would have been impossible anyway; and on my humble scale it must often have consisted of almost infinitesimal concessions, often in kind, especially when daily provisions were purchased. It must be understood that Chinese domestic servants buy their own food with their wages. This makes their already minuscule earnings so tiny, in terms of how to eke out an existence not only for themselves but for their families as well, that one can well understand why the early Jesuits did not consider, under such circumstances, that normal squeeze could be construed as sin. Without it, indeed, the established order could never have been maintained.

Chinese servants are also aware in great detail of exactly how much money their masters are using to live on; and mine must have been so even more than most, since economies had to be rigorous and unfailing if my way of life—free of all impediment, so that I could remain on in Peking year after year, to study—was to be maintained. I early made this clear to them in their own language—here I had a definite advantage over the average foreigner—and from time to time I conferred on how certain details of my establishment were to develop.

Yet, since I was running a Chinese and not a foreign variety of household, I took special care to compensate for this strictness, and for our regular financial accountings (kept in Chinese, in a little book brought in from the kitchen) by always presenting to them their winter and summer clothes, of good stuff, on the major feast days. Such was the old custom, which almost no Westerner observed; and they appreciated it. I also used their "little names," Chinese fashion, at home, never calling them coldly by their surnames, or "Number One" and "Number Two," or most barbarous of all, indiscriminately, "Boy!" As my Chinese improved, this habit and the use of other similar forms of speech, overheard by our neighbors, incidentally gave us locally most face of all. Nods of approval would then come even from the aged in the lanes.

Beyond the customary double pay for the last month of the Chinese lunar year, about mid-February (so that everyone could "cross the boundary" financially at holiday time), I also helped with their children's schooling, in time of illness, and by always being on hand for those occasions of major and public importance in Chinese life: birth, marriage, and death. Money might then suddenly become a matter of urgent concern; and of course their reserves, from a Western point of view, were pitifully slender. The Chinese, however, can smile blandly with unbudgeable composure when calamity is only half a step away.

All together we thus lived a dignified if thoroughly local existence; and its satisfactions were good. Nothing I ever did in China took me nearer to the simple joys and sorrows of the people, or made me more a part of the very alley in which I lived, than a readiness thus to participate as heavily as my purse would bear in all the *ta shih* or "great events" of my servants', and also of their families', lives. We knew what we were about, all of us; and for years we sailed our common craft in consequence without mishap.

As I have already said, I deliberately chose two servants who spoke no English. This had a double advantage: I had no pretension from below, and I could also observe the native system working with a minimum of adaptation to fit in with foreign fancies. Their names, which will often occur in these pages, were Wên-Pin, "Simple-yet-Eloquent Letters," an upstanding young lackey once trained in the then vanished czarist Russian Embassy, whose character was of touching purity and singular incorruptibility; and Hsü Jung, "Hsü-the-Glorious," my minor servant, smaller, somewhat older, much more plebeian and less honest, but full of interest in life. Hsü Jung was obviously not so well brought up; he was far less concerned with matters involving ethical correctness than was Wên-Pin. For the latter, whose family name was Chia, came from a completely self-respecting household, that is, one properly grounded in Confucian precepts. The origins of Hsü Jung were by contrast indefinite. He was vaguely Buddhist, much more superstitious, but most of all merely full of the pleasures and excitements of living. His zest could reach marvelous intensity.

From the first we were three human beings, come together. They so naturally expected me to be interested in their characteristics, and that they should observe mine, that the unconscious rudeness of the conventional Western system, which generally assumes that neither party will pay too much attention to the humanity of the other, and the coldness or hypocrisy of the resulting relation, have struck me forcibly ever since.

I had chosen these two to serve me separately before I learned that nothing could have produced a more complex situation, since it cut across the cardinal principle that there must be a hierarchy in service, with a direct devolution of authority. During seven years we never solved this problem; we lived with it. It required a nice distinction to assign minor tasks, specifying them myself, since this they could not do alone. For although one was superior and one inferior, there was no formal chief, one who had "called upon" the other, to serve under him.

Occasionally, in the first years, there would be an explosion, a raging typhoon after a long spell of good weather. At such times silences would become very vocal, or one would appear from the kitchen and I would even be told that the problem was insoluble. "One must, it is necessary, confer with 'him' " [the other]! A day or two of resentment would grip us all. Yet I think we finally learned that as my first decision had been made, thus—time having already gone by—it now must continue. Decorum finally made the thought of change no longer seriously to be considered; but not until we had been through the usual threats of dismissal or resignation several times.

So I found out how Chinese solidarity worked, even when there was no sympathy of temperament to support it. Like two parties in an unsuccessful marriage, Wên-Pin never grew to like Hsü Jung spontaneously, and this feeling was reciprocated. Yet it never interfered except triflingly with co-operation in line of duty. If in the early days I specified who was to do a routine task, perhaps at an awkward moment when the servant whom I had named was not there, I would blandly be told, "He has mounted the great causeway to buy a packet of tea leaves." This pretext of absence to shop for a trifle merely meant that the affair was not of my business; what I needed would always be properly attended to anyway. Perhaps at that moment, calculating from some previous statement that I had planned to be away, the servant in question had gone on a round of visits; or else was sitting entranced in a Chinese theater, listening to the falsetto lament of some improbably noble character in a romance from the chivalric histories of the Three Kingdoms. There were no days, not even hours, off: this was really the better system.

Or, if a servant became ill, or had exceptionally to go off to attend to some piece of private business, to my constant wonder he provided upon his own initiative a substitute, usually some member of his family. Nothing ever interrupted service; and yet private life was not sacrificed in the process. All the intolerable strain of ducking in and out for working hours such as we know it in the West, of racing to work merely to be found present at a given moment, simply did not exist. I know how comfortable the afternoon visitings must have been, because guests gradually also appeared in my own kitchen, staying there quietly by the hour. If I entered, or the broad leaves of the door were ajar, I would receive a dignified bow; manners were always unconsciously good. There was dignity, no shame, no desire to avoid observation. This was tranquil enjoyment of a right.

The mutual credit system had really astonishing ramifications. Later, as "expert," I occasionally was called in to exhort or discharge a servant in other households, run by foreigners who observed other conventions. We then would invariably have an hour of drama, in which I had to learn to play my part.

"Well, then," I would finally decide, "since things have come to this pass, unfortunately you must go!"

The offender was never dismayed. He only smiled more intently, quite willing.

"I shall indeed depart promptly," he would reply.

Why? Because that would be his vacation! He had helped with his own wages when members of his family had encountered similar misadventure. Now he would rest, now it was he who would be carried on their backs; and by the time he had used up his own invisible credit within the family system, a new job—hopefully perhaps even a better one—would no doubt appear. The smiles were therefore strangely real.

Also, if work suddenly multiplied or entertainment were afoot, surely and without fail new and willing hands would be present in the kitchen. Brothers or other relatives got wind of the enterprise mysteriously; and they would arrive in the best of humor, to *pang mang,* a familiar phrase, to "help our haste." This was absolutely counted on by my own two; and thus with powers such as they could dispose of within their own circle, no familiar task was too difficult for them. They in turn would occasionally go elsewhere, summoned in the same underground fashion; and I know that the challenge was pleasurable.

If I invited more people to a dinner party than could be cared for easily, someone in the kitchen would be helping to *pang mang*; at our own holiday times, or if I celebrated a Chinese feast, there were always hands to *pang mang*. My face was involved, they wordlessly told me. All of us must do well what we were committed to do; and to pay off social obligation handsomely was one of the solid satisfactions of life.

Of course I inevitably entered their credit system, too, for specially excellent and thoughtful arrangements put me, contentedly enough, quite properly in their debt. At all such times, though, my household— even down to my dog—enjoyed itself hugely. Within the barrier gate the bustle was pleasurable; an air of confidence and good cheer put one in an excellent mood for the moment when it would enthusiastically be announced, everything ready, that the guests' rickshas were at the door. This backing never failed me, even once! One can see why Chinese parties are so glowingly remembered by those fortunate enough to have known them at their best.

Do not imagine, however, that in China only the rich can thus entertain. I have seen humble folk, even ricksha boys, give elaborate parties in their own tumbledown courtyards, complete with catering, for nearly a hundred guests. How can they possibly afford this? Well, if it is to be a marriage, the whole neighborhood, not to speak of the two families involved, must be invited anyway. The *p'êng*—or matshed—maker is first called in. Within a few hours tall bamboo poles have been set up, and a large structure, the *p'êng* itself, forming a roof over the whole court, is lashed with stout twine to this framework. The host now has his large room for a day or two.

I remember one such party, the wedding of a friend's ricksha boy. In spite of the difficulty of finding a good bride for someone in this occupation—which was considered unsteady—we were informed that the matchmaker had picked out a very suitable young lady. Would we come and see?

As the guests arrived, each presented with both hands a rose-crimson envelope, containing a gift of paper money. Aware of the custom in advance, this we did properly also. I later learned that to within a few Chinese dollars these gifts had covered the cost of the food served at the party. There was also hire for the varnished tables and stools, there was the *p'êng* itself of course, and there were minor expenses. But even while the feasting was in progress some old uncle was doing the accounts. All was entered into a ledger; and the new groom made his first courtesy calls upon those who had given most. Face thus became an extra reward for generosity.

The experience and powerful stimulation of large-scale entertaining is thus not denied even to the very humble in China. This is what it means to belong to a people who have had perhaps the longest unbroken social experience on our globe. Public good manners, on such occasions, seem to be instinctive; everyone knew the cues—in Peking —and seemingly wanted only the chance to display with ease and charming gracefulness a role well-mastered long ago.

Another thing I learned, as time went on, was how rapidly news could travel among the uneducated. My servants were by no means illiterate; indeed they read the almanac constantly. It was their guide book through the lunar year, giving directions even about what days were best for washing the hair. They reveled also in long novels full of Chinese deeds of derring-do, with heroes leaping to housetops, brandishing huge swords and making bold speeches. To their amusement I occasionally borrowed their books, which I found were also surprisingly familiar to my teacher. Yet it was comment upon what occurred immediately about them, the living and contemporary scene, that gave life its savor. The real world in their eyes was of vastly more interest than the shadowy pastime of reading.

The kitchen was naturally the center for communication; and newsbearing there never ceased. The sturdy Shantung water carrier who daily filled my glazed earthenware cistern—for we had no well of our own, still less "self-arriving" water—was always ready to deliver himself of a hearty sentence. The coal-balls for my brick kitchen stove, high and platform-like, came in with a further bit of gossip. Or the barber would arrive, put down his carrying pole, set up his little red-painted portable bench and place a brass basin upon a high wooden stand that he also brought with him. Then, for one of the servants, would begin a long and leisurely session, with a shave over the whole scalp, followed by rinsing and ear-picking. This gossip was prized as among the best, for barbers of course went everywhere. Or members of the family would quietly and simply be there (I came to know a great number of them well by sight). One could never tell just why they had arrived, but news was always passing, being digested and commented upon; and obviously it kept coming promptly and fresh from its source.

This was specially true of the messengers who delivered "chits," the local name for our notes that replaced Western telephone calls. When foreigners were in close relation, such messengers might be on the road constantly. Each chit was entered into a chit-book (I have mine yet); and its receipt was attested, if the master was away from home, by a rubber stamp or else by the ordinary house seal pressed into it. The latter was esteemed more formal and therefore in better taste. If the message was received personally the master might scrawl his initials, foreign fashion, beside his own name. In this way we could nearly always tell quite accurately what had happened to every document.

When only a word of acknowledgement was needed, it was often added in this place. "Would you perhaps like to come picnicking on the lakes next Thursday evening?"—"With pleasure."—"Do you care to see the Devil Dancers tomorrow in the Lama Temple?"—"Drop by my house first!"

These messengers came from other households; they were all known to each other; and they usually sat quietly in the kitchen, chatting and sipping tea while a return message was being devised within. Chits were often frisky; nearly everyone enjoyed the arrangement, not least the messenger himself. Sensing his role, he sat recounting the latest, or hearing our own news; and it never took long for anything of remark to spread over the town. A messenger with five notes to deliver knew by heart who had dined with whom the night before, how it had all gone, and so on, in the whole of his master's circle, by the time he returned home with his chit-book again. Further, since we were all said to have nicknames in these regions, the literal sentences must at times have been somewhat curious. One Westerner, who had a weakness for visiting hostesses just before meal hours, was known simply as the "Want-Food One." There were "Old Virgins" and Great or Small "Very-Verys" (older or younger married women) in numbers.

If that special rupture of the amenities commonly known as a "Peking quarrel" were bubbling, and they often did, the messenger's role would become more active. I do not know whether these altercations sprang from pride confronting pride, since on however small a scale each was sovereign in his own scrap of kingdom; or from exasperation when an adversary of one's own kind began to set bounds, to limit one's power. These were traits that life in courtyards engendered. Even the Chinese were aware of a common temptation to "bolt the door and set oneself up as Emperor."

Here I stumbled upon what must have been a wellspring of classical Chinese intrigue. Especially during love affairs, the messenger had a chance to make so much personal face, which he was not at all loath to seize, that drama sprang into being full-fledged. The household servants were informed: "As she wrote that chit, her *amah* [maid] told me that she appeared to . . ." etc. This would be relayed within; and although I sternly discouraged such gossip, from time to time the situation would explode if my servants felt that I ought to know something of importance to myself (as they considered it), and therefore to all of us—before I penned my reply. After all they were my small army, and in the world ambush was inevitable. One must be prepared.

Or perhaps some genial party was going forward, perhaps arrangements were being made in fine weather for an excursion to a distant temple; and the preparations—food, crockery, and transportation— were being divided. A message would come, and after domestic consultation I would select a sheet of paper. Finally I would put my envelope into the chit-book, adding on my line the words "Reply herewith." Meanwhile the messenger had kept his own liaison unbroken, sitting comfortably in the kitchen. The oral system worked quite as well, on his level, to keep him in touch with such affairs, as did for us our own writing. Connection was therefore double, and from the Chinese point of view now secure.

One other creature joined this small company of a student bachelor with his two servants, a little dog so wise and graceful, so unreal, that at times it seemed as if he were one of the traditional sculptured lion-dogs come to life. He was indeed a lion-dog, and the breed had come from Lhassa; so his forbears had been Tibetan. Erh Niu was his enigmatic name. It meant merely "Bullock Two," or else "Bull the Second." Perhaps he had been called a little bull because someone had fancied a resemblance; perhaps there had also been a number of pup-pies in his litter, and as is the Chinese custom, they had all been num-bered. In China even children are named in this way; and I was later to meet a man of distinction whose name was "Cloud Five." The four elder cloud brothers are less well-known.

Erh Niu had an excellent pedigree. He had been presented to a China-born foreign woman by a eunuch of high rank, living in retire-ment at the Eunuch Temple—as we called it—an elegant and well-administered establishment near the Eight Precious Hills (where the Westerners played golf). Eunuchs solaced themselves in their old age, when most of them became noticeably frail, with their pets; and they were known always to possess the best of the breed.

This dignified miniature bullock, with his thick silken coat of several tawny colors, and long hair forever concealing his eyes, was generously ceded to me after I had once admired him, and then came to spend his existence in my own courtyards. For the first few days he crawled under low furniture whenever possible, and was generally miserable. Yet this wore off nicely, and Hsü-the-Glorious, who had a quick taste for everything living, from pet crickets (which he kept in little wicker cages over the kitchen stove) to the passing monkeys in street shows, and who was much more interested in my new acquisition than the Confucian-minded Wên-Pin, soon loved Erh Niu with a devoted admiration that the dog found frankly satisfying.

He responded to such a degree that even when he was being

bathed, bedraggled and with his wet head shrunk to squirrel-like proportions, all his fur drenched and soapy, he knew that Hsü Jung was doing what was proper. The daily combings to fluff out his fur became highly comical; Erh Niu took interest in telling us, stroke by stroke—with extra whimpers *ad libitum*—just how it was going.

My teacher definitely did not approve of too much interest, and even less of any ecstasies. In his fixed tenets any such inordinate love of beasts was undignified for man. It was merely one more proof of Western frivolity! So there was an exchange of recognition between himself and the dog, with a mutually intended distance left between them.

Erh Niu took his duties seriously. He was often bored, to the point of heaving repeated sighs when life was dull; and he expressed a knowledge of gradations in rank and intimacy that I have never seen in any other animal: men before women, Chinese before foreigners, eunuchs of course above all, and finally my friends before casual acquaintances.

How he sensed my boredom on those rare occasions when a half-stranger had to be shown the house was a mystery; yet after such a visit he was always completely aware of my relief to be free again. When a eunuch toddled in on a formal call, or when the tall old wine merchant, my landlord's intermediary (whose shop was nearby at the rear gate of the Imperial City), arrived for some visit-of-affairs, Erh Niu's pleasure was so great that he would actually crawl under their robes, trying to lie flat and quite concealed. Only with difficulty could he then be extricated.

Yet if some Westerner fresh to Peking from a tourist ship, armed with a letter and passing through for a mere five days, came by hired ricksha from one of the big hotels, to have a cup of tea, Erh Niu's violent barking could only be stopped by his physical removal to the kitchen, in the arms of the secretly delighted Hsü Jung. Then, when the visit was over, and the faded red door of my outer barrier gate had banged shut of its own weight after the departing guest, an invariable and quite complicated ceremony would begin. First the dog would leap wildly over the two intermediate thresholds to rejoin me as I was returning to my inner courtyard, kicking his legs back-

ward and steeplechasing over the high Chinese sills. A ritual of purification followed, round and round the court, as vigorously as he
could run and in the largest possible circles, stopping only to cough
up the hair he had caught in his throat. The same circling, with
renewed scrambling, would be resumed a time or two further. Finally
he would come to me, and stretching himself by a sweeping bow,
very low in front, regard me from under his mop of hair as if clearly
to say: "You really give me almost more than I can bear; yet, as you
see, I perform it!" He would then trot promptly to a comfortable
corner, his duty done, and subside, incredibly flat, his head glued to
the ground. A final sigh or two, and we savored domestic peace, as
I resumed work on a Chinese lesson and life returned again to proper
tranquillity.

Hsü Jung not being Confucian, cared much less for appearances than
did Wên-Pin. So he continued to adore the dog, and many times
solemnly told me with an air of deep belief that the animal understood
everything and could do everything, except speak. On Chinese holidays he dressed Erh Niu's hair elaborately; and over the years a
variety of pigtails and topknots appeared, often resembling the tight
wool-bound brushes or erect fronds on small children's partly shaved
heads, as the Chinese love them. I would often know of a morning
that some feast day had actually arrived because Erh Niu would
appear, trotting self-consciously beside my morning bowl of tea,
decorated with perhaps several high tufts, tight bound in bright-red
or cochineal-pink wool.

The dog took all this as his due; it was we who were the animals
if we did not concede him his dignity. He had only one race of
natural enemies—the marauding cats. If one of these silently appeared
on the curving roofs, he would break into a fury of barking. Mistress
Cat would usually look silently down in disdain, then walk com-
posedly to some other place.

When the days of the war with the Japanese came on, Hsü Jung
invented a new amusement because of this. After the first abortive air
raid (when on a dark midnight my servants roused me by lantern
light, reporting how in the lane it was being passed about that we
should quickly smear Chinese mustard about our nostrils, as an anti-

dote to mustard gas), in time we became quite used to Japanese air-
planes passing in flight over the still peaceful city, bent on more distant
missions with their deadly cargoes. At such times Hsü Jung would hug
Erh Niu tight, or go over to him as he lay in his round basket, and
pointing to the airplane cry: "There are cats, CATS, within the Sun-Root
People's flying boat!" (The Japanese lived in the east, which is, of
course, the quarter of origin of the sun.) Erh Niu never failed to try
to frighten them off, and this always cheered us all. For we loved
our dog, and of course we knew the Chinese proverb: "Cats shift
houses (in time of adversity); dogs do not shift houses."

Erh Niu never lost awareness of his superior identity. He ate with
more moderation, with more decency and cleanliness, than many a
human being. He could be playful, and he could condescend to
special moods of indulgence and tolerance. Yet he always remembered
"who he was"; and his sense of our common property and mutual
duties was ingrained. It was as if the lessons had been learned forever
on the roof of the Asiatic world while in the West, we must presume,
barbarians were still painting themselves—and perhaps even their
dogs—blue.

When I had to leave China, when the fortunes of war had finally
crushed down all our hope for any pattern of life as we could know
it together in Peking, Hsü Jung came to me one day to assure me
that, when I was gone and the dog should become his, if he had anything to eat, Erh Niu also should have something to eat. The good man
made this offer solemnly, knowing how uncertain it might become
who would or who could, eat—in the days that were coming—and
what!

Besides my town residence, in that time of abundance, I also had
one in the country. It lay in the fields several miles from the west wall,
on the way to the "Race Horse Ground," P'ao Ma Ch'ang, where
under the leadership of the British were held the winter paper-chases,
with Mongolian ponies, pink coats, velvet caps and all, in a few of
which I occasionally joined. P'ao Ma Ch'ang itself even boasted of
several poorly imitated half-timbered English cottages, including one—

half club and half dormitory for hunting visitors—that as a whim had been named "The Honourable Week End."

My country house was a small Buddhist temple at some distance from these creations. It consisted of two courts only, a rustic forecourt, much littered with country gear and farm produce, and a spacious inner one. This was shorn of its principal hall, which long ago had collapsed. The space in front of the platform to it, nevertheless, still provided quite enough shelter in the existing side-houses to make it a most comfortable place for withdrawal and country quiet. I could even invite guests, since there had been built, as a modern addition, a separate high-walled enclosure, off center to the rear, with three small extra rooms.

It was not my temple at all, but that of an Englishwoman who left China from time to time on journeys to other parts of the world; and while she was away I kept an eye on it for her and at the same time enjoyed its use. It had originally been occupied by some czarist Russians who had come out to administer the affairs of the Trans-Siberian railway when this had first been put through, so the property had been sufficiently altered, with a well and water supply, wooden flooring and glass windows, to adapt it to the foreigner.

A terraced half-wild external garden, European in concept, opened out from a small back gate. Within this lower walled enclosure, on a bent wood Russian reclining chair, I used to pass hours in the grateful spring sunshine, aware of the passing of time only from the moving shadows of the still bare branches upon the stone-paved walks.

The courtyard within was oddly arranged. After the collapse of the main hall, low brick-bordered terraces had been made from the rubble, following the lines of the original walls. Upon these were set out growing plants, and the shape of the building was thus retained. There was further a curious central structure, really a square brick tower one story high, also built of the rubble, over what once had been the main altar. Steps led to the top; and in the good time of the year, all here was floral greenery with plants in pots, everything open to the sky and a fine view of the tranquil countryside beyond. This place became specially alluring in late summer when the tossing wheat was bleached to light yellow, and the blue-clothed peasants, stooping at their work in near or more distant fields, reminded one strikingly of scenes by Breughel the Elder. Indeed, "Breughel-outside-the-Walls" I named the whole region.

An old guardian lived in one part of the east house; and the few Buddhist images still left, powdered with dust, were kept by him next door in a cluttered storeroom that also was used to house guests' rickshas. He gave these gods a few meager sticks of incense morning and evening, with three blows upon a dirty gong; this was apparently quite sufficient for them.

Behind the guardian's lodging there was further a Chinese greenhouse, half sunken pit and half mud wall, the slanting frames on its sunward side covered with Korean paper. Out of this primitive contrivance, with the slightest of heating from a tiny smudge stove in winter, the guardian's assistant, a simple soul, drew numerous and thriving flowers. In good weather they were transferred in tubs or pots to the tower, or else to the low platforms under it where Buddhas and Lohan had once been enthroned.

Across the tree-paved court, finally, was the west house, where I usually lived when I came out alone. This consisted of an inner bedroom, and beyond it, through an improvised bathroom pleasantly cool and shady in summer, a quite spacious main living room. This my English friend had arranged with the greatest charm. Numerous fantastic mythological Chinese animals—"beasties" as she called them— pranced gaily on scrolls upon its walls. A sure eye for color had made every other object complete their harmonies; and soft opalescent rugs from Kansu covered the floor. The excellent simple Chinese furniture that she had transported from town, was arranged to perfection in this setting.

Whenever the weather lured me, summer or winter, I bicycled to this place from my Wax Storehouse, often stopping to break my journey at the first of the "traveling palaces"—or stations for the Emperor's progresses—outside the walls. This was known to all of us as the Fishing Terrace, since it included a charming pavilion for this purpose, set on a high stone base projecting into an artificial lake. The property had been ceded to one of the last of the imperial Grand

Tutors, and was quite tolerably cared for. It had an extensive tangled garden with some fine rockery and old planting, and a well-drained system of canals intermittently flowing with very clear water.

The Fishing Terrace was the best place, for miles around, from which to watch the cheerful havoc that autumn played with the leaves from ancient trees, spared only in such properties. In the days of crystal purity, of a blessed and almost holy gaiety, that mark the autumn in Peking, sudden heavy showers of leaves would batter one during a walk, coming down as from the sky at some carnival of the immortals. China, in moods such as this, gave more than a foretaste of heaven.

When I finally reached the temple, quiet would gratefully descend. Often, before my tea, I would feel the compelling need of sleep; and from the depths of it I would wake as to another world. I could move about rooms slowly; simple gestures became so deliberate that they recalled archaic elegance. Perhaps I would determine to break the spell, to mount the brick tower and see what was happening to the "Breughel world" outside. Yet a new and even sweeter invitation to meditate would sweep over me, and an hour later I would find myself still comfortably reclining on the divan under the "beasties," my tea tray rung for and brought in, beside me still undisturbed.

It was in this place that I learned how little, in our modern world, we know of simple physical peace. After a day or so of such solitude and repose, even the bones and muscles of my body set themselves differently. Reading or study, instead of knocking for entrance at rigid and half-barred gates to the mind, tranquilly took on simple clarity of meaning.

I could also go on long country walks, from the back gate across the fields. I went partly for the pleasure of seeing what was afoot—man always perfectly matched with nature, at whatever season of the year—but in part also for the mere sensuous pleasure of my return, exercised and relaxed, to this haven of silent peace.

The pottering kindly man who was guardian had been trained to "do for me" alone; and fortunately I liked the simple food that he could cook. We occasionally added to it when I sent him to a nearby hamlet for a handful of some such delicacy as dried mushrooms, or pungent Chinese sausage, to flavor his well-prepared rice. His very age kept the spell intact; neither of us were at all dependent upon the world; and by this arrangement we enjoyed a common freedom from its confusions. In these almost mystic spells of withdrawal, especially on tranquil starlit nights, as I paced the courtyard beside my lamp-lighted shelter within, I knew deeply that here was a better life.

At about this time I was reading the great T'ang philosopher poet, Tu Fu, and also the verses of Po Chu-i, both of whom had much to say about just such impressions and such resolves. Surely their tenderness and detachment, their smiling disillusion with life, and their pity and understanding of how ill it goes for most of us, never could have been apprehended in a better setting.

Ruin, in an ancient country like China, amid appealing simplicity like this, can be accepted smilingly; even the final and greatest ruin of death. Further, since in imagination human beings can prefigure this last irreparable loss, and then retrospectively assay once more the transitoriness of mortal existence, one learns not to reproach oneself excessively for errors of the past, and conceding ultimate defeat, to consult one's intimate moods, one's own quiet and small desires.

The enjoyment of these precious gifts, one learns, the gods will often sanction, however grimly they may trace for us the larger pattern. Under such circumstances man is finally returned, whole, to himself. "So let me live," said the farmer-poet T'ao Yüan-Ming, over fifteen hundred years ago, "thus should I be content to live and die, and without questionings of the heart gladly accept the will of Heaven."

CHAPTER V *Peking: The Grand Design*

IN GENERAL, of course, I dwelt not in the country, but as a townsman, within the walls. Yet even this existence was different from urban life elsewhere. Of all the great cities of the world none can rival Peking for the regularity and harmony of its plan. As a design, it reflects clearly the social scheme that called it into being. And although that scheme has now slipped forever into the past, so powerful and enduring was its expression in terms of space and enclosure, of axis and perspective, that a curious illusion is produced: somewhere, it seems, even if now invisible, the system that created such a marvel must continue. All the citizens of Peking, Chinese or foreign, are conscious of the city's majesty; the sheer breadth of the setting enhances composure and lends dignity to everyday manners.

The plan is composed about a single straight line, drawn north and south through the center of the city. The massive surrounding walls are so regular, except for a single bend at the northwest corner, to accommodate them to a watercourse there, that if one were to fold a map along this north and south line, the east and west sections would very nearly match. Along this riving line formerly went all the authority in the capital, for placed squarely upon it was the so-called Purple Forbidden City, the palace itself. This Great Within, as it was familiarly named, is a perfect oblong, more than half a mile long, and almost half a mile wide. The power of a whole empire had once radiated from this central cell.

About this innermost area is the so-called Imperial City, once completely walled behind a further enclosure of its own, and created for the needs of the palace. Cell thus contains cell. Outside these two ordinary citizens could live; yet a distinction was made between the two great divisions of the population, conquerors and conquered, when the Manchu rulers replaced the native Ming dynasty in 1644. At that time, the new privileged class completely took over a third and outermost enclosing cell, reaching from the Imperial City to the fortified walls; and this is still named after them the Tartar City. The Chinese proper were commanded to live in front of, and therefore "below," the gates to this triple arrangement of cell within cell. The humbler zone was vast, however, and protected by an outer set of walls of its own. It was also slightly broader, so that its ends overlapped a part of the hollow rectangle given to the Manchus. Such is the so-called Chinese City, populous, less well-built, and lacking the spacious palace properties to be found in the Tartar City.

Thus in Peking there are always walls within walls, moat within moat, and gates—pierced by great boulevards—leading to still further gates. The walls themselves, of time-hardened brick, are the pride of the city. Nobly high, massively thick, widening toward their base, and crowned with battlemented parapets like a medieval fortress, they contain the town. Their similarity to European fortification invariably causes surprise; but in its day feudal warfare was much the same all over the world, and attack and defense with archery, in time of siege, everywhere brought about similar forms. So broad are the causeways laid out upon the walls that when they were in good repair, it is said, a number of horsemen could gallop abreast over the top. I have also been told that to make a complete circuit, marking all the bounds, requires a walk of some twenty-five miles. Marines in the American garrison would occasionally set out to do this, timing it as a challenge.

The effect of living within this vast enclosure, so handsomely protected, is definite. The local population trusts the system in spite of all the evidence of modern warfare. Insensibly, one comes to do so oneself. Each of the great gates is solemnly closed at nightfall, to open only at dawn again the next morning. Whatever may befall the following day, the citizen thus feels safe during the watches of the night.

In the center of a more ancient scheme, an even larger city planned by the Mongols, but now north of the Forbidden City, are the Drum Tower and Bell Tower. The drums once thrummed regularly at nightfall from their high platform—old Chinese have described to me the great sound spreading over the rooftops—to tell the burgher that curfew had come. In time of alarm the tocsin could also be sounded from the even loftier Bell Tower, sending its warning to the whole area within the walls. Chinese cities were historically planned in this way whenever possible, the two towers being placed ideally at the intersection of diagonals from the corners of the foursquare walls. This arrangement can be found in Chinese antiquity.

The gates also were important traditionally. Since the Chinese make use of walls, I have once heard it expressed, to "govern by prestige," progress from one zone to another is to any Chinese a matter of importance. At each opening he is quick to sense whether he is to be advanced or stopped. Chinese history and Chinese historical novels abound in critical incidents occurring at such and such a gate. Their names were carefully chosen; their position determined by the laws of geomancy; and even Chinese of only moderate learning know by heart the names of many of the chief gates of their ancient capitals.

Peking, in this most splendid, has gates arranged with the greatest regularity. In the south wall of the Tartar City there are three, including the majestic Ta Ch'ien Mên or Great Front Gate, which gives on to a broad esplanade leading through the center of the city straight to the enclosure of the palace itelf. The Chinese City has the same number, only these are lower, less imposing, and farther away to the south. Each of the east, west, and north sides of the main rectangle has two gates apiece.

So important are these in Chinese eyes that their demolition would rob Peking of something fundamental. Yet the westernmost gate in the enclosing northern wall, alas, has lost its outer tower and barbican. Once, when Wên-Pin was talking of the old days, and of how when the person of the Emperor was in its proper place, the center of the whole grand hive, all had gone so much better, he sighed and said:

"Yet even if he could be put back on his throne again, how could this any longer be made right? Is not the Tê Shêng Mên, the Gate of Triumphant Virtue, now ruined?" This gate, it should be said, is more than two miles as the crow flies from where the Emperor hypothetically would have sat enthroned. So sensitive is the Chinese feeling for symmetry!

The fortification of these largest gates in the outer wall was made as complete as the military science of the age could contrive. A broad moat, further, encircled the whole. By imperial command nearby fields were to be plowed so that the direction of their furrows might impede, rather than advance, invading horsemen.

Militarily, Peking is thus an almost perfect expression of the old Chinese system that evolved it. As the capital, moreover, it had also to be set in proper relation with the whole of the world about, even to the planets. This concern with the entire firmament has no parallel that I know of. Orientation, once complete, was to achieve no less than a complete harmony of man with nature. The Temple of the Sun, therefore, was set within its great enclosure outside the walls and to the east; that of the Moon, its somewhat lesser counterpart, lies—exactly as one would expect—to the west, opposite. The familiar Temple of Heaven is to the south, balanced across the main axis by the Temple of Agriculture, with which it thus creates a pair. It is given its true counterpart to the north, however, where was placed the Altar of the Earth, lying outside the walls. As one moves about within and without the metropolis, the sun and moon, the heavens and earth, are thus constantly in mind. Imagination plays upon these symbols even in daily routine. This is one of the charms of Peking to be found in no other Chinese city.

Color, too, plays a symbolic role. Yellow was for the Emperor, or what was the Emperor's, alone. If one sees it on the cresting of a palace wall, that palace was for imperial use; if it is the color of the glazed tiles of the main hall of a temple, that building also was once designated as imperial. Green came second; it was the princely color, and was used exactly as yellow but of course alway subordinate to it. The common subject used plain earthenware tiles for his roofs— glaze was never permitted—of the ordinary deep gray that is also the color of Peking house walls. Indeed, this neutral gray makes every-where a constant foil to the brilliance of the glazes on the sloping roofs of buildings of consequence. There are also temples named after their symbolic colors. Such are the Black Temple, and the Yellow Temple, north of the city, the roofs of which are of these colors. None of this was ever accidental. Condign punishment overtook those who im-prudently committed follies.

Thus was contrived the grand design; moat enclosing moat, wall behind wall, and compartment opening within compartment, a hierarchy reflecting every gradation of power and influence, a sym-bolism finally embracing the heavens themselves. If architecture in-fluences men unconsciously, is it a wonder that the inhabitants of such a city were indeed more enlightened, more truly cultivated, than those of any other in China? The citizen of Peking is however quite aware that from birth to death he moves in a splendid world of human planning; and because of his familiarity with imperial prescriptions and imperial scale for all such matters, even today he is given special respect throughout the provinces. In this sense Peking remains un-changingly the true capital of China, generally loved, looked up to and admired. If one inquires concerning almost any amenity, one will invariably hear in conversation: "In Peking they arrange it thus and so." That is the criterion.

To describe the whole vast enclosure in detail, neighborhood by neighborhood, would weary the reader. Yet as one went about various regions within the walls, one entered many quarters both diverse and individual.

There was, for example, the aerial purity of the circular Temple of Heaven, crowned with a triple tiled roof of deepest sapphire blue; its flat circular white marble altar, also triple, lay open to the sky. Here, at times of high ceremony, the Emperor knelt to take upon his mortal shoulders responsibility for the welfare of the whole empire. This was a place to return to, remembering Chinese history, at chang-ing seasons of the year. Mist or moonlight, rain or snow, would en-hance one aspect or another of its symbolism.

The Chai Kung, or Palace of Retirement, within this enclosure, was always for me a place of special significance. Here before each sacrifice the Emperor withdrew for several days of purification. A hush always seemed to surround these now empty courts; indeed the whole enclosure of the Temple of Heaven was eternally still. Its broad alleys, planted regularly with cypress trees, were laid out formally somewhat after the manner of a French forest, offering unbroken long perspectives. In snow and sun, with the curving brilliant roofs rising against a pure sky at the end of a vista, the sight could be dazzling.

The Temple of Agriculture, in a separate enclosure across the central line of the city, was its terrestrial counterpart. Here the chief altar was square, since—as every Chinese knows—that is the shape of the earth, in contrast with the round for heaven. The Emperor came to these grounds every spring to plow the first furrow. Symbolically, this readied the whole empire for a new cycle of sowing and planting. The Empress had her corresponding duty to the north, in the grounds of the imperial lakes, where she plucked the first mulberry leaves to feed the cocoons which yielded silk and thus made possible civilized clothing. Like the ceremonies of the Emperor, hers also took place long before dawn: the first man and the first woman of the civilized world must be about their important tasks early, to show the way to feed and clothe mankind. During the bleached hot days of summer, the grounds of the Temple of Agriculture were so abandoned, so utterly deserted, yet still remained so green and shaded, that they then became one of my preferred places for study. Leaving my house by bicycle in the cool of the early morning, I often spent whole days there quietly reading or reflecting.

The plan of the city, of course, provided ample space for religious building. The Temple of Confucius, with its cavernous and empty halls, was placed to the north, where its spacious courts were far removed from the perpetual clamor of the commercial region about the Ch'ien Mên. Not far from the Confucianists dwelt the wild and stormy-looking Lama priests, in the brooding courts of their complex lamasery. The chief Taoists lived outside the city, as if to emphasize their minor place in the trilogy. These I shall describe later. Throughout all the "Cities," however, and especially within the Forbidden City itself, there were temple halls everywhere, shrines and altars in such numbers as are possible only in an ancient capital, where foundations had been lavish and long sustained. How many courtyards could one visit thronged on the great holidays, incense smoking in great bronze censers and gongs striking by the minute; or else private shrines quiet in the sunshine, fragrant with lotus or with peonies.

Then there were the boulevards, the broad avenues that ran almost from wall to wall, especially the long straight ones traversing the Tartar City. Two chief arteries, going north and south, pierced through the residential quarters on either side ôf the palace. At the intersection of these with similar ones running east and west, were Chinese triumphal arches with brightly painted wooden framing propping up high banks of glazed and colored tile. These were the familiar *p'ai-lou*. A Single Arch in the East and West Cities marked the crossings at the level of the outer courts of the Forbidden City. A hollow square of Four Arches, east and west, was erected at more northerly intersections of the main boulevards. These four points, the East and West Single Arches and East and West Four Arches, were the centers for commerce and trade in the Tartar City.

"To have your new foreign pipe fitted with a silver band and then properly engraved," Wên-Pin might say—my teacher had recently named it "Floating Clouds"—"I must go to that good silversmith's at the East Four Arches."

Or Hsü Jung would be having dreams of wealth: "I hear that there will be a great silk sale tomorrow, at the new shop about to open near the West Single Arch."

The trade of the whole Tartar City, and also of the cells within it, clustered obstinately about these four points. When a native of Peking becomes nostalgic, he is not thinking of the Great Within, or wishing himself back in some splendid temple courtyard; more probably he is longing for the savor of brisk trade, the crush of prosperous crowds amid the cheerful babble of native voices, somewhere near one of these familiar *p'ai-lou*. Here ricksha boys must walk their vehicles; here if one glimpses a friend, one must salute promptly before he is borne past on the milling stream. This is Chinese urban happiness.

I had selected a much quieter part of the town to live in, north of the palace. To it—I was later told—most of the serious Western scholars eventually moved. There were good reasons for this; the neighborhood was indeed congenial. Here the half-deserted palace properties were magnificent, tall trees spreading above long unbroken stretches of high wall in the tranquil lanes. Vague regions, in part heaps of rubble, but in part also laid out as little kitchen gardens, often bounded these walls. Here common folk lived in small tumbledown huts, within the fortifications yet almost as if they were in the country. There were also many unpretentious houses like my own, with no gardens attached, yet far less cramped than those for example in the distant Chinese City. In time I came to distinguish quite clearly, as did all true Pekingese, between the manners, even almost the accent, of my own part of town and places as little distant as the East and West Single Arches.

In early summer, in the North City, there were hours when one could hear the insects buzzing in the linden trees, against a background of silence like that of a small country town. The vendors of refreshments settled comfortably under their blue cloth canopies for the long day, completely unhurried, not even seeking trade. Conversation was more tranquil, voices melodious. Occasionally there passed faces of great purity. Life here flowed traditionally; this was my part of town.

At the opposite pole from this was the curiosity of Peking known as the Legation Quarter, an oblong area of some size under the shadow of the south wall of the Tartar City. Here had been erected, much after the manner of an international exhibition, a whole collection of small palaces with adjoining villas and minor appurtenances, arranged for the practice of Western diplomacy. This had grown up as a planned quarter, on land divided among the various foreign powers after 1901; and it presented a most oddly assorted juxtaposition of architectural *tranches de gâteau*.

The buildings of each legation—in my time gradually these became embassies—looked as if lifted bodily from their own country to be set down here in China. Not only were the styles all different, the very hardware on the windows would be French, or Dutch, or British; the plumbing, the tiling, all had been transported at the expense of the state to which the building belonged, to be combined with grosser Chinese materials at hand.

Legation Street, running through the quarter from end to end, with its own iron barrier gates that could be closed in time of stress, presented a succession of the largest of these buildings. Yet there were others in further broad tree-lined streets, named after Marco Polo or other more modern European worthies. Perhaps the culmination of the non-diplomatic buildings was the large, balconied, German hospital, in stern Teutonic Gothic, with an entrance doorway as for some hostel of Knights Templars. It gave on to roomy corridors, where hung highly-colored framed Chinese votive tablets commending the skill of some German surgeon, announcing in calligraphy or even embroidery, for example, how "Spring has returned at the touch of his Wonderful Hands."

The German nursing sisters were dignified women. Their spacious tiled pharmacy, their white-curtained hospital beds, their very embroidered sofa cushions or well-laundered tray cloths, all set and kept high quite different standards from those of the Chinese about them. Many-colored petunias throve in their window boxes; delicious small spiced cakes arrived with the afternoon coffee.

A war lord could rent a suite of hospital rooms here, if he wished to retire for a temporary illness; and then delicately painted concubines, perhaps in garish satin tubular gowns recently purchased in Shanghai, caused no flurry whatever if they shuffled past on their small feet in the broad cool-paved green corridors. It was even rumored that if a patient were accustomed to his daily pipe of opium, this too was conceded. Yet the German Christmas music sung each year in these echoing halls was the best that I ever heard in Peking.

To return to the lordly embassies, the crown of all was of course that occupied by the British. The dinners there, if not the most interesting gastronomically, were the most formal and of course the best served. The very lion and unicorn on the impeccable gilt-edged Bristol of the place cards guaranteed this. The buildings themselves were nondescript, and the general plan of the irregular large "compound" methodless. Yet there were well-maintained and comfortable small houses, glossily painted, with small parlors and small stairs, tiled hearths and much chintz, good books and cheerful fires, rear gardens and stables, all clustered about the ambassador's much larger residence. There was daily also a miniature changing of the guard, with British sentries wearing thick hobnailed boots looking properly wooden as they stood motionless before their sentry boxes at the main gate.

At the French Embassy, the cipher "RF" for République Française was placed over a large archway in late and poor neo-classical style, much like the entrance to some "modern hotel" *de luxe* in a French watering place. There always seemed more glassed-in galleries and echoing passageways here than elsewhere; and one soon became conscious of the click of foreign heels on French parquet. The rooms to which one came for business had French telephones; they rang with French vivacity, French logic, French interruptions.

The Germans had in their time possessed a little Germany, baronially heavy in style; the Dutch lived in commodious red brick houses with white marble trim, everything quite as well scrubbed as was to be expected; and the Belgians had reproduced for themselves a tawny brick villa with the high steep-pitched roofs of medieval Flanders, ornamented with elaborate wrought ironwork. This, we were told, was a replica of one that old King Léopold formerly had presented to the beautiful Cléo de Mérode.

Its example meant little, of course, to the Italians, whose broad and flat-topped regular façades were corniced, rosy, and serene. A handsome campanile soared above their chapel, transported from other skies. The Spanish, less wealthy, had suspended a large gilt shield, flanked with the columns of Hercules and bearing the device "Nec Plus Ultra," in the center of a conventional Chinese gate with crimson doors and lacquer columns, leading inward toward their temporary Spain; and in the main bathroom of one Latin-American house I remember an almost life-sized crucifix, realistically modeled and colored, sharing one wall with an expensive American bath scale.

White Russians, in my time, inhabited the ex-Austrian Legation, dragging out miserable but dignified ends to ruined existences in suites of high-ceilinged rooms heated with glazed porcelain stoves of delicate cream color, which might have come straight from Schönbrunn. In the echoing marble entrance hall below, tablets incised in Latin told him who might stop to puzzle out their sense, vague facts about Franciscus Josephus, Rex et Imperator. In one side court, much overgrown, a Baltic baron, now immersed in Buddhistic studies, once showed me a diagonally striped sentry box, *ci-devant* imperial, straight as if from a toy opera, assuring me solemnly that it was the last of its kind in the world.

The well-heated, large-windowed American buildings took up much space. They included service buildings with dynamos, a tall radio mast, a large drill ground, and well-installed barracks for our Marines, as well as an indoor basketball court that once did duty as a buzzing courtroom when an American judge on circuit came to Peking for the trial of some local *cause célèbre*. The Ambassador's residence was not pretentious, but ample and comfortable, with a portrait of Washington and also a frequently chiming grandfather's clock in its large green-carpeted central hall.

Rumor had it that in planning the houses of the lesser Secretaries of Embassy, a harassed government architect had in his difficulties simply sent out working drawings of local American post offices, which were then reproduced in detail here under the Tartar City walls. One could trace where mailbags might be hauled in at side entrances, and where grilles and counters could be installed, if this were ever required. The tale must surely have been an invention; but the facts fitted.

Entertainment in the various houses belonging to the American staff became under constantly changing personnel much what it would have been in their different local worlds at home. Annually on the Fourth of July, however, converging in rickshas from all quarters of the city, surprising numbers of the patriotic faithful—ranging from lean and serious up-country missionaries to thick-set plethoric tobacco or oil salesmen—would foregather at the Embassy. This was the holiday of the year for a general turnout. Heavily laden tables of refreshment were set out on the lawn, there was lavish ice cream with many sweet cakes; and the Marine brass band, in dress uniform, played through the heat of the long afternoon, heaving up one patriotic song after another, in slowest tempo. My servants used to see me provided with a specially stiff starched white suit, and then stand approvingly to watch me off at the door, in a hired ricksha, on my way to this ceremony.

The local banks, whether American or European, were most catholic in their arrangements for celebration. They all closed not only on both the Fourth and the Fourteenth of July, and indifferently too for the birthdays of the British King, Confucius and Sun Yat-Sen, or even the Emperor of Japan, but also on May Day (for the modern Germans), and above all on the important sporting "fixture dates"— bye-days, the gymkhana, and of course all the horse races, at P'ao Ma Ch'ang.

Grouped about all these disparate buildings was a collection of small shops. Here were the imported materials from which foreign life of Peking was made. The *coiffeur*'s salon was tended by White Russians; I remember once seeing icons and many lighted candles through a rear door that was ajar. My friend, the old-timer Italian wine merchant, was prosperous and paunchy; he also had a large family of half-Chinese children. The cleanly serious photographer came from Germany. His superior shop was large and orderly. Work was accurately done; and his assistants addressed him respectfully in very good Chinese-German. At the tailor's, invisible native workmen using British thread—if one had remembered to specify it—stitched Scotch tweeds for the sports jackets to be adjusted by the polite and talkative English fitter. A complacent and slow-moving French *marchand de comestibles* would calmly sell you *haricots verts en conserve,* in small tins with brass labels, or else great blocks of *savon de Marseille* with the true Castile smell.

So it went; in each embassy one ate the cheese, one drank the

wines, of that country and no other. The table silver, the linens, even
the flower vases, all were from across the seas. Those who lived in
"the Diplomatic," with notable but uncommon exceptions, would
eventually decide to buy fairly dull and expensive porcelains, or to
acquire garish Mandarin robes, which they condemned to the oddest
uses; or they would have Georgian tea services "reproduced" outside
the Ch'ien Mên, since this was considered an "economy." Much of such
dull loot eventually went back, I suppose, to overfurnished European
flats, or else on to further international posts. China, to them, was
not in any way what it had become to me.

It was necessary, however, to make an adjustment with this world,
which wanted me for its dinner parties, in part, I fancy, simply because by education I was obviously a convenient gramophone for use
with multilingual records. Compromise was uneasy, especially by the
time I was attending classes in the university, and obligated to appear
there early each morning—and sitting on a hard wooden bench in a
Chinese gown to listen perhaps to comment on the structure of early
Buddhist society. The two worlds obviously did not mix.

Once, in replying to the repeated invitations of an importunate
hostess, I was sorely tempted to send her merely the trousers to my
dinner suit—wrapped in fresh tissue paper, in a neat Vuitton suitcase
—instead of an answer increasingly difficult to word. My visiting card
could so easily have been placed on top, merely inscribed, "I knew you
wanted these!" Yet I thought better of the dubious prank: Peking
quarrels could easily become violent, and it seemed better to avoid a
stupid entrance to one, the more so because by this time I was already
remote in spirit, journeying happily in better lands by far than those
of diplomatic entertaining.

I was given the name of "The Oyster" for such behavior; yet I knew
the pearl of price that I must not thoughtlessly divulge—and this
nickname did fortunately discourage assault by repetition. I fear, therefore, that I am no source of information for the major dinners of
Peking.

CHAPTER VI

The Face of the Capital

THOSE in the Legation Quarter who lived in foreign-style houses may have had the benefit of sash windows and of laid floors, of plastered walls and even radiators for steam heat, yet they missed much. If such dwellings, moreover, were the property of their own governments which they themselves served, their lives moved as in another sphere. In these asphalted streets the multitudinous sights and sounds of the old capital did not exist. Trees were planted along their well-swept borders as in some model European city; and local peddlers and hawkers were excluded by special police guarding the entrance barriers. The clangor, the vociferousness, the energy of the cheerful and roistering proletariat were here replaced by something restricted. As a mixture it was not alluring.

How different things were in the Wax Storehouse! Here activity was unceasing from before dawn until late at night; the sheer continuity of it rang in my ears. Here was argument, laughter, anger, noisy quarreling—every emotion constantly finding its expression. I was immersed in the life of my own neighborhood, of my own alley. Next door, a young bride, dressed in red like a little idol, might mount her embroidered sedan chair, moved to uncontrollable tears in the last moment of parting from her family. Or a prolonged funeral over the wall would make us much aware of Buddhist ritual, with prayers and chanting through many nights, and routine family wailings during sacrifice times.

I learned much about Chinese ideals of filial piety and family senti-ment—from the doings of neighbors represented to me by my servants as all that these were *not*. On one occasion I even saw a woman wild with indignation "curse the public thoroughfare" as the phrase went, to tell the world with all the energy in her lungs how insupportable had become her circumstances. This was an extreme measure. Yet perspec-tives of local existence from birth to death became familiar to me in many variants during the succeeding years. Finally I could deduce, from my eyes and ears alone, much that cannot be understood until one has lived long as an inhabitant of one of those curious islands, a small neighborhood within a great metropolis.

My dwelling was in the region of the Imperial City called Within the Rear Gate—far indeed from the diplomatic quarter or those side streets in the eastern part of the Tartar City popular among West-erners, where foreign-style houses rose above Chinese walls. The Rear Gate itself was on the central axis. Through it passed a broad boule-vard leading south to the rose-walled, cypress-planted enclosure where dead emperors formerly lay in state after they had been borne for the last time from the adjoining Forbidden City.

From this artery, a lateral opening called the Gate of the Yellow Flowers, or else the Decorated Yellow Gate (both translations fit), led into a maze of smaller lanes, which often were as crooked as the great avenues were straight. Here were the Porcelain Storehouse, the Awning Storehouse, and others, and also my own Wax Storehouse; all once used for provisioning the imperial palace. Entering these lanes, one progressed between blind walls, turning many corners. The un-pretentious shops were small, often not more than open counters, with a room behind them stocked with goods for local needs.

Only when I had lived in Peking for some time did I realize how my servants divided shopping in general. The most superior manner of purchase, the most intelligent as well as most face-conferring, was the private display of articles not shown in a shop at all. They were brought to the house on appointment by a merchant who usually came with an assistant, his wares wrapped in the large blue cloth bundles, or *pao-fu,* that one so often saw in the streets. In the old days, when women did not leave their houses to make purchases, this was the manner in which silks and satins were submitted to the lady of a household. Even in my time, antiques, pictures—mounted as scrolls—and other precious articles were generally sold in this way.

The merchant, or several rival merchants, all familiar with each other, would wait patiently in the kitchen until the master's pleasure was announced. In palaces, special side-rooms near the front gate were set aside for this purpose. They were then ushered into one of the larger living rooms, where they artfully spread out their wares, always saving the best, of course, until the last.

Everything was done with leisure. What was to be considered for acquisition was discussed casually and finally set apart. Purchase was seldom made on the spot, and I do not believe that the merchants actually liked this: it invisibly robbed them of their standing. So while desire—and price—were still only sketchily defined, objects were inspected, and the buyer could reflect on them in what might be their ultimate setting. Such a system kept the "silver man," or the "bead man," or the embroidery or silk merchant, continually on the road; but it also presented insidious temptation to purchasers. In the course of a year fairly large amounts changed hands in this way. The most agreeable form of purchase that I have ever known was a generous show of this kind, or even a double one, after lunch, with surprises perhaps already hopefully installed to await the moment when a group of people, guests together and in good humor, would come from the table.

There were in Peking, however, plenty of superior public shops selling only a single commodity or article. Wên-Pin and Hsü Jung knew the names of the best, as if they were on some Chinese equivalent of Bond Street or the rue de la Paix. In such shops could be bought the best fur hats for winter, of expensive otter skin, or neat white-soled black cloth slippers, or lanterns, or fans, or drugs or tea; each carried goods of quality only. Competitors might be clustered along a single street; thus we knew of Lantern Street, Jade Street, Brass Street, and of big and little Furniture Street. Above all there was the Liu-li Ch'ang, the old glass works, long ago deserted by the glass blowers, but taken over by the best antiquaries and booksellers in the city. These were shops for men of education only.

The larger and more general store, especially for modern silks and other fabrics, had come to exist even in Peking; but it remained a not too well-assimilated newcomer. It never had anything of the solid quality of a dignified old Chinese tea shop, for instance, reputed with justice for its varieties of dried leaves in great canisters, with fresh jasmine or dried chrysanthemum flowers to be added to them. Some of the best tea shops had elaborately carved façades and fine old-fashioned interiors. One was first seated on a stool at a large lacquer table; and preliminary talk with the long-gowned and venerable proprietor, attended by a bevy of younger assistants, had to be unhurried if one were not to be considered uncouth. Finally, some sample or other of the tea recommended was brewed, so that one might try it at leisure before making one's choice.

My servants knew perfectly which shop by reputation produced the best hemispherical black satin men's hats; which one made the most prized thick-soled boots, also of black satin, of a model such as formerly had been used at court. From time to time the Elder Born also told me tales of lavish buying by the *grands seigneurs,* in the time of the princes (when his own family had been prosperous); and of happy inventions—even if only a clever technique to slice mutton wafer-thin, for the popular Mohammedan restaurants—that had made a sudden reputation, as well as a fortune, for some humble shopkeeper.

Auspicious shop names, usually of three characters each, with involved meanings stating that they were "ever flourishing" or "broadly ample" were legion; but the best known became for me—as for everyone locally—merely syllables run off the tongue, pronounced unthinkingly as are familiar shop names in any large city.

The best-known establishments were managed with as confident an air as were even superior restaurants where high officials were accustomed to congregate daily. In any good shop it was unthinkable not to be asked to be seated, while a young apprentice first brought tea. Upon my return to the West I found that unconsciously I had become so accustomed to this amenity that the lack of it struck me forcibly.

Good shopping in China, though, involved much else besides tea drinking. There were many conventions, a number of formulae to be mastered; but the best wares were never shown to hasty barbarians, and if observing custom took time, everyone of consequence had *that*! Visiting shops was perhaps not the richest man's technique for acquisition; but the merchants who were proprietors of a long-established house were secure in their self-respect. Indeed—when they were Philistines—they could at times be comically smug.

All such shopping was far above the local level. With a few exceptions at the Rear Gate, our small examples near the Wax Storehouse were much more like mere provision counters, to which one could run for a candle or a dipper of sesamum oil, for a farthing's worth of pepper or of mustard. Even more immediate was purchase from the armies of hawkers and peddlers, shouting themselves hoarse so that their voices would penetrate into even the most secluded courtyards. Here I had to acquire a new pair of ears to understand what my servants heard unconsciously. Wên-Pin would suddenly appear, to ask if perhaps I wanted to buy some of the large fresh shrimps or new flowering plants that had just gone by my door. Or Hsü Jung would arrive to ask: "Would K'ê the Elder Born [my Chinese name and form of address] enjoy an almanac or calendar like those we ourselves have recently bought?" We could call the peddler back. Did I not hear him, at that very moment, still only leaving my lane?

There were proper times of day for the offering of certain merchandise. It was only after a number of years that I learned by chance that chamber pots were never to be sold in the daylight. To have hawked them thus would have been shamelessly unfitting. So one had to know their cry, and also that their vendor came only by night.

For the many who rose early, there were special hot potations sold at daybreak. One in particular that I much liked was called almond tea; although it really had nothing in common with ordinary tea and was much more like a very hot liquid cornstarch pudding with a fresh almond flavoring. In the frost of a winter morning in Peking, when the wind blew frozenly as if straight from the fastness of Central Asia, this would begin the day as did nothing else. There were also newly fried dough-rings—blown up like *pommes soufflées*—curling and blistery as they arrived crisp from the iron cauldron; or round wheaten cakes, tasting doughy because still hot, their browned tops covered with crumbly sesamum seeds. I learned many cries for the good things to be eaten as the day began, winter and summer; and it made early rising, for study, something of a pleasant conspiracy.

Then would begin the morning roar of Peking. One could listen for it, as for the roar of a distant lion. The din was greater than is easily described; for once the morning fires had been lighted in this unindustrialized city of a million and a half, everywhere near and far there began bargaining and buying, hawking and vending—all at once. It was a cacophony, a pandemonium, that had no counterpart in Europe, even in the noisiest southern marketplace. In China the tone is much more sonorous, the calls more singing, more prolonged. It would swell to a great chorus of rhythmic metropolitan altercation, with every soloist vocal in his turn. Kindling, or cabbages, garlic and leeks, each had its own motif; each had its special praises lifted insistently for a moment above the continuing background of sound.

What in China do the millions who are the poor purchase from the poor? How does one manage busines with no capital? An early start is made from the country with fresh vegetables, let us say; sturdy legs bring them within the walls at a smart pace, in springing baskets suspended from the inevitable carrying pole. Trade is on immediately! He who sells first walks laden least far. Yet if he sells too cheap, when the day is done his coppers will be few. It was touching sometimes to come across a peddler resting because he was obviously weary, or to hear fatigue in some anxious voice, cracking a little as the hours drew on. The desire to outshout, to sell rapidly, made the clamor only more vociferous.

Every edible product, every small necessary, had its peculiar cry, delivered with an intonation like no other. That for fresh persimmons was one thing; that for needles and skeins of thread completely different. There were also ingenious small instruments to produce odd penetrating noises, and thus help in the differentiation. At times the effects strikingly resembled modern music. Small drums on sticks were beaten with weights attached to strings, which twirled to hit their double membranes a smart blow—and then reversed to strike again. The barber twanged a giant tuning fork of unusual penetrating power. There were wooden clappers, trumpets of many varieties, heavy clanging plates of jointed metal for the tinker or the knife grinder. At times the sound swelled to make a canon, or a round of many parts, moving, crossing and recrossing, distant and near.

The clamor was at first distracting. Although I never became quite so oblivious to it as were my servants, yet the day came when I, too, could be quite unconscious of any of the varied sounds continuing to float about me. And yet as some delectable sweetmeat came by, candied translucent grapes impaled on slender sticks, or walnuts alternating with tiny crab apples, glacéed in sugar, at that moment my ear would pick up the sound, and I would send a servant to the gate.

Late in the tranquil nights of summer, one vendor with a broad barrow would often station himself nearby in my lane. He sold a number of cooling drinks, the best of which I thought was cold boiled prune juice, with some of the prune left floating in it—icy, tart, thirst-slaking, and with a remarkably satisfying bitter aftertaste. This peddler jingled in his palm two small brass bowls, one inside the other. The sound, kept up for hours, through association infallibly ended by making me thirsty. So I might send for something from one of his large porcelain jars. On their carts, these men used good, indeed occasionally excellent, porcelain, always badly damaged but stoutly riveted together again, to make a good show.

Such buying and selling was in terms of merely a few coppers. There was always a little argument first, some chaffer; but the conclusion generally came promptly. The poor, I observed, had constantly to recalculate their purchasing power, in the face of such hourly temptations. Yet they often indulged themselves with a ha'penny worth of some little delicacy or other; and this must have helped to compensate for a diet in general monotonous, except during fresh vegetable season in the spring, which everyone publicly enjoyed.

As I reflect on the good-natured bargaining and the interest with which all this went on, the warm sounds of North Chinese voices come floating again to my ears. Even here, the traditional good manners of the capital, of a civilized people, were observed. As vendor and buyer stood in the lane, a ricksha boy might wish to pass by, progressing rapidly. He would shout ahead, "Draw to the side, draw to the side!" or else, "Lend me light, lend me light!" (by removing yourself from my path), with proper politeness, to give adequate warning. All things could be done nicely, was the unspoken premise; and such human needs are always simple enough to be sensed promptly.

Even in the deepest courtyards, in the grandest houses, the sounds of the world outside were never completely hushed. But in such places they became, as it were, a motif familiar in another part of the symphony, vibrant elsewhere but here repeated pianissimo, to enrich a further melody in a changed and beautiful setting.

There were also the shows of the street, the ever-changing spectacle of the great city. Here, too, I had to learn what I was seeing; some explanation beyond what met the eye was essential. At funerals, for instance, the chief mourner, dressed in unhemmed and unbleached coarse white stuff—to show how grief had abased him—his long wand in hand, headed a procession in front of the catafalque. He customarily stopped briefly at several, or even at quite a number of places along the route, where an unsteady table with crockery for tea had been set up, often hastily and only a few minutes before. There followed mutual bowing, prostration on a mat casually flung out for him; the cups were drained and the procession resumed. What precisely did this mean?

At grander funerals it all came clear. The friends of the dead man, being civilized, were concerned to offer refreshment to his mourners on their sorrowful journey. The best *ch'a p'êng*, or tea sheds, for this purpose were still of matting, to be sure, but they had elaborate roof ornaments simulating those on temples, and the furnishings within might include large altar sets of heavy cloisonné, rented for the occasion. Here the ceremonies proceeded with decorum. Yet if subsequently one saw the mourners of a humble funeral stopping at several merchants' door fronts, and small tables whisked into place with only a few minutes to spare, later to be just as promptly removed again, one now knew the reason.

Funerals and weddings, of course, were the great public shows. My servants followed both, indifferently, with unflagging interest. The bellowing of the deep horns and the almost continuous thunder of the drums were so alike that Wên-Pin or Hsü Jung were themselves occasionally uncertain, and would have to run out to make sure. For funerals, the fact of importance was the number of bearers of the catafalque. They came in multiples of eight, such as sixteens, thirty-twos, or the very grand sixty-four. It took this number of men to support the red-lacquered poles, with their crossbeams, under the heavy framework. When sixty-four bearers were used, yoked to some great swaying superstructure, people often left their work for a little and went to look on.

Nothing so large as this biggest catafalque, with embroidered satin curtains swinging from its lofty curving roof, would fit into a small lane. The accommodating entrepreneurs, however, had a remedy for this. On the day of the funeral, or even one or two earlier, two cata-falques would be sent to the family patronizing them. The first, or great one, was delivered to some open spot near the dead man's house, where it was set down empty on scarlet lacquered wooden horses, to be admired for its stateliness by the neighbors. Then a smaller one went up the lane; and the funeral would begin—with concerted violent weeping among the mourners—by the respectful transfer to it of the coffin of the deceased, through his own doorway. The further change, and the formation of the larger procession, occurred in full view of the town. So relatives were not debarred from offering this posthumous satisfaction even to those who lived within "little gates."

Some of the largest funeral processions stretched literally over several miles. I remember a monstrous one that brought the whole traffic of Peking to a standstill for the better part of a morning, with a catafalque so high that the electric trolley lines had to be propped up to let it through. A war lord, distinguished also for his patronage of culture, was being buried.

"To him who hath," in such cases, were also now given many further gifts. They were of paper, to be sure, and made only to be burnt; but they still might help a former patron or friend to enjoy a foreign motor car or a brass bed—or even in these latter days, his own radio cabinet—as soon as they caught up with him in the spirit world after becoming invisible in the flames.

One of the most interesting processions that I ever saw was for the obsequies of an old prince. It was in completely old-fashioned style; and one day I unexpectedly found it marching along in an out-of-the-way part of town. Besides the usual paper models, there had also been included for this aristocrat the whole panoply of what seemed to me completely medieval hunting. Only this, for some obscure reason, was real. There were camels with folded tents lashed to their backs; there were several falcons, hooded, on the wrists of marching falconers; there were even a few very thin hunting dogs, all passing in procession.

The Chinese delight in such a show. It usually was headed by a professional major domo who knew how to keep moving, or how to stop, the whole unwieldy train behind him. The signaling was complicated. With him also went men bearing large banners, on which were two great characters reading K'AI TAO or "open the road." The regalia that followed—rented of course—was of gilded lacquer, showy and effective, including pairs of arresting symbols such as upright human hands, mounted on high poles. These were invariably borne by poor devils, or remarkably dirty and ragged urchins, dressed in flapping funeral livery of blue or green coarse cloth picked out with large white disks. They were eventually paid a few coppers for their rather disorderly participation; and they were known in general to be a nuisance.

Preceding the coffin walked the company of male mourners, the chief of them usually pale from much night watching and ceremonial kowtowing. At the rear followed a string of rented glass coaches, horse drawn "foreign-style" vehicles, bearing the female mourners, also in unhemmed clothes and with curious thickly platted headbands of the same coarse white stuff. These women were usually rocking with grief and weeping loudly. It was of course in part a customary demonstration, but in part it was uncontrolled sorrow. Funerals always achieved this perplexing mixture of worldly display combined with unrepressed emotion.

Wedding processions gave a somewhat similar effect, although on the whole they were less elaborate. They also could set up a curious intensity of emotion in the spectator, with the constant blaring of

trumpets and the dinning rumble of the drums. One never saw the
bride, since the embroidered curtains of the phoenix chair—hers for
that single day of her life—were always tightly closed (and everyone
wondered how she felt inside). Certain female relatives of maturer
years in charge of matters, however, were customarily carried home
from the ceremonies, later in the day, in chairs that were partly open
in front. Their uncovered glossy hair was invariably dressed with
precision; they were in their immaculate best silks; and everyone
looked on, realizing that they had been upon serious business.

After I had been invited to a few weddings, I learned what happened indoors. It was long and complicated. The bride, that very day
presented for the first time to her husband, was always unbelievably
modest and respectful. Tradition demanded that she keep her head
down, from humility, when spoken to; but she usually let it droop,
literally, under its elaborate phoenix headdress. These days the headdress is usually of chemically dyed crimson chenille, an intense color,
cheaply trimmed with glass pearls. In all her finery, the bride makes
herself as self-effacing as possible. I never saw one who did not seem
painfully weary from fullness of emotion.

In my lane, I heard of course constant talk of weddings and of
matchmaking in general. Criticisms of suitability, and blunt and unabashed curiosity about the outcome, were perennial matters for
gossip. A wedding, like a funeral, was definitely one of life's "big
affairs," as the Chinese classify them; and other people's destinies
always made good material by which to appraise one's own. Was not
traditional Chinese marriage, further, the most hazardous gamble of
all—even to a people deeply fond of gambling?

The street, however, had more to offer than these major shows,
surviving so little altered from the traditional past. There were smaller
processions too. The bride's gifts, for example, were usually carried
openly to her future home a day or two before she herself was borne
there. Among the wealthy this was often made an opportunity for a
very pretty public display. Lacquer-framed vitrines, like glass coffins
in a fairy tale, held all the new finery; everything in pairs when
possible, and arranged to show to advantage as it went through the

streets. Porcelain ornaments usually followed the silks and satins; and the larger objects, cupboards and beds, tables and chairs, all the installation of the future household, also walked along, on porters' legs, drawing up the rear.

Or some grateful patient, attributing his recovery from an illness to the skill of his Chinese doctor, would present a laudatory inscription, usually of four large characters carved or painted on a large oblong board, to add to a collection probably already suspended outside the latter's gate. Certain doctors had so many that they must have contrived to make the process cumulative; they were compared to famous healers of old, even to sages and immortals. What "face" this gave! Perhaps one would hear a merry jingling in the distance, and soon large tiered food boxes, many layers high, would also appear borne springily along. The presentation would therefore, we knew, include a banquet. By tradition little flags and bells were attached to these boxes, to express with what joy the feast they contained was offered. The whole paraphernalia was customarily rented.

I came too late, of course, to see the Manchu Bannermen, in brocade coats simulating more virile armor, or any of the imperial archers; and I only heard tales of the Emperor's processions, when the whole length of the route had first carefully to be sanded in imperial yellow. Yet since the Eastern and the Western tombs— where lay the sepulchers of the last reigning house—were several days' journey afoot from the capital, one can imagine the scale of preparations for an imperial funeral. An aging missionary friend had as a boy stood on a hill near the neighboring city of T'ung-chou to watch one of the last of these, which he described to me. Every dignitary in the land who could possibly manage it was in the select company immediately accompanying the catafalque. They must have constituted a portrait group of the highest ministers of state, as they walked slowly along.

Emperors who lived to old age also had great birthday celebrations. Occasionally, on the grandest of these such as a sixtieth—which completes a full cycle, as Chinese time is reckoned—they might be borne in a partly open chair for a part of a journey, perhaps from the Summer to the Winter Palace. Since everyone had nevertheless to touch his head to the ground as the procession passed, this cannot have afforded the population a prolonged view.

In one of the halls of the Forbidden City I used often to examine several giant scrolls, each many yards in length, representing such festivities. On them were shown in detail the booths and platforms erected for plays and other public shows, each contributed by some local guild, or by various provinces and cities throughout the Empire. None of this, of course, would ever occur again.

Yet I just managed to catch the last vestiges of princely scale, first in a three-day birthday party, complete with elaborate threatricals, for the venerated mother of a deeply filial prince of the imperial house; and later at her funeral, for which, although already more than half ruined, her son determined to provide every satisfaction in the next world that a Chinese funeral can give. On this occasion, the same private theater that had served for the earlier one was transformed into a mortuary chapel. While waiting for a first procession to leave the palace, bearing a great paper spirit boat to be burned at a cross-roads—a ceremony to which a number of foreigners had been invited—we sat drinking tea at the very same tables that had earlier served for the more cheerful festival. Thus I knew at least a little how some of these larger shows must once have been managed.

There were other ceremonies that one also was never to see again: for instance, the return from early morning audiences in the For-bidden City, customarily held before dawn. At that hour, my Elder Born explained to me, it was obvious that men's minds were at their keenest, just awakened from sleep, to take counsel on affairs of state. This was the fitting time for audience; did I not feel it within myself? Each courtier had a bodyservant, a *kên-pan-ti*, who waited at the palace gates. Master and man both were mounted; and as they rode away from the palace, and the sun rose, the master customarily divested himself of his long necklace of court beads and his topmost layers of clothing. These were literally thrown to the *kên-pan-ti*, riding after him, and they had to be properly caught. The servant first ex-tended his arm to catch the beads; the clothes were next taken over, and even folded as the ride continued. Thus the whole became a display of pride and insouciance on the one hand, and of skill on the other.

It was not easy to imagine the brilliance and dignity of the old reunions, I was told, with everyone apparelled in fine stuffs, in brocades and satins, or in summer in fine gauzes, with embroidered hems of rainbow colors. I have seen Mongols so dressed, riding their ponies over the high plains; and the effect was that of a magnificently illustrated storybook come to life. How much the modern world has lost by choosing dull black for formal male costume!

At the season of the Chinese New Year, one could occasionally see venerable Peking conservatives, making their rounds of calls, still wearing old-fashioned clothing. Its rich color showed how the major notes had once been struck. What must it have been, though, when the groupings were not of individuals only, but of hundreds? It was always told to me further that the Manchu aristocracy traditionally dressed with the greatest care and neatness; and that they particularly prided themselves on the colored sashes of rank that could be worn by them alone.

There was one convention about the use of color that even in my time had not fallen into neglect: the young usually wore the brightest, the old the softest and most muted shades. Little babies were given brilliant quilted coats, often made with a hundred different pieces of silk—all begged from neighbors—to deceive the jealous spirits into making errors of mistaken identity. Small children, carried like idols on the arms of proud parents, would also be bundled into little capes of vivid scarlet or vibrant green, with a whole collection of gold *repoussé* images on their small headdresses. The old, on the contrary, wore shades of dull blue, or dark plum color, or dim grays like the estuary of a river in a fog. For them, these were considered fitting, dignity matching dignity, in their final years.

I have seen old gentlemen riding silently in glass-paned coaches, a footman leaping down from behind to guide the horses round a corner, who were living examples of what seventy or eighty years of the old-fashioned discipline finally could do, in China, to the human frame. They might be bowed with the years, shrunken even, but majesty dwelt consciously upon their white heads. They invariably wore such colors as darkest green, the browns and grays of tree bark, or dull steel, or else a quite indefinable purple-blue-black; relieving the simple cut of their gowns usually with a single idiosyncratic touch, as for example in summer a fan made of eagle's feathers, with perhaps a crystal pendant swinging from its spotted bamboo handle, or a spectacle case of green sharkskin or of black satin embroidered with metal thread.

I have never seen old age more grandly self-respecting, or more self-justifying. The modern Westerner loses enormously by not comprehending what high ranges, both of appearance and conduct, are accessible to those who have actually cultivated their later years. This single mistake, and the consequent mismanagement of all our possibilities from middle age onward, puts us worlds apart from those Chinese within the traditional system. We wax happily, but wane with ineptitude. The last part of life we tend to abandon even to despair, whereas for the Chinese it is a summit, for the very reason that it has been built by human wisdom alone upon a notoriously fragile and transitory base.

These hard-won honors of longevity could not be assumed too lightly by anyone without severe censure. My servants would quickly comment if a man only in his forties began to cultivate his beard. "It is not fitting for So-and-So," they would say, "to stop being clean-shaven, and to affect drooping whiskers, when the time for these has not yet arrived!"

The city's show never ceased. Sometimes there would appear in the streets country people in mule drawn, slow-moving, two-wheeled "Peking carts." These had once been quite ordinary vehicles; but the fashion had passed, and they were now used only by prosperous and conservative provincial folk. The stout framework of such a cart was in general heavily ornamented with metal bosses; and its small square of flooring might be covered with several layers of thick-piled carpet, woven to size, to make sitting cross-legged within more comfortable. (Even at that Peking carts almost jolted the breath out of one's lungs; I know it because in the country I have used them.) Cloth awnings were made fast to the long shafts, and the cloth cover for the arched hood of the cart itself often also had elaborate cut-out scroll work stitched in contrasting color at the corners. A fitted Peking cart thus rolled at one, on its lumbering high wheels, straight as if from the Middle Ages.

These were the anachronistic touches. The modern city moved in quite another type of vehicle, the go-cart of late invention, ill-balanced on its two rubber-tired wheels, known to the Chinese as a *jên-li-ch'ê* or "man-strength-vehicle." From Japan, where it was apparently contrived, we have borrowed a similar word for it, jin-ricksha; and then shortened this by docking the first syllable. These existed in Peking in every stage of newness or disrepair; they swarmed over the city and the adjacent countryside. One saw them polished and shining, all of glossy black brass-trimmed lacquer, with perhaps a fat merchant being jostled rapidly along "topside," lighted from below at night by his own gleaming carriage lamps, pressing a clanging bell set in the carpeted floor with his slippered foot to clear the way for speedier passage. Or one saw wretched and tottering old men who had to walk rather than run, so decrepit were they, dragging creaking wrecks unevenly loaded with every conceivable object.

This use of men as beasts of burden, however, was not so cruel as we in the West too readily may assume. I remember how an early teacher told me: "A younger puller is always careful, if people are riding in pairs, never to outdistance an older partner. Would not this be disrespect to old age?" Further, in all my years in Peking, I never saw a Chinese peremptorily order a ricksha boy to go faster than the pace that he himself had set; although Westerners, always in a hurry, occasionally did. Conversation, also, between the Chinese passenger and his human motive power was frequent, voluble, and unabashed.

Yet it was known to be a hard life. The men were often wet through from exertion, in rain or snow, at times when they could not change clothing. In bad weather, while waiting for fares at corners, they crouched miserably on the floor of their vehicles, between the shafts, unprotected except for a canvas hood drawn over the seat in back, forced to endure whatever the season presented. Also, their coppers had to be earned first to pay rent on their vehicles, which they seldom owned. Life thus often became an unending and bitter struggle with debt.

I remember, however, one beautiful spring evening, after a hard winter, when the transparent night sky had taken on an effect of finest satin, with a moon scudding between banks of soft fleecy clouds. In a quiet open place by a temple wall not far from my gate, spring breezes intermittently lifted the tender streamers of a large weeping willow. Under its great trunk sat a ricksha boy, whom I wanted to hire. He would not pull me, though, and he made it clear. His time had come for a mood of reminiscence; winter was over and this luxury he would have. Later, when the vendors of night foods would tempt him with their clinking brass bowls, and he might feel that a steaming portion of hot savory noodles would be worth further effort, he would move. At the moment, though, he was at peace with the world. He politely and quietly waved me away.

There were other curiosities upon the street peculiar to a North Chinese city. Toplofty camels were our local beasts of burden. It was they who delivered our coal, mined not far away. Coal itself, of course, had been used by the Chinese for centuries. Marco Polo, in recounting his travels, at the end of our thirteenth, has a detailed passage expressing his wonder at the "black stones" that the Chinese "dig out and burn like firewood." In Peking I learned not to be surprised to find my whole lane blocked from time to time by a string of laden animals, resting solemnly on the ground, having recently traveled with their burdens up from the mines.

In the spring, when their thick coats peeled, the camels became repulsively mangy; and as the weather grew warmer, whole trains of them, now looking as if they were made of badly scorched leather, made for the uplands, where the climate agreed with them better. Yet autumn would see them back; and as the days turned cold their good camel hair grew in again, reminding us that winter was ahead. Beyond the walls it was a common sight to see long lines on the march in single file, padding slowly against the horizon like some picture of Bible lands. Country merchants who owned them had the gates to their farmyards cut broader at the top, so that the laden beasts could pass through with their swelling loads high in the air.

Horses, in this much-used land where grazing was an expensive luxury—indeed nonexistent in the form we know it—were of course much more costly than the more familiar mules and donkeys, and they were never used by the people generally. The Mongol ponies that we saw in Peking, imported from the uplands, were kept chiefly by Westerners for polo, or for exercising on the *glacis* surrounding the Legation Quarter. This, in Chinese eyes, was merely one more unaccountable foreign habit, gratuitous and therefore quite foolish exertion on the part of the obviously rich. The ponies were small and quick, but they betrayed their untutored origins by the bad habit of stumbling, on ground unfamiliar to them after their high untrammeled pastures.

It is man himself, however, who in China is the beast of burden. The role of the animals has apparently always been subsidiary. The cow was neither liked nor easily cared for; where was there pasturage for it? Through the breadth of the land it was the scavenger animals, pigs and chickens, which fitted best with the native economy. In Peking, pigs were sold alive in a thriving market, perhaps half a mile from my lane; and on a windless day their prolonged squealing, during the market hours, was borne to us from the scene of their sorrows. They were often wheeled there trussed up in filthy rickshas, slightly too human to be regarded comfortably. Yet, for contrast—such was China—even at that moment an aeolian orchestra of pigeons might be wheeling overhead, light bamboo whistles attached to their tails fluting through the air with graceful sound.

Man made no protest at what seemed to him his place in this destined order of things. Those of stouter frame earned their living with their bodies, their natural capital. So much of the routine of daily living was made of simple muscular labor that it gave a curious and quite archaic beauty to the life of the city. The water carriers, staggering with heavy barrows along every bumpy lane, were typical. They came almost always from Shantung, where men are stocky. A broad leather strap attached to the wooden handles of the creaking barrow passed over their shoulders; and it required great strength and care to keep a laden and sloppy cart from tipping on the uneven ground. Courtyards might be paved, this was part of their value in

Chinese eyes; but the open thoroughfare where men struggled and labored was normally of earth and earth only.

Men also carried all heavy objects, when possible on their heads. How often did one see a massive piece of furniture with only a bent torso and straining legs beneath it, coming gravely down a street, like some monster—half cabinet and half man—invented by Hieronymus Bosch. These porters were never talkative as they waited for employment; their livelihood must have schooled them to patience, for loads were bulky and progress slow. Yet damage rarely came to an article thus transported; and whole households might be transferred at will, without packing—everything going upon the road in this manner.

There were also familiar artisans, the men whose occupations could be told at a glance, if one were acquainted with the tools of their trade. The carpenter carried his box of saws; but they were not like ours. The tinker came to work in one's own court, arriving to solder metals or to rivet porcelain. On his shoulder pole, somewhat like the barber, he carried both his work bench and balancing it a small cabinet, usually much brass-ornamented and provided with rows of small drawers. This he would also sit on when he began to work.

There were musicians, both seeing and blind, whom one could hire to come and deliver ballads within one's own courts. A certain cheerful troupe sang them even while dancing on stilts, men taking the women's roles, with suggestions of costume. There were trained animals, for shows in the lane itself, with a collection to be taken from bystanders at the end of the performance. Or one could summon them also to one's own court, as an amusement for friends. There were trained goats, trained dogs or monkeys, and even trained mice who ran up ladders to flag-topped towers, and then down again. Witty speeches to the animals always made up a part of the performance; and the simulated dialogues never failed to draw laughter from the gaping crowds.

There was one man who sometimes came to our neighborhood with a traveling library of picture books for children. He carried these, with a diminutive table as well as tiny stools to go round it, all upon his own shoulders. Wherever he set up shop, the children invariably gathered. For a penny they could have their books, at which one might find them sitting, with much chatter, under some familiar tree not far from one's own door. This, though, was a summer amusement only.

Men made candy figures of spun brown sugar; or they modeled wax, or molded other toys, as one looked on. A goose might go by imprisoned in a wicker cage, its projecting neck and head dyed deep pink, for identification from other flocks in the country ponds whence it had come. This meant that a betrothal was going forward. The prospective groom, in old-fashioned families, always sent one of these birds to his unseen fiancée, to have it express by its cries his own longing for the consummation of the match!

Old men in wide-cut garments would come gravely walking along swinging pairs of large circular bird cages in each hand. They were taking their favorites for exercise; this, we were told, made their song better. They invariably congregated in special tea houses for bird fanciers, which were always thronged. In the open spaces near the city walls, falcons were trained to fly aloft for seed flung into the air by the spring of a curious demountable bamboo rod, with a little horn cup attached to its end. Their talons were so sharp that they were allowed to perch only on heavily padded guards on the forearms of their owners.

Then there were the lusty or crippled beggars, all surprisingly cheerful; or else women overtaken by some calamity, and burdened with their children. The history of their sad case, written in large Chinese characters, would be set out on a sheet of dirty paper weighted with stones and spread upon the ground before them. One read; and left a copper or two. Or there would be the rag woman, usually incredibly wispy herself, searching everywhere like a witch for snippets of old cloth, which she carted off in a coarse osier basket adjusted upon her back, giving poor little boxes of most inferior sulphur matches in exchange. This cloth was later soaked and pasted upon large boards, layer upon layer, to thicken and dry in the sun and later be cut off to make coarse soles for the cheapest grade of slippers.

Ingenuity, in a thousand ways, made use of everything conceivable. Fresh lotus leaves, for instance, in summer commonly served us for wrapping food. One might dine in an outlying restaurant, and liking the fare, ask to have a sample of some dish to take home. (This was often done: what had been ordered belonged to the guest.) Nothing was easier than to oblige; and a great pancake of living green leaf, gathered in with bright magenta hempen cord, served as a wrapper.

A striking contrast to this panorama of the profane world was made by the priests, either Buddhist or Taoist. Because the cut of their clothes was so old-fashioned, and so much ampler than that of even ordinary Chinese dress, they always stood out along the street. They never seemed to impose any intentional disparagement; but they brought with them a sense of another world. The Buddhist gowns for street wear were black, and cut like Japanese kimonos at the throat. Indeed, centuries before, the latter had been the customary Chinese garment, and had been copied in the islands. Taoists wore curious hollow hats, their long hair drawn through the brims and gathered into topknots kept in place with jade or wooden pins; this was a most archaic arrangement. They also generally went about in half-length coats, wadded in winter, made up of a number of black and blue patches. Many were exceedingly poor, and some wandered perpetually; yet for a priest who had been properly ordained there was always the assurance of at least three nights' food and shelter, in any monastery the length and breadth of China. This was the custom.

Whether Buddhist or Taoist, these were familiar figures; although the Confucianists, as moralists, had no priests. During the Japanese occupation, the conquerors brought with them another, proselytizing, variety. These were also Buddhist; they went about the streets in pairs, wearing curious limp caps of dark pleated cloth, and coats shorter than was usual in China. Their thick leg muscles were some-how also very Japanese. They tapped ceaselessly on small drums making a most hollow, otherworldly, sound. Its measured rhythm was insistent: "Come away! Come away! Hence, hence!" again and again, it seemed to say.

The blind, too, moved in a world of their own, never stirring with-out constantly striking a gong that easily identified them. So sonorous was it that one could hear a blind man through his whole course in a neighborhood. There were pathetically many; but this was as nothing, my servants said, to what it had been in the old days, when the small-pox had raged. "Fate has granted happiness to some; to others this destiny!" they explained. The world was made that way.

I thus began to comprehend, by a thousand sights and sounds, the unceasing life of the city. Clothing also gradually revealed many shadings; but it took time until I could interpret these correctly. The fluttering old-fashioned garters tying in an old man's trousers at the ankles, perhaps of cerulean blue to contrast with his dignified black silk clothing; or the handkerchief tucked in at the nape of a country girl's neck, to keep her pomaded and shiny back-knot from soiling a new and carefully pressed blue cotton-wadded gown: each of such details came to suggest a local, finally some familiar circumstance. Scraps of sentences, facial expression, also became increasingly intelligible. The street was speaking its familiar tongue; and as time went on I knew that I could understand it.

It was of course for everybody. When the spectacle was not free—as formerly when the Emperor moved abroad—then looking on was specifically forbidden, at the risk of grave punishment. Otherwise the assembly of even a large crowd, actively engaged in remarking upon whatever curious sight had collected it, was never in Chinese eyes cause for offense. The street, the world, was public property. This was the poor man's great show; and also his education.

CHAPTER VII   *The Forbidden City*

IN THE center of all this activity, at the focus of the plan, was the
incomparable, the majestically "Forbidden" City. Stately walls, rising foursquare from a broad surrounding moat, here closed in the
marvel of all China. Madder rose, a natural soil color, dyed its plaster
walls a purplish pink; and its roof tiles were glazed in deep imperial
mustard yellow. Add to this the shimmering foliage of trees in summer, or a frosting of glittering snow on the sparkling roofs when
winter had come, all under the immaculate blue sky of North China,
and the color scheme is complete.

We have seen how the Forbidden City was itself the innermost of
three inscribed rectangles comprising the chief area of Peking. First
came the giant brick walls of the Tartar City proper. Then, already
far within, was the enclosure of the Imperial City, once provided with
complete circuit of its own rose walls, now in great part torn down—
although the entrance gates remain. These were topped with green tile,
the secondary color. Within this already special reserve was finally
the palace itself, the "Purple Forbidden City"; purple either in allusion to a constellation that includes the pole star—round which all the
others turn—or else directly to its color.

It was forbidden very literally. If access during the day was a
special privilege to those highest in rank in the empire, after dusk
and until dawn again, except for eunuchs on service, the Emperor
was literally the only male within its miles of avenues and corridors.

While the system that created it continued, nothing within those haughty curtain walls was ever to be glimpsed by a subject unless—most improbably—he were specially to be summoned. Here was the most strictly guarded soil in the Central Kingdom.

I arrived in Peking, of course, when all this already belonged to the past and the empty shell alone remained. It had been divided to make two museums, administered by the state. Yet the ambition was soon burning brightly within me to explore all that I still could of its mysteries. Even if it required much planning, and great patience, I was determined to get to every corner possible. This continuing desire received its final rewards only after years had passed.

The maze was itself a wonderful puzzle. Progressing northward and inward from the swarming Chinese City, through the Great Front Gate, one had first to traverse a long and broad esplanade. One then crossed a first row of five marble bridges, passing through a further massive gate to arrive at an enormous forecourt. Towering at the back of the open space were finally the palace walls. Here was the entrance to the hive of some rare species of insect; and as if to emphasize this, within every roof turned to imperial yellow.

The main portal was the Wu Mên, or Noon Gate, facing due south. It must surely have been the finest in the empire, as was fitting. Here the massive rose walls were pierced with five deep barrel-vaulted tunnels. Above the battlements rose a group of harmonious, yellow-roofed pavilions so large that a whole historical museum was later installed within them. The five entrances below were arranged as follows: the central one was for the Emperor alone; no one could use it except himself, or those in his immediate train. A vaulted passageway to the east, pierced in the same wall, was for civil officials, who thus held the Chinese place of honor, on the left. A symmetrical passageway to the west was reserved for the military. These two were for the great officers of the land. Two minor entrances, finally, one at each side, served for lesser functionaries. At the main entrance to the "Great Within," a five-fold division of rank was thus established.

From his throne, any one of the number of them placed in hall after hall along the central axis, theoretically the Emperor could see from this entrance through the Tartar City, through the great Ch'ien

Mên, or Front Gate, and then further to the wall of the Chinese City with its own gate, and open country beyond—all down a central avenue straight as a hair. This part of Peking was as if laid out on a chessboard.

The east wall of the palace had a single entrance, the East Flowery Gate. This was used by civil officials when they came to their special Hall of Audience within, for the courts customarily held before dawn when the Emperor was in residence. The west wall of the Forbidden City also had its symmetrically placed entrance, the West Flowery Gate, for the military when they came to their hall, also before dawn.

The Emperor never saw these officials; they prostrated themselves far from the throne room, which was distant within. Only the very highest officers were ever granted personal audience. Distance thus symbolized humble respect. However strange this may seem today, one must not refuse to take seriously a system that while it lasted commanded the respect of millions of loyal subjects, men who regarded their nation not as one among many, but as the civilized and true center of the world, the Middle Kingdom.

Within the perfect rectangle to which these gates gave access were courtyards without number. Broad high-walled palace avenues, treeless and paved, separated the main blocks. Only at the rear, in the center of the north wall, was there a further and last gate, towering behind a final zone of highly artificial garden. This was known as the Shên Wu Mên, the Gate of Divine Martial Vigor. There were no other entrances—still less any asymmetrical wicket or postern gates. Behind a broad moat, the imperial bodyguard could protect these four entries, one for each point of the compass, in security.

How was the interior planned; what principles determined the subdivisions? Once one had grasped its chief purposes, the scheme was not complicated, but remarkably simple. The Great Within was divided into three parts. To the south were the chief halls for public audience or public acts; to the north was the private area of dwelling palaces, not only for the Emperor and his Empresses—since he might have several—but also for the numerous concubines, whose persons were referred to obliquely and politely, in China, as "Side-Houses" because of this very arrangement.

Then, between the public and private areas, and to provide isolation for the latter, was what I always thought of as a "Courtyard of Separation" with only low buildings of its own, but with many lateral entrance-ways and ramps. Its paved area was vast and open. To present distance was apparently its single function. Covered with snow in winter or under the hot summer sun, it represented simply an interposition of space, on a magnificent scale, to divide the Emperor's private from his public life.

Each of these three areas had little-known courts or buildings to be explored, or offered details peculiar to itself alone, as I shall explain. Yet one feature was common to all: the central axis. This invisible line was the Emperor's, and his only. When he was in complete privacy, perhaps with his ladies walking in the paved rear garden of the palace, or else during the day with relatives in one of the more tranquil side courts; or when he moved forward to the outer palaces for a ceremony in one of the so-called "Three Great Halls," his presence was always significant directly in proportion with his nearness to, or his position upon, this central line.

Each palace hall was raised a formally prescribed distance from the ground level, upon its own platform. Height emphasized dignity, and triple terraces with white marble balustrades elevated the chief buildings. So ingeniously planned were these raised terraces in relation to the backdrop of Coal Hill to the north—rising steep and high above every wall, planted with fine old white-barked pine trees, and crowned with five varicolored tile-roofed pleasure pavilions—that from them one could look abroad and see nothing but imperial roofs and behind them distant landscape. To the west, in the nearer distance, were the tree-lined shores of the artificial imperial lakes. Beyond were the purple Western Hills. All signs of urban life were so completely erased that from what met the eye they did not exist. The magic that had raised this fantastic enclosure had simply made the teeming city about it vanish.

In all my wanderings I had never surmised a marvel like this! So I set out to discover every mood, to wrest every secret from the wonderful assemblage. It was a pursuit, almost a wooing; it carried me through seasons; it became an absorption. It had in it, too, a great element of luck. After two or three years, some weed-overgrown courtyard, apparently destined to remain sealed forever with a rusty Chinese padlock, through chinks in whose rotting doorways I had long peered in vain, would one day be wide open, while unconcerned masons went about some simple task. My reward would then be great. It was an imperial hunt, also, silent, subtle, unpredictable. As an exercise in patience, with rich prizes after long watchfulness, it was unique. I stalked it with an architectural passion, and I was willing to wait long; but I was determined to secure a perfect return.

So now I can remember hidden courts, remote corners, deserted unfamiliar regions; and I can recall them under the sailing clouds of high summer, or in the frozen mists of winter, under barbaric wind or pardoning rain. Memory opens these imperial perspectives once more, and to the rose and yellow of walls and roofs are added the lapis blue and emerald green of the painted beams, delicate flowering trees in their season; with here a figure and there a figure, some frank and smiling guard at a familiar corner, the pottering coolie who used to bring a huge and steaming wadded tea jug to the sentries on duty, or a tall and inscrutable dignified old eunuch who acted as custodian at one of the shrines, probably all now vanished from the site.

The whole was so beautiful that it washed vision clean, yet so soberly proportioned that it never startled but only soothed the beholder. If China was indeed grouped about Peking, and all Peking about this palace, this was only as it should have been. The center represented, in microcosm, the essence of the whole.

I should never have discovered many of the details that I did, had it not been for the leisure that I was able to devote to this place. I knew the days when mist hung motionless, and the rain dripped for hours in courts that no one ever came to see. I knew, too, how on certain blessed summer days buoyant clouds sailed happily hour by hour over the glittering expanse of yellow tiled roofs. In the portico of the gatehouse before the largest hall of all, the Palace of Extreme Harmony, in good weather one could sit at little tables and have tea, with breezes pouring through its shady recesses. Here, when the weather was at its best, at moments one felt superbly afloat, aloof in a world made only of the cerulean heavens and of Chinese classical architecture.

So many, even among those who deeply admired the palace, came only from time to time, and then followed unprotestingly the conventional routes laid out for visitors. Any day, I could afford to arrive early, or stay late, depending upon sun and sky. I could spend a whole spring morning sitting under an old flowering apple tree, in a corner I knew, or beside some fragrant lilacs near an abandoned bridge. There were occasions when by some lapse in the regulation of the moment, I was free to mount to the surrounding wall. Then, looking inward I would plan how to get to some place perhaps never glimpsed until that moment. I had eternally to review my packs of character cards, of course, or to busy myself in one way or another with my attack upon the language, yet I was always at leisure to savor each charm in its transient hours.

Wise orientation and the perfect rectangularity of the plan made it possible to observe in detail the progress of the sun through each day. Each season, too, recorded changes in terms of light and shade. China, one understood, had been long-lasting for the very reason that her life was keyed to the earth's rhythms. Even now, when I see a photograph of the palace interior, I can tell by the way the light falls at what time of day it was taken. For at noon all shadows were always cast straight north; and the angle of deviation, morning and afternoon, is marked clear on the properly oriented walls.

From the top of the Wu Mên one could look outward over the town. There was comparatively little of it to be seen, however, except smoke from some distant chimneys to the south. Immediately below, along the main axis, was the great forecourt so broad and spacious that it was said several thousand troops could be marshaled within it.

On the left, or east, was the T'ai Miao, or Ancestor Temple, for the last ruling house. Its lofty halls, now open and empty, contained the ghostly spirit thrones of deceased emperors and their consorts, strangely narrow—since they were for the dead—but nevertheless all provided with imperial yellow satin "throw-overs." These buildings were set within a grove of *arbor vitae,* gnarled and twisted old trees. A row of them had even been planted down the center of the main avenue, leading south, to indicate symbolically that here, for the comings and goings of the dead, human roads were no longer of use. Whole families of cranes, curious mature birds, nested in an enclosure of these trees off to one side; this was the only quarter of the capital where one ever saw them.

To the west, symmetrical with the Ancestor Temple and thus also adjoining the palace, was a similar enclosure which we knew in English simply as "Central Park." It had originally been a kind of Earth Temple, for sacrifices now abandoned; and it still possessed a strange outdoor altar, raised and square, each side made of tiles glazed a different color. Since the fall of the Manchu house, this site had been converted into a "modern" public garden. Some poor cemented fountains, Western novelties, and several atrocious bronze statues of war lords, strutting horribly on small pedestals, defaced it; and two long rows of outdoor restaurants, between tea houses and photographers' shops, bordered a broad walk near the rear. Here in the late afternoon, especially when the peonies that were one of the attractions of the place were in bloom, willowy Chinese girls, the local belles, were accustomed to promenade in the midst of their families to show off their lovely figures, encased in far less lovely Shanghai brocades and silks. Their flat slippered feet detracted somewhat from the picture, but they were often thin and graceful as antelopes.

At the rear of both the Ancestor Temple and "Central Park" were broad terraces, planted with rows of ancient trees, bordering the moat behind which rose the walls of the palace. These, being to the north, were shaded places to which one could retreat on languid summer afternoons, with the inevitable tea and melon seeds set out on wicker tables and served from a neighboring matshed. Shimmering dragon-flies would dart between the lotus and the water; and the heavy scent of the large pink flowers would finally fuse all together in a single impression of soporific peace. One might linger until a moon began to appear through the motionless cypress branches, not a breeze stirring, nothing to break the spell.

Within the Forbidden City itself, though, what buildings were most extraordinary? The reader will not here find descriptions; and this is not because the splendors of the Three Great Halls, for example, did not attain the maximum of objective impressiveness—as had been planned by their anonymous architects. Nevertheless, unpeopled cells of a now empty hive, they held little for the seeker of a vanished past, which I had now become.

To be sure, one could wander into the foremost of them, the finest single building in the whole enclosure, and gaze aloft at the gilded coffering of its fine ceiling, supported upon columns made from the tallest trees in the empire. Yet there was a sense of emptiness, and in the general desertion it was the trivial remarks of the Chinese or foreign visitors that inevitably branded themselves in the mind.

Formerly small "mountains" of bronze—somewhat like large door-stops—had been placed at intervals on the once mirror-glossy black brick surface of the now bare floor, to indicate a "thus-far-and-no-farther" to the assembled officials of the first, or second, or lower ranks, who had come here to prostrate themselves. Yet the throne was now not only deserted but even visibly dusty; the mandarins long since departed; and the guides hovered about indifferently delivering glib misinformation, in Chinese or English, to those who came to gape and then soon turned away again.

The second of the three great halls was square rather than oblong, and was planned as a smaller, intermediate, building. It had once been used to house the great seals of state, heavy squares of jade elaborately carved with writhing dragons. These, long since looted or stolen, were now represented merely by rows of high empty boxes, each on its separate pedestal and covered over with orange-yellow cloth. The great seal of the Emperor, as the saying went, "transmitted the state"; but that variety of state no longer existed to be given in succession, either peacefully or bitterly disputed at the risk of life itself, without scruple and finally even by murder.

A great water clock, which long ago had ceased to function, once marked the hours here, as water dripped slowly from tank to tank, poured into the topmost from a ladder at the back. Its floating gauge rose from the lowest tank of all, on a level with the spectator. Pendant to this Chinese clock was a Western one, with a big round face, equipped with a small stair at the side which one could mount to wind it. East and West thus formed a pair: Chinese symmetry as usual providing symbols by balancing opposites.

The third great hall was oblong, and also oriented broadside to the south upon a high marble terrace. Its internal arrangement was similar to that of the Hall of Extreme Harmony. Everything about it, though, was somewhat smaller in scale, as befitted a rear hall for secondary ceremonies. Since it was a little more deserted, more naturally forgotten, it was a much pleasanter place in which to loiter.

Yet these three halls never revealed any surprises. They had been too important once, and their proper function was now utterly obliterated, converted as they had been into exhibition halls for large and rather gaudy palace trappings. It proved much more satisfactory to look at them from distant vantage points—perhaps recalling lines of court poems—and muse upon the power that once had drawn within them the talents of an empire.

There were, however, courtyards that did retain a special quality, some spell or other that would lure me again and again. The Chai Kung, or Hall of Abstinence was in one of these. Before any sacrifice of importance, in the old China, ritual demanded that the Emperor go into retirement, to purify himself. These periods of withdrawal might last for several days, during which he fasted. There were also other prescriptions, including obligatory bathing.

The court before this hall was open and unadorned, quite bare of trees. Within, besides the usual apartments, was an inner room, once completely secluded, with a sunken tank for the ceremonial bathing at one end. How often must an Emperor have withdrawn here, temporarily to sever his ties with the outer world, and in spite of all the powers conferred by absolute sovereignty in an Oriental country still have felt himself, like all clay, what Maeterlinck has called, I think, *"un pauvre petit être mystérieux"*! For him, also, one day his rank would be of no avail; he too must in the end face the insoluble problems familiar to the humblest of his subjects.

When the Forbidden City was converted into a museum, this hall was set aside for the exhibition of various jades. Large showcases of "mutton fat" or "spinach green" were consequently placed against almost every wall. Yet a sense of the original use of the place lingered on, too personal somehow to give way to present vicissitude.

There was another court that seemed to possess an even more sensitive and indefinable vibration. It was small and open, indeed merely four quite low plain rose walls, with simple gates, each with a pair of leaves, at opposite ends; and two rows of young trees running its length to shelter a pleasant stretch of broad paving between. It was at its best in winter, when a slight fall of snow powdered their crystalline branches. Then so perfect seemed its proportions, so profound its utter simplicity, that just to pass through it stirred in me a mysterious pleasure. There must have been a harmony of proportion so perfect that half a foot, one way or another, would have destroyed the effect. So far as I could learn, the place was in no way to be distinguished from half a dozen others somewhat like it. It thus became, as I privately named it, the "Magic Court," since I never was able to analyze, but could always feel again, its peculiar spell.

A scar existed on the face of the Forbidden City—in the northwest corner. Here, one came abruptly to a screen of "natural" rockery, guarding not a further palace, but outlined stark against the open sky. Behind it were now only foundations where obviously fine buildings once had stood.

These had been lost in a curious fire. The last Emperor but one had allowed himself, it was said, the imprudence of an altercation with the whole body of the court eunuchs. He had issued a command to inventory his possessions in a number of places, hoping to stop— or at least to stem—the peculation that eventually, dynasty after dynasty, always grew intolerable. Here he courted defeat. For the eunuchs were formidable in number and in entrenched privilege. Heads would fall if this went on! So one night a fire broke out that consumed so much treasure, and made so much more untraceable, that thenceforth there was an end to further inventorying. The scar was thus a double rebuke, and one loss had engendered another.

It must not be thought that I wandered thus about various sections of the palace, merely to enjoy such pleasures. There were two libraries to which I went quite regularly for work, especially after some years had gone by and I had been granted a special pass. I was very proud of this. Except for one other American, Dr. J. C. Ferguson (the venerable adviser first to the throne and then to succeeding presidents), who was dean of our local colony, I believe that no other foreigner possessed the little diptych—with its Chinese text—that opened these inner gates to me. I had received it at the request of this compatriot, much trusted by the Chinese, who had kindly exerted himself on my behalf; and no privilege ever accorded to me in China gave me more pleasure.

Soldiers on guard came to know me; and I could proceed perhaps a quarter of a mile farther than could regular visitors, into unexplored parts of the maze between long avenues, quite deserted. Finally, after returning several respectful salutes on the way, I would reach either, on the east, the Palace Archives, or on the west, a library arranged for the administrators of the Palace Museum.

They were very different places. An air of unhurried and tranquil scholarship hung over the reading room of the Archives. It was of course only another converted palace hall, yet it had better furniture than most—the archivists had a nice sense of these things—and its hardwood chairs were placed with undeviating symmetry about the walls or at heavy central tables. Complete silence surrounded this room. A courteously attentive white-haired servant first smilingly brought tea; and one always further entered upon a little conversation with the official or two present, about trifles. These became important chiefly as a medium for a preliminary exchange of moods, before broaching the object of one's visit. It was pleasant, living as I did, really to be in no hurry; I still feel that haste might have ruined all.

"Would one, then, perhaps like"—finally—"to see that treasure, the Great Map of Peking, the original one of the reign of Ch'ien Lung?"

"If no trouble, yes indeed!"

(This was a map so large that it indicated almost every single building in the whole city as it had existed in the eighteenth century.)

So the wished-for section would be brought from some storehouse at the rear, beyond a further court, and then spread out over the whole of the large tables for me to pore over. In my studies I was by now resurrecting part after part of the old capital; and not only palaces and temples but also the imperial stables, the mews, the kennels, the archery fields, the barracks, even the icehouses, all were there.

Damp and bookworms had been at work in the two centuries intervening, and they had caused no little damage. One or two identifications, of much importance to me, hung by holes in the labeling—or rather by the fortunate absence of them. The vanished Temple of the Pole Star was here shown facing to the north. Early Jesuit churches, later destroyed, could here be seen with their baroque façades neatly delineated in elevation. There were always new surprises; or the exciting confirmation of past surmise. Our talk remained hushed, the joy of discovery respected. When it came time to go back along the deserted rose passageways again, I was often glad of their length, for such success was heady, and this made more comfortable the return to actuality.

The Museum Library was in quite another region of the palace, in the opposite direction. Here the conversation was invariably a little more brisk, more contemporary. It would run to such subjects as the re-edition of imperial catalogues or the need of photography, with negatives and prints, and hopes for reproduction and publication.

In days that now seem far off, before the Japanese arrived, here was a center of learned work, held—one now sees—like a sand fort against an advancing tide. Yet the projects were far-reaching, some of them positively dazzling. There was so much of beauty to preserve, to codify and if possible to give to the world. Even then, though, with the threat of war, most of the furs and jades, the porcelains and pictures of the museum had already been shipped to the distant South; and during my time in Peking one often talked sadly about what was in hiding in faraway caves, treasures that one hoped were being preserved against a better day, which never came.

It was specially in the company of the staff of this library that I learned how little the West can hope to know of the great bulk of Chinese culture. With a flick of the hand, some biographical dictionary or gazetteer would be consulted; and as several interested participants gathered round to discuss the findings, some three thousand years of genius—vanished men and noble cities—would be touched on, a word here and a word there, with such lightness and familiarity that a spectator like myself, counting his very limited store, felt how hopeless would be any attempt to achieve even a summation of what the great past of China had produced. Here one heard formulated in terms of clear and powerful vision many novel aspects of what this civilization once had offered; yet to those learned men it all was as obvious —the Chinese so phrase it—as a pearl in the palm of one's hand.

There were certain scrolls of painting, or detailed photographs of them, left here even at the end. (These served admirably, I learned, to catalyze discussion.) One outstanding example was very long. It represented a passage through the old Sung capital of K'ai-Fêng along its waterways. Beginning quietly in the country, pollarded willows bordering open canals in the fields, as the painting was unrolled, one arrived at the walls of the city. Here the press of boats became very great; goods were being loaded and unloaded. Once within, one progressed along canals into every kind of urban quarter. The grain merchants', the dyers', a small square with a fair in progress, the acrobats drawing a crowd, taverns with gardens bordering the water's edge: all were shown with every detail of circumstance.

Finally a hush seemed to come over the bustle on the waterways; one had entered the fairyland of the palace enclosure, the forbidden region. Here were lapis rocks, and malachite verdure; here all was refinement and elegance. One passed through groves of pines, concubines in fluted skirts with fluttering sashes making here and there a charming group, and finally one came out on the shores of the imperial lake. Floating there was the largest barge of all, of two stories. Upon its upper deck had been placed a throne, brocade-covered yet empty, through respect. Then suddenly a great rock in the foreground closed the whole. On it, like a carved epitaph, were inscription and signature, and the identifying seals. This was said to be a copy, dating from the eighteenth century, of a scroll so famous that in the Sung dynasty one imperial minister had finally not scrupled to commit murder, to obtain it as his possession.

It was strange how many different regions were fitted into the simple rectangle of the Forbidden City's bounding walls. The courtyards, and especially the gardens, at the rear, might well have been in some other palace, so dissimilar were they from the great buildings lying far to the south. Much of the difference was due, I feel upon reflection, to changing scale. Chinese formal arrangement, as exemplified in Peking, demanded that the great courts of any palace be majestic, so in the beginning space was used lavishly. Then, as one progressed inward, approaching nearer and nearer to the rear wall, the units became gradually shallower, to squeeze in all that had been planned. At the very back there was almost always a little crowding. The Forbidden City itself was no exception to this rule.

There were also certain halls in the private zone of the palace, on the central axis, used for Manchu household purposes. Weddings were held here; and the quite asymmetrical plan of the largest of them included a "kitchen" for private sacrifices, and also space for witch dancing and exorcism. A high mast stood in one of these courts, to present meat to the crows, in commemoration of an old Manchu legend. For one of their national heroes, in a time of great peril, fleeing from his enemies had hidden in a tree. There the crows instead of cawing, had remained quite still as if to protect him.

There was further in this region a pair of most attractive so-called "warm rooms," spacious sunny chambers, with various dependencies, all heated for winter residence by flues and conduits under the floor. These reminded one of the northern origins of the last ruling house, and recalled the much smaller palace in Mukden, which had been their earlier capital before the conquest. On either side of the main courts, at this level, were other spacious ones assigned to the principal concubines. These were consciously elegant in highly individual ways, all still handsomely roofed with deep yellow glazed tiles.

Then the garden began, so ornamented and set about with odd arrangements of rock, or sponge coral formations set upon ornately carved marble bases, so built up with small pavilions like jewel caskets, or highly decorated shrines and temples, that it was a long while before I could learn to think of it as a garden at all.

To be sure, there were trees, many cypresses, their twisting trunks thrust upward through the paving, which was often enriched with bands of small pebbles laid to form elaborate patterns. At one place, on axis, two of the oldest trees had been grafted together, making a forked arch; and this the Chinese much admired. There were also flowering bushes, planted within paved squares, the most famous of them a flourishing mock orange specially cherished by the Empress Dowager. It was said by the Chinese to have come from a distance, and bore the magniloquent name of "Flower of Peace." Americans, though, always recognized it as common enough, almost a suburban plant at home. Where, though, does distance not lend enchantment?

In spite of all this artificiality, the rear garden was a most agreeable place. The altars of its many religious buildings—streamers of many-colored faded brocade hanging low behind their open doors—were still furnished with quantities of dusty gilded objects. Banners and scrolls still covered their walls. To inspect these was an invitation to gentle wandering. There were also odd "porches," "studies," and "cabinets," fancifully decorated and painted in unconventional colors; with gal-vanized sheet-iron roofing now over their once open small courts— a nineteenth-century touch! In these, it was said, the last Emperor had received his foreign guests more informally than anywhere else in the whole palace. Typically, though, he was here as far away as pos-sible from the main throne halls.

One or two of the garden pavilions were elaborate, running to several stories. Here the last Emperor's tutor, Sir Reginald Johnston, and also the young American girl who taught English to the last Empress, Miss Isabel Ingram, would meet together, after morning lessons, for small luncheon parties of four. The young Empress took a liking for the foreign name of Elizabeth, which she wished used for herself on such occasions. Thus the wan children who were the last sovereigns played pathetically. Their time, and that of the order they nominally headed, had already run out.

To make the Englishman feel at home, one of these houses had been arranged for his personal use, with a thoroughgoing and quite fright-ful installation of Victorian furnishings. Axminster carpets with large cabbage roses covered the floor; cheap Nottingham lace curtains still hung at the windows; and rickety sofas and deplorably ugly fancy chairs had been placed about "foreign style" in the small rooms.

In these rear buildings the palace eunuchs had apparently installed the most magpie-like collection of all their misguided purchases—al-

Old-fashioned gentleman, Peking

Adding the titles to a Chinese book

Hsi Pien Mên in snow, Peking

Late snack barrow, Peking

The persimmon seller; autumn scene
outside the Forbidden City, Peking

View through a moon gate in the Pei Hai, Peking, north over the Bell and Drum Towers

Temple scene, Ta Chüeh Ssŭ, in the Western Hills near Peking

Chinese date seller

Street kitchen, Peking

Balustrade and incense burners, Forbidden City, Peking

*Camel-back Bridge,
Summer Palace,
Peking*

though some of the assorted wares were gifts from diplomats or missionaries. Thin and feeble *art nouveau* chandeliers hung from the ceilings; there were quantities of swollen-veined Tiffany glass dishes, boxes of paper-wrapped French toilet soap, even bottles of a familiar brand of American antiseptic mouth wash. The last were placed on side tables pell-mell with fine jade and porcelain ornaments.

I even remember one cheap drinking mug, considered correct by someone for imperial presentation, embellished in decalcomania with the legend FOR A GOOD BOY! When the museum was first arranged, these objects were not removed. Everything had been permanently sealed, by order, within the apartments through the glass windows of which one now peered. Even dried-up plants still remained in their decorated *cache-pots*, their soil bone-dry and cracked with age.

Nowhere more than here did one sense a basic fact that first strained credulity: as this last dynasty approached nearer and nearer to its ignominious end, the Chinese completely lost their once excellent taste. Horrors abounded, even in the choice and forms of the simplest native objects. Finally one saw the last cherished importations, early gramophones with painted morning-glory horns, or cheap bicycles displayed in front of inferior embroidered Japanese screens. There was even a deep enameled bathtub, with no plumbing attached, set into an alcove hung with ugly pink satin curtains. It was a descent indeed from the splendors that had traditionally surrounded the dragon throne.

There was one last band of rockery, and one came out finally to the last paved court within the palace. Through one more tall crimson spirit screen one could reach the outer world again. The gate tower looming high above was used as a storage place for the many sedan chairs and litters, and all the elaborate regalia formerly necessary in court processions.

The shows for which they once had served were now to be reconstructed in the imagination only, of course; and to animate the scene one had to people it with numbers of serving eunuchs, dressed in their rainbow-colored robes, servitors of a variety that still gives one a slight shudder if one looks through old photographs. One could then fancy the much-feared old Empress Dowager in her chair, borne on some minor errand within the palace, with perhaps the ill-fated favorite consort of her son forced to follow in a smaller chair—the poor "Pearl Concubine" who at the end had been thrust into a well by these self-same eunuchs, not far from this rear gate, in what was apparently a well-planned "suicide." The glittering insects who figured in such court dramas could be poisonous indeed.

If one lingered a little overlong, reflecting on such matters, the freedom of the open street between this rear gate and the grounds of Coal Hill—with perhaps some simple sight such as a laughing colloquy between two running ricksha boys—became a consolation. In China also, the sadness of palaces had weighed heavy indeed upon those for whom they had become prisons; and the burden of helpless sorrow, of humiliation amid imperial luxury, had moved many a poet through the dynasties.

Coal Hill itself, which was not strictly within the palace enclosure but formed instead a separate one behind it, has surely been described in many books before this. Yet I should like to reserve a place for it here also. In form it was related to the crescent-shaped tomb mounds that were always placed to the rear, and whenever possible to the north, of large sepulchers. Like these it was also supposed to protect the palace from baleful influences always feared from this quarter. Coal may possibly have been the foundation of its five high crests, each topped with an elaborate tile-roofed pavilion; and were this so it might have provided ample stores in time of siege. Yet fruitless digging was once attempted; and this English name is almost surely a misnomer, a mistranslation due to a local variant in the Chinese tone of its name. It is much more probable that Coal Hill was originally only called "Beautiful."

The pavilions crowning it were designed to be a splendid termination to a unique area of the palace region. They rose symmetrically each upon its separate eminence, with white-barked evergreens planted between, and verdure spread below. Conscious variety of shape enriched their design; their decoration was also of bright color. The outermost pair was circular, the middle ones polygonal, and the central one, the largest of all, broad and square, with sturdy red lacquer columns supporting a high double-tiered roof topped with a button of imperial yellow tall as a man. All this was flung, as on the crest of an advancing, steep, wave, high against the sky.

From this place, above and behind the center of the palace, the view was like no other in the capital. One was so high, and the region one overlooked, even down to the forecourts in the distance, was so vast! The plan was of course uncompromisingly rectilinear; yet the graceful curve of every roof, the unbroken harmony of cheerful color gave so much simple pleasure that even here the final effect was still gentle rather than overwhelming. I know of no other architecture that can produce such an impression, on such a scale.

From Coal Hill, in the old days, one could survey large parts of the North City, behind it, as from an eyrie perched high in a wood. One unexpected effect of Chinese arrangements for domestic building, always with low structures about internal courtyards, was that from a distant height, as here, in summer their walls became completely invisible under the foliage of trees planted within. Today not a few scars mar this effect, projecting cement buildings in rigid "foreign style," bare and with window-pierced walls. There was quite enough left, however, to make clear how once in the very center of this metropolis, one could look out toward battlemented fortifications across an unbroken area of green foliage, under which human habitation was so concealed that one was reduced to guessing where all but the main arteries lay.

Directly behind Coal Hill and still within its bounding walls, lay the closed halls to be used only when an Emperor in death had by regulation to be separated from the living, while preparations were being completed for his funeral. The mausoleum in the hills had usually been built far in advance, either at the Eastern or the Western Tombs. The final procession always took several days to reach either place; and its scale was invariably mammoth. One Ming Emperor in Nanking, I was told, had even had arranged five simultaneous funerals for himself, which started out for as many tombs. This was done through fear of grave-robbing—in China a most ancient occupation. The funeral halls behind Coal Hill were thus only a temporary

resting place. The trees grew thick there, however, and quiet surrounded it, empty and deserted, during all my days in Peking.

Finally an open broad avenue, still along the central line, led away
north toward the Rear Gate through the walls of the Imperial City.
Thence one could continue still on axis toward the Drum and Bell
Towers, quite far north, which served as landmarks for the whole
region. From many distant places one could see them isolated and
majestic, often catching the late light. A poor municipal branch library
languished under the balconies from which once had pealed the
drums; and the closed Bell Tower was as deserted as if in a country
town. Yet looked at from afar, they were proud witness of how many
centuries had been spent perfecting the traditional plan. Here in
Peking it had reached a superb culmination only just before—as centuries go—modernity came to rob it of all significance.

There was one area of the palace, imposing on the map, that always
remained closed. We were told that it was so overgrown that it literally could no longer be shown; even the labor of clearing a path
through it was beyond the power of the authorities. Season after season this explanation had to suffice. Yet a small group of us from the
Language School finally determined to attack the problem frontally.
I well remember waiting—with the inevitable cups of tea—in the
anteroom of the man in authority himself, wondering if such a plan
could bring success. Our small delegation was unhurried and courteous,
in carefully phrased Chinese. He too was courteous. Finally we pre-
vailed—very much I believe through this demonstration of our knowledge of Chinese composure. A visit was permitted.

We had to wait for some weeks before the clearing away was announced as accomplished; but the time did come, and a handful of
Westerners passed through gates that long had been sealed. Truly,
much had had to be cut away! There were sharp ends of lopped-off
thorns in crevices upon the marble steps; wisps of hay were still drying
where they had been flung aside to clear a path for us.

There rapidly began an afternoon of exciting adventure. We hastened
here and there, discovering what it was like to see palace apartments
long uncared for, and apparently abandoned in some haste at the end.

There were still, for example, several large bundles wrapped in orange cloth lying on the dusty floor of a locked upstairs library, a room with paneling inlaid with unusually precious materials. Caught in the sealing, they had been left behind, who knows by whom, and who knows why?

Nothing had ever been restored, nothing, obviously, put back into order; this we could see under the thick dust everywhere, as we hastened to look through traceried doors and windows, long without their usual paper. It became obvious that one reason why it had taken so long to convince the authorities of our scholarly desires was that they were losing face by letting us peer into these untidy and deserted rooms. What we saw left a strange impression.

The structural fabric was still in tolerable repair; the architecture and decoration could easily be assigned to a time corresponding with our own late eighteenth century. Large carved jade animals, even a jade goldfish bowl, were still neatly in place on the overgrown paths, out-of-door ornaments. There were no signs of major violence. What finally had strangled the whole seemed the ramification of property itself! One was assailed by weariness merely to contemplate the administration of possessions as numerous as these had become. There had been such quantities that even the uprooting was incomplete; all afternoon we kept seeing chances the marauders had missed.

Paint was everywhere cracked or peeling, and lacquer disintegrating; that of course was to be expected. The charm of such an extended setting, untampered with, made us accept this ruin easily. Yet we saw so many places from which objects, probably all precious, must have been summarily carted away, and we could observe that originally there must have been such numbers of them, that by the end of a long afternoon we found ourselves fatigued with a sense of almost personal evisceration.

So it was from courtyards like these that palace loot had come! This was the setting for the largest and most expensive "curios" that finally reached the West. What we had seen hitherto elsewhere in the Forbidden City was, then, merely a rearrangement, an awkward putting back and substitution, a glossing over! This was what palaces became when the rodents that are men had finished nibbling. Property is hard to guard, anywhere. Yet there must have been vaster amounts here than I believe one could find in any similar Western palace, and it had suffered a condign fate more irrevocably. These disorderly and tattered rooms had been the mine from which the suave dealers had enriched themselves; this, finally, was the disorder left when a great and proud system succumbed.

The Emperor, then, how had the Emperor felt? One thing came struggling to clarity. The Emperor of China in that time of prosperity had owned so many examples of every known object under heaven that paradoxically he became an almost propertyless man, moving everywhere and forever through an endless maze of almost impersonal possession. Nothing really could add much, or even subtract much, from what was always about him—until the arrival of a final catastrophe. The joy of simple ownership given to ordinary mortals, who can dream of acquiring, struggle to possess, and then fondle some new object: this could not exist for him. A nation of five hundred million, aesthetically talented, had for centuries been heaping up quantities of treasure, for every use and of every variety; and all the best flowed regularly to the court, much of it even to the palace, for the use of this One Man. He perpetually lacked, therefore, Emperor because he was, any sense of fluctuation, any of the satisfaction in small human desires fulfilled that is also one of the treasures of the humble. Perspectives of almost terrifying abnormality kept opening before me that afternoon.

These courtyards, we were told, were planned for the extreme old age of the great eighteenth-century monarch, Ch'ien Lung; and in one place we found a curious symbol of this. There was one large court, quite as regular as all the others; but in the center—strangely replacing the usual paving of cut stone—almost filling it full, choking up the empty space, was a great hollow mound of porous rock. It was so high that from the top of it, on one side, a tiny flying marble bridge leapt across to a second-story gallery. Deep underneath had been contrived artificial caves; and we groped about in their windings, discovering the arrangement and observing how the dim light, seeming always about to fail, would ever at the last moment be eked out by some artfully contrived funnel or aperture. This, though, was an old garden trick.

At several places upon this artificial mountain, stones had been set to make rustic flights of steps, by which one could ascend to the summit. Here, crowning the center of this courtyard for old age, was an allegory subtly contrived for those who could read it. A circular pavilion, using plum color and green for its tiling and woodwork, became the place for an aged Emperor to be led, falteringly, to catch the last rays of sunlight. It was a patriarch's journey, near and yet far, dignified, too, as the thoughts of the old.

Every detail of this little pavilion, the thin "cracked ice" of its window tracery, the carved borders of its marble flooring, and its painted beam-work, played upon a single theme, the fragile plum blossoms that in cold weather spring from the gnarled branches of an old tree. To Chinese eyes the meaning was as clear as if written: "May there thus be small flowers of enjoyment in your old age, delicate and fated to bloom only in the cold; yet also pure and fair, sprung from branches that have weathered the storms of time."

CHAPTER VIII   *Princely Men and Little*

WE HAVE examined the setting of life in Peking; and watched
—a little—how life passed there through the moving seasons.
What of the people who so unfailingly animated this scene? What were
they like?

To attempt a summation of Chinese character is like trying to
draw a net through the sea: not only is the task of leviathan magnitude, but some of the agile small fry of thought must always escape.
How can one ever state "The Chinese are thus and so," when for
every general statement somewhere its complete reverse is also true?
No two men, indeed, can find the same traits of character in any
country, because at bottom as we look at the world, we find only ourselves. What I shall say here will perhaps be the opposite of what
was discovered and then stated in complete good faith by a missionary, or a diplomat, or some Western oil or tobacco agent; yet all these
impressions originally were drawn from the same broad field of objective reality. China's very size, of course, has added to the dis-
crepancies.

Yet these intangibles must be put down; and I wish to qualify the
next two chapters in this book with only a single statement. The
China that I saw was, in so far as possible, the traditional China, which
I was able to observe with a minimum of the deviation in vision that
is caused by self-interest. I practiced no profession; I was not forced
into relationship with any group; I asked for no special privileges—

inevitably to be paid back in other coin. Above all I neither earned nor spent in that country any significant sums of money. Thus I was able to be receptive yet self-contained, curious yet leisurely. I had ample time to allow the pattern to form itself, no need to force it to a desired shape. What I have set out below, therefore, are my own conclusions after they had gone through the usual preliminary extremes of oscillation; as they finally fixed themselves in my mind with the passage of tranquil years, which were indeed so blissful personally as surely to have conferred upon the whole its sanguine and happy stamp. This then is my truth. My statements have about them nothing so pretentious as a claim to general validity.

Now unless one is to produce mere snapshots of impression, to read the character of the inhabitants of any country does require living there long. This is specially true if the underlying ethic is as different as are, in China, Confucianism, Buddhism, and Taoism from familiar types of Christianity in the West. Time is also required for the study of men as well as books. One cannot take matters at their face value. It would be an error to believe, for instance, that because we announce the news of a death with a grave face, and the Chinese smiles, he is therefore a monster. Here we permit a feeling to show which, because of quite another standard of behavior, he instinctively hides or converts into something else. I early realized that for a long while all my findings had carefully to be labeled "Strictly Provisional. Handle with Care"! Only after I had both read and discussed much, and with various persons, concerning the aspects of Chinese character set out below, did I begin to feel that I could make some attempt to classify them.

In this chapter, I should like to confine myself very much to the individual; although there were many abstract qualities woven through the texture of Chinese life—such as, especially in Peking, a pervading grandeur and gentleness—that I hope to deal with later. The individual, though, may by chance appear in the guise of some venerable official, a Buddhist monk, a Taoist wanderer, an old functionary, or perhaps a modern student. Who, exactly, is he? Let me say at once that granting all the variation in single destinies, the overt social relations of Chinese life seem to me predominately Confucian. Confucianism, indeed, is just this—the broad accepted rules of public conduct evolved for the relation of Chinese with each other. They are wholly a product of the Chinese mind, one that came to birth on Chinese soil. Unlike Buddhism they are not a complex, imaginative, importation. Indeed it may well be argued that Confucianism in its studious refusal to concern itself with the supernatural, is finally not a religion at all. The general acceptance and the enormous prestige of its code for so many centuries, however, have given it a validity undisputed even in spheres where its basic assumptions are not recognized.

Confucius himself, who lived about twenty-five centuries ago, was a gentleman, a very great if at times a rather pedantic gentleman. With pious reverence he gathered all the details of ceremony and etiquette as they had been practiced in the courts and by the worthies of previous ages, by the great who had preceded him. He obviously set much value on these matters. By the time of the death of Mencius, nearly two centuries later, the codification had become permanent. It furnished a complete guide to human relations. It has never changed since.

What is this ideal, so long-established, so genuinely and profoundly revered? The system that it engendered was given most solemn state recognition until almost our own day—when a serious reaction has set in. That critics did early and often object is true; but through the long ages their carping faultfinding with something so stable and so practical always smacked a little of flippancy, if not of heresy.

Fundamentally, Confucius wished to establish the gentleman as the ruler of the state. Given scrupulous and ethical standards of personal conduct, and granted only a general willingness to put such men in power and then to abide by their decisions, the problems of the world, thought Confucius, could finally be solved. All the rest was bloody struggle and anarchy, or else intellectual frivolity. Yet the gentleman, of course, was not made way for; and objectively Confucius' policy was a great failure. Struggle and anarchy have indelibly marked China's long history; but, then, where have they not?

It is remarkable that down the ages this detailed character of the gentleman has endured. It has indeed so kept its original form that even today it bears Confucius' recognizable stamp, across twenty-five centuries. It is still the accepted norm by which Chinese man, in his social relationships, measures others and is in turn measured by them.

What, then, is this gentleman like? Even the popular Western caricature of the "heathen Chinee" bears some of the stamp of truth. The patriarchal old man is the ideal. He salutes gravely. He possesses indeed a whole code of bowing, from a slight dignified nod to the repeated prostrations of the deep kowtow—or head-knocking, as the word means literally. He clasps his own hands and smiles. He delivers hoary proverbs, or quaint platitudes. Yet his wisdom is profound, and—an important difference from certain Western varieties—it is cheerful and not bitter. So this stock figure comes near to the truth. The Chinese ideal does set tremendous emphasis on maturity and decorum, on etiquette. Yet it is always surprisingly good-humored, reasonable rather than rigid in its consideration of human problems. Typically, too, the solution sought is invariably practical rather than theological.

Confucius himself has given us maxims in plenty. He tells us, for instance, that the gentleman's society is "clear and plain as water"; it is altogether free of that emotional coloring which the ill-bred man perpetually gives to it, either through what he does or what he leaves undone. Indeed it is because of this very limpidity of conduct that the character of the gentleman is never quite comprehended by coarser natures. He must, above all things, be careful to pass muster at the bar of his own judgment rather than at that of others. When he meets with adversity, Confucius recommends, typically, that he "curl himself up within his own nature." When things go wrong he must always "seek the cause within himself," and not try to fasten blame upon others. As one can see, the standard is exacting and high.

Confucius' gentleman is also a gentleman in our own sense of that delicate word. Above all he must never actively seek his own self-interest, or place himself in any way before others if to do so would contravene strict ethical justice. It is such ingrained courtesies that make the old-type Chinese so respected and superior a figure.

In his pronouncements Confucius never leaves us in any doubt about precisely what he considers that a gentleman is and what he does. The moral is drawn as clearly as in a Victorian novel. Good is good, finally and definitely; and bad is bad. Here are no mocking and subtle Taoist paradoxes; here also is no excess of delusive Buddhist emotion. There is the Princely Man, a paragon of virtue, in every way superior; and contrasted with him the Little Man, small in character and mean in action. In the Chinese Classics these two are usually displayed together in contrasting formulae, made of short sentences regular in meter, easy to memorize—and thus to carry through life. The recorded sayings of the sage abound in them. "The Princely Man is harmonious and independent: the Little Man takes sides and is not agreeable"; and so on. Examples run into dozens. One could always know exactly where rectitude lay, commit its precepts to memory, and then observe how it contrasted with inferior behavior.

Let us try, briefly, to define the Princely Man, this pre-eminent man of breeding. What were his ideals? *Li*—decorum, politeness, proper manners—was one of the essentials. How is one to stand, or sit; when, and where? Upon what occasions does one use the deep prostration of the kowtow, and then how many times? When does one yield place to another? How far to the outer gate does one escort a parting guest, and through what number of courtyards? These are, to the practicing Confucian, matters of importance.

There are many refinements. There must never be touching of persons, no physical contact. Above all one should avoid immature, offensive, enthusiasm. A Chinese, be it remembered, used formerly to shake his own hands, not yours. Even today, to offer a Chinese of the old school a chair so recently used by another as still to retain a little human warmth is socially a gesture quite unacceptable. The proper management of one's breathing is also essential. To a Chinese any breath can offend. At the old court ceremonies most elaborate precautions were taken lest a subject so contaminate the Emperor. The ivory tablets, held upright with both hands, shown so frequently in Chinese paintings of scenes of audience, were used primarily for this purpose, to shield the mouth; although the ivory besides being presumably endowed with natural purifying qualities, was also used as a convenient surface to write upon. I have had it told to me, by one of my teachers, that courtiers could thus conveniently have within eye-range a most surprising command of facts, if the Emperor were suddenly to require information.

Every circumstance was similarly prepared for, and a polite manner evolved of managing otherwise awkward situations. To give an example, on an official visit to a government bureau, or yamen, the superior officer, whether host or guest, held by rank the privilege of ending an interview. How could this be done so as never to be brusque, yet to call a halt at the moment when the superior wished it. The method, although indirect, was simplicity itself. Tea was of course served when the visit began, as an elementary politeness. And the first cup or two could be drunk, upon invitation, without constraint.

When the time came to end a conversation, however, after a pause in the tea-drinking, the superior officer, whether host or guest, merely raised his cup to his lips. This was the signal; and reputedly the waiting servants were so well trained, and this was all so much a convention, that even as the cup was touched one could hear the cry relayed outside to the entrance courtyards: "The chair of the Honorable So-and-So!" There were thus never awkward pauses, no inept pleas of shortage of time, or other engagements. Social movement progressed evenly and smoothly. This is typical of formal Chinese manners; they furnish a sure path if one is duly instructed. Here are no upsetting dangers to face, no risk of the impromptu going astray.

Chinese anecdotes abound with examples of how, to every human situation, there must exist an elegant solution, or failing this at least a conventional withdrawal—like a classical move in chess—by which decorum still can safely be preserved. Over the centuries this has produced a certain petrification, as might be expected; but instructive examples of such behavior, precious anecdotes illuminating the long range of Chinese history, are often marvelously concise and effective. Their expression has not seldom been given final form in a single phrase, in which one variety of human experience has been so condensed as to remain henceforth imperishable. This is what it means to have ever at hand the garnered experience of centuries of high civilization.

I shall give a single instance of such a petrifact. A common short phrase, a compact group of four Chinese characters only, to illustrate a common human situation in marital relations, runs simply "to *cast water* [in] *front* [of a] *horse.*" What can this mean; what is the riddle?

The anecdote is as follows. Once a poor man and his wife disagreed, and she selfishly abandoned him before he rose high in the world. Years later, repenting, to shame him and thus force him to take her back, she appeared at his yamen announcing herself as his rightful wife, and requesting admission.

The wily husband was not now thus to be caught. Yet he was aware that he must receive her. Summoning his full retinue, therefore, he mounted his horse, and gave orders to have her enter the main court. His position was one of dignity. Would he take her back? Yes, he would indeed consent. But first he bade a servant bring a basin of water. Then, using the gesture as an allegory, before the entire assembly he cast the water to the ground in front of his horse. "I bid you only dutifully to gather this basin of water back again," he said, "and then you are still my rightful wife!"

In the theater, at the storytellers', in reading or conversation, the Chinese seem to find special enjoyment in such examples, incidents gleaned from this or that heroic tale, or else from the action of some clever actor on the stage of life. Thus they may learn deft procedure, which although never departing from strict decorum may still make it possible to have one's way in the world.

There is another facet. Familiar euphemisms to circumvent the ugly facts of life abound. If a child, for example, dies in infancy, within a few days of its birth, its parents may save face, in what they consider their embarrassingly frustrated appearance to the world, merely by announcing: "We threw the baby away!" ("We, therefore, did not want it!") If an Emperor died of smallpox, the official announcement calmly proclaimed that "he had come out with heavenly flowers, and has now ascended the dragon throne." Everyone knew exactly what was meant; yet it sounded well. Such obliquity can occasionally quite shock a Westerner by a callous glossing over of evil, only negligently concealed in grandiloquent travesty.

Yet the intention is not always cynical. However ill a friend may be, if one inquires concerning his condition, his family invariably replies: "He is better, a little." This goes on even when his end is obviously near; indeed his death may then be announced with a broad smile. In the whole language, for public statement, there are no Chinese words for bad and ugly. The nearest one can come to them, except in vulgar speech, is to state that something "not good" or "not beauti- ful." Thus the ordinary Chinese saves appearances; and these are of great importance to him. He would not know how to act otherwise in public without being guilty of some shaming breach of precious *li*, which serves him as a decent covering, almost as a second skin. For a Westerner no amount of intimacy with Chinese of the polite classes will break this down. It is best by far merely to accede to the conven- tions, and much more restful.

The Princely Man, further, must be magnanimous. The Chinese are very sensitive to breadth of character and largeness of action. They love to contemplate *han yang* or "elevated nurture," and its expression in tranquil composure. One scene in a popular play, where a cele- brated general receives the news of a great victory through a message that finds him in the midst of a game of chess, and never budges by so much as a hair to indicate its contents until the game's end—out of perfect courtesy to his opponent—seems literally always to fascinate the audience. This is obviously their ideal of a magnificent gesture, of completed character.

As in other lands, this magnanimity at its finest takes the form of forgiveness, even of forgetfulness, of past injuries, of scrupulous re- straint in the very circumstances that would be seized upon by meaner characters. In contention, the Princely Man "never snatches away what another holds dear"—avoiding action, finally, until if possible he can control it after his own manner.

In following this ideal, there is even among simple people a curious group effort to spur an erring member of a community to better con- duct. If his character has in it some glaring defect, if he gambles, or drinks to excess, for example, his circle of friends may arrange to give him what is tantamount to a surprise banquet. All goes well; every- one assembles with good will and cheer. Then, when the company is in high spirits, and conviviality is general, he is presented with a ring. On it will be engraved a Chinese character naming the virtue that through love of him they now wish him to acquire. Such *chieh* or "avoidance" rings bid him abstain from a shortcoming below his best self. The token in such a form is also to remind him constantly how to improve himself with the best wishes of his friends. I remember once seeing a bus inspector, in a small and very crowded vehicle, squeezing about trying to verify fares. On his hand I happened to notice one of these rings: the Chinese character on it read "Patience."

How opposed, how indifferent to all these endeavors is the character of the Little Man! Here is no meliorism, no concern with the flavor of goodness, or openness to the spell cast by magnanimous behavior. The Little Man, in China, is simply a gross and self-centered Sancho Panza, in contrast to whatever may be quixotic, or unworkable, in the Confucian ideal. Certainly he is of the earth, and at times he can be very earthy indeed.

To begin with, he lives very much by, and for, his gut. This seems his chief sensory organ; and a well-filled one is obviously for him the most reliable satisfaction in life. It may here not be out of place to attempt to explain this a little. In a society such as the Chinese, where even today living remains most elementary, the need to procure food is imperative. Eating, if possible pleasurable eating, comes before all else. There is everyday insistence upon this, and obvious satisfaction in consuming food in large groups.

Banqueting, even gorging, helps to relieve a latent major fear—that of some time, in some circumstance, going hungry. The Chinese promptly insist that if you are their friend you will eat with them; and they very soon begin hoping that in return you will also give them a banquet. Thus are profitable relations cemented. It is because of the underlying insecurity of their economy, I believe, and also because of the agricultural pattern of the Chinese community generally, that such parties for eating together are by all odds the most important and the most frequent in Chinese society; indeed once the eating stops the party breaks up. The amount of total income spent on food in China becomes, because of this, very much greater than with us. From high to low, everyone expects it, and knows that it is expected of him in return.

No Chinese, whatever his nurture, needs convincing of the prime rank of the actual pleasures of the table. They all enjoy food enormously, eat in general every edible product—except milk and beef—

known to man; and they talk about food incessantly. (One does not say "How do you do?" as a greeting, but "Have you eaten?") The Princely Man, even in this superior, does watch his table manners; but all the rest have few or almost none—at least of our kind. Ceremony, at the table, is chiefly concerned with one's place about it, and not overmuch with niceties in conveying food to or from the mouth. Confucius, indeed, did give certain quite careful directions for conduct at meals—although personally I never saw them much observed. The etiquette of seating, however, and above all of urging one's companions to a better place, remains elaborate. Once precedence has been determined, though, one senses that the average Chinese feels that nothing further should be permitted to constrain him from taking proper pleasure in his food.

Surely this wholehearted enjoyment is reasonable; some of the happiest hours of life in China, as in any other land, are spent convivially at table. Indeed Chinese pleasure in food is so gleeful, and the long banquets are so broken up with games, with jests and good cheer generally, that one must leave Confucius far behind, with his rigid advocacy of silence during meals, if one wishes to be merry in China as she is! Puritan deprecation of this continuous insistence upon food and the preoccupation with eating it in the company of friends may free one from some of the Little Men; but it would be a rather solitary China one would choose to dwell in.

Drunkenness, on the other hand, is quite rare—especially public drunkenness. (In Japan circumstances are different.) One is told, or reads, of stupendous bouts; but when one hears such proverbs as "If one dislike a man, half a bowl is too much; if there is a true affinity one hundred are too few," one must remember that a Chinese wine bowl is after all of miniature size. By our present-day standards, most of the heated rice wine is also not very powerful. Moreover, Chinese banquets last for so long, and vociferous games such as the ever-popular "guess finger"—like our own "scissors cut paper"—are continued so lustily, played with so much shouting and laughter, that one literally wears off the effects of the wine progressively.

Westerners have been known to return from a Chinese feast apparently replete; then, after a few hours, the chopped and highly flavored food already half digested when served, prepared moreover to be eaten chiefly for taste, with the mild wine, leave them wondering themselves at how little they feel satisfied. In matters both of food and drink, we in the West have quite other methods of replenishing our energies than have the more sensitive, the less heroic and more delicate, Chinese.

Let us continue, though, with the Little Man's defects, not to uncover the seamy side so much as to make our picture true to life. The instinctive interest that the Chinese take in the material goods of this world, their absorption with and pleasure in the properties of even the most trivial objects, have led to quite contrasting results. On the one hand this sensitiveness has made them one of the great artistic nations. The Chinese eye, and Chinese hands, seem in the past to have been capable of drawing from matter, any matter, charmed beauty that is unrivaled. Contrariwise their insistence on the material has also made them, in the affairs of daily life, a mercenary people.

In considering this last result, one is at the outset confronted with a curious and far-reaching paradox. This nation, which so enjoys the possession of physical property, takes abominable care of it. Upkeep, in general, is simply nonexistent. There are almost no exceptions to this. Whether or not they may plead extenuating circumstances, the Chinese allow everything to run down. Palaces are not renewed or repainted; their furnishings literally fall to pieces. Highly original effects, in every branch of the arts, planned with care and executed with patience, once achieved then seem no longer of interest. Disorder, neglect, major degradation of property, supervene everywhere. Everything finally becomes a litter, tatters, wisps, and shreds; material is first run down and then run out of existence. There are moments when this produces revulsion in Western breasts.

The Chinese know this of themselves. They know how their enthusiasm comes always at the beginning of an enterprise, and is only with difficulty sustained through it: "The head of the dragon; the tail of a snake" goes a familiar proverb. So everything runs down; and in the hands of the poor, constantly pressing upon the bare means of subsistence, property is literally used until it vanishes. Yet these forces are at work through the whole social structure. Here the Chinese are at absolutely opposite poles from a cleanly, foresighted, and provident people like, for example, the Dutch in Europe. Rather than undergo the drudgery of daily care, rather than subject oneself to the constant discipline of proper upkeep, one will always do with worse; finally one will actually do without!

Anyone who has kept house in China knows how unceasing is the exhortation necessary for the simplest tasks demanding routine effort. If the project is new, and therefore interesting, the dragon's head will appear at once, all splendid with horns and fangs, the beast curvetting and breathing noble vapor! Yet ask to have a foreign-style hardwood floor regularly waxed, as did my missionary friends, or order that a piece of machinery be carefully wiped so that it will not rust in damp weather, and the snake's tail will slide away from under the door.

One result of this, as the prosperity that marked the long reign of Ch'ien Lung declined and then vanished in the agonies of the nine-teenth century, was a lowering of living standards so drastic that those who have only read of China and its splendors in books, and have never actually lived in the country, cannot conceive of it. The first shock is a major one. In Peking there was apparently not a single family, even among those in easy circumstances, that lived in what we should call basic comfort, or even general amenity! Here and there one aspect or another might be stressed; one collector would have a fine array of seals; another might be found enjoying his goldfish. But to have everything well maintained, above all to keep carefully ap-pointed property in good condition and in smart order; this apparently never really enters Chinese heads. To the average Chinese, moreover, the Western determination to achieve just this seems actually a de-plorable and most uncomfortable waste of energy.

So everything tumbled down, neglect brought ruin even in places where it ill could be afforded; and the Chinese lived on, ineffectively and cheerfully, in complete disorder. Worst of all, from a practical point of view, no one could be made to give sustained attention to any project—a railway, the installation of a piece of important machinery, or even the upkeep of a single object—if its maintenance required con-tinuing and disciplined labor. (This fact, as much as any, explains why there is no modern Chinese navy.)

Yet for all this, physical property and above all the money with which to buy it were almost never absent from Chinese minds. In walking along a street, perhaps a majority of the conversations one overheard involved questions of price or value. "How much was this?" "What did you spend for that?" "How much, today, can one buy it for?" "How much salary do you now earn?"

One's salary is never long a secret, by the way, in China. Li Hung-Ch'ang, her great emissary to the West at the end of the last century, consistently followed his native custom, it is said, in his relations with those whom he met in foreign countries. He had two habitual questions. If he was presented to a woman: "How old is she?" If a man was introduced to him: "What, then, is he worth?" The Chinese among themselves talk perpetually, unashamedly, of money; many of their best dreams must be made perfect by its appearance!

Yet one must not be without understanding. Life presses constantly upon a population overlarge even for the vast area—although often not too rich geographically—that it occupies. It is no wonder that the prime safeguard against sudden catastrophe, the best remedy if it should arrive, is indeed just this: material possession, or better still, portable wealth in any and every form. There are certain grateful and glowing exceptions. The literary man, especially if he is a Confucian scholar, can at times show a moral disinterestedness that many Westerners might envy. By his education he has been made aware of how lovely, in its calm detachment, is the sensation of perfect internal purity.

For a handful of such men, nevertheless, there are thousands of coarser clay, the porcine, the groundlings. The merchant classes, identifiable at a glance, especially when they have achieved prosperity, and all their families, seem to think only on the material plane. This grossness is vast; and can be very repellent. The poetry of life seems scarcely to touch such individuals, perpetually occupied with bargaining and trading, with buying and selling; and there is enough of this attitude in all classes to give Chinese society, in retrospect, a rather brazen ring.

Another characteristic that every Chinese I have ever known possesses, bred into his fiber, is his sense of belonging to an order of things loftier, by far, than any introduced to China from the West. I have never observed a single exception to this attitude; it engenders a doctrinaire conviction of superiority as by birth, quite irrespective of whether pertinent facts are in glaring contradiction or not. At its best this gives complete self-respect to one of the large divisions of mankind; at its worst it degenerates into quite unjustifiable conceit.

The young college student in China is in general absolutely sure that everything he studies about the West only proves that it cannot achieve what his own country has already enjoyed in past centuries. He therefore sooner or later finds one part of his intellect in violent conflict with another; and he is fortunate if he does not at some stage develop, as one of the maladies of his intellectual adolescence, a case of virulent anti-foreignism. What he can never understand is why the West, since it is so obviously and basically inferior, has yet achieved such ascendancy.

At times his progress may lead to ludicrous episodes. In the period immediately preceding the Japanese occupation, in a foreign-administered institution of learning near Peking, the undergraduates decided that as in Western colleges they too should have that novelty, a Reserve Officers' Training Corps, to school themselves in the art of defying their hated enemy. The head of this "dragon" immediately became magnificent. These young men were going to show, with uniforms also, how in every way they were adequate even to the military standards of the strong if untutored West, which they were momentarily condescending to copy.

All went well for a brief time, until the actuality of Spartan rising for early drill became insupportable for the intelligent young men that these young men knew themselves to be. A planned adjustment or *fa-tzŭ*—about which we shall hear later—got them out of their predicament. Their local bugler was bribed, no less, to take punishment, if this should be inflicted, for "forgetting" to sound reveille. Their own faces would remain without a flaw, for if they were questioned about their non-appearance, had they not a most plausible excuse?

The bugler first did not blow; but then was ordered to blow again. This continued intermittently, until they decided at a meeting held to consider the problem, to abandon an experiment that—it was obvious—was continually being interrupted by this unfortunate hitch.

Such was their variety of intelligence; and yet they probably still wondered why the coarse Westerner had more power.

Nothing seems to shake the conviction that the superiority is innate. It drove the diplomats of the nineteenth century to distraction. Illiterate coolies in rags have it; the very dogs of China have it, to the last mongrel in the lane. (The lofty breed of Pekingese self-consciously refuses even to consider the question.) To both man and beast, foreigners obviously have only imperfect information concerning the proper order of the world, an order which all of them, as by divine right, simply know.

This makes true friendship with Chinese so difficult as to be almost non-existent, whatever wishful tales one may hear to the contrary. No matter how much courtesy, how much enlightened self-interest a Chinese brings to the affair, he is constantly making comparisons which are either invidious, or worse still, necessitate placing part of his own superiority in the realm of the invisible—where it does not rest easy in times like our own.

A further irritant is Western vitality, only too obvious, too bouncing and bounding. This offends his sense of the fitting; but it also wearies him physically. If one can restrict the area of friendship to suave courtesies and the gentler phases of life, the Chinese are among the most civilized and charming companions in the world. The very gradation of their smiles puts to shame our cruder variety. The andante tempo of the whole relationship—as I have heard it expressed—brings with it the balm of repose. But let there arise some incident calling for sterner stuff, and a certain evasiveness, a retractility that I shall presently discuss, soon appears, however ingeniously framed are pretexts and excuses.

One must understand this with some sympathy even if, as a good Westerner, one cannot but deplore it. Westerners seem to possess more ready, as opposed to enduring, vitality, than the slighter Chinese—if perhaps only because of their stronger frame and richer diet. This is important. The Chinese survive hardily, not even finding conditions too distressing, where we should soon perish; but for daily use they can seldom muster, and then waste, so much violent and expendable energy. Westerners are also in general accustomed to live under conditions of much greater personal safety, even today, than are the Chinese; and their habitually more light-hearted attitude constantly reflects this. The Westerner further has habits of frankness, whatever the situation, of action *sic volo sic jubeo,* that to a Chinese are inexplicable even when they are not in his eyes extremely rash.

The ready way in which one Westerner attacks another and is attacked in turn, in the ordinary give and take of social life, obviously neither fearing to lose face nor at all alarmed lest relations be imperiled by such sallies, is to the Chinese a strange business. "Draw in on an adversary only if you are absolutely sure that you can demolish him; and who can be positive?" they seem to reflect. "If not, though, leave room for the turns of fortune, for compromise. Do not offend!"

In the common relations of friendship the two parties, Eastern and Western, therefore do not want the same thing. So it is small wonder if intimacy usually fails to develop, unless there is in Chinese eyes a chance of continuing profit in it; and then one may witness prodigies of loyalty and personal devotion. This alone may explain why so many who have lived in the East never have done praising their household servants. A few fine souls, of course, will maintain the highest standards even when it is not to their interest. This is rare among a nation of individualists; but, then, surely it is rare anywhere.

The time comes inevitably when the Westerner and the Chinese part. Sooner or later the Westerner leaves the land where even legally he is only a guest—for until most recently he could not purchase outright an inch of Chinese soil. He has also probably been treated as an undisciplined even if amusing, romping, child, and a very spoiled one at that; but this has been in part by the force of temporary circumstances. Then, some day, he returns to his own "external country," leaving the local Chinese, in their own estimation, where they have been all along, in the "central" one.

This last, be it here remarked, is the only name the Chinese have for China. Even the republic, today, is still officially named the Central Flowery People's Country. Here politeness, contrary to custom, concedes no superiority to what belongs to another: this matter is vital.

China is the center; and there is to be no doubt of it. The postulate remains strictly true for all except the thinnest fringe of educated Chinese university students; and they, in public estimation, are beings with destinies apart, no longer completely members of the larger body public.

Unhappily inspired is the Westerner who attempts to demonstrate to simple folk how little this corresponds with present-day facts. Smiles of superficial "polite" assent—with no knowledge of geography to bring upsetting doubts—are often made bright from a light of amusement within. "How *can* any other people pretend to anything like the grand design of Chinese millennial civilization; especially those who know no characters, who have obviously acquired only a most imperfect sense of 'ruler-and-compass,' or decorum and politeness, who constantly stalk wildly about in truncated clothes instead of moving evenly and with dignity in proper long ones—who act in short much like excitable madmen?"

The very physical characteristics of the Westerner, hair that is often red or yellow, not even hair color—which is of course black—prove this to him. Their physical smell, reminding him of mutton, nauseates him; at times violently, so that it is difficult to control. Their bodies, large and coarsely shaped, are horrid with fuzz, quite unlike his own smooth skin; their prominent bony noses are also not like his, delicately flat and spreading; their strange-colored eyes—"tiger eyes"— prove that nature has made them, whatever their present ascendancy, permanently inferior to his own brethren, who at least have more human appearance and are aware of proper deportment.

Westerners in China actually do often appear an indecent, coarse, bright or else turgid rose, laced with purple. The light makes fine Chinese skin, by contrast, seem not so yellow but instead a much more agreeable color. All people look—and also smell—much less pleasant away from their own soil. No Chinese has ever seemed to me half so natural and attractive in the West as in his own land. In a Western sack suit, aping Western brusqueness and cultivating a businesslike manner, the student loses half his charm. Even his facial expression changes; he no longer represents the best of his breed. Why should not the reverse of this, as it affects the impression we make upon the Chinese when in their country, also be true?

Here is another Great Wall, immense in extent, but like the real one a barrier that has never kept out conquerors determined seriously to breach it—in their time of might. The average Chinese, however, is resigned to this. By now in almost every part of his own land he has seen "external country" men. Yet he rests secure. No matter what the times have brought, however violent may have been recent irruptions, it is his feeling that some day the tide is bound to recede. Thus it has always been since the events of far-off history. The Chinese, being superior, even to the obvious physical details of their bodies, must eventually, even passively, triumph. This is a conviction.

There is another trait in Chinese character to which I was able to apply a more or less fitting word only after a long search. This I have called, for want of any existing and more familiar expression, retractility. The Chinese variety of sensitiveness is more like that of the herbivores than the carnivores: safety through flight is its first law. At the slightest sign of danger, if he can do so an ordinary Chinese will promptly remove himself physically from the spot. "Of the thirty-six ways of handling all possible human situations," runs a common saying, "flight is safest!" This is a tempting, and surely a prudent course of action, in lands where private liberty is not guaranteed by law, as with us. For if a personal mishap occurs, no intransigeant appeal to abstract justice is possible, at least practically. We must understand this before we condemn.

Even in trivial matters, however, if a remote possibility of danger is sensed, it is second nature for a Chinese to draw in at once. "There will always be time," he seems to tell himself, "to come to an actual engagement with an adversary, later, when more is known." Meanwhile avoidance is instinctive. The consequence, in Chinese life, is a constant maneuvering for temporary position, an ingrained unwillingness to face any definite issue squarely and bluntly. This perpetual motility with its finely calculated variants of conduct makes the Chinese a very subtle people. As a technique it is understood and is used by absolutely everybody; it works with almost reflex promptness.

In social relations I never discovered but one counter-maneuver; for to advance while a Chinese was retreating would merely have made him decide to retire still more rapidly—as far back into his defenses as was physically possible. If, however, one let him understand that his withdrawal was clearly perceived, and if with sensitiveness at the same time one also withdrew into one's own territory, just so much and also no more, one might arrest and finally even stop his withdrawal. It was reassuring to him to discover in a Westerner an awareness similar to his own, which perhaps he had not anticipated; and he would perhaps reflect that complete withdrawal, no longer urgently necessary, might end by destroying a relation he wished to preserve, even in the hope that its price would eventually be paid by his adversary.

Then, in cases that ran smoothly, each could afford to advance once more; and if mutual timing were good, it was often possible to end with enhanced confidence and in complete accord. One false step during the preliminary retractile period, however, and like an untamed and shy animal, a timid Chinese might never again be persuaded to go near ground where once he had been frightened. As time went on, I learned that by employing this technique of slow motion, and by never overwhelming anyone with a sudden release of energy, I kept my Chinese friends, where other extremely goodhearted although excessively forthright Westerners might lack them.

Yet at best there were sharp limits to Chinese friendship. One of the chief of them, I believe, came from mutual lack of intellectual esteem, even when a personal balance had finally been established. This caused many East-West friendships gradually to wilt. The Chinese began with internal condescension. Then the Westerner, conscious of his unassailable mechanical superiority, if nothing else, sooner or later, refined or coarse, began himself to soliloquize somewhat contemptuously about the whole race when dealing with them on this level. Inevitably the Chinese sensed this; he in the course of the relation had been measuring Western action by *his* standards, and usually had also found it lacking. He might then think his own thoughts, maintaining an ambiguous attitude, half politeness and half rejection, which it was almost impossible, certainly very difficult, to penetrate. In the world, invariably, the Westerner somehow had the advantage, certainly every economic advantage. In Chinese eyes, however, he used his valuable power for puerile amusement, and—finally—he lacked all sense of a proper scale by which true civilization must be measured. If language formed a still further barrier, while no actual conflict might occur the two camps almost inevitably ended by losing touch as time wore away the novelty of the relation.

There was another aspect of Chinese relations to which one also had to give earnest attention: the necessity of constant precaution lest one harm another's "face." The West has long known this. Politically, and at their worst, the Chinese have habitually used their pride as an outer barbican, erected purposely to impede. Yet an extreme sensitiveness about personal dignity is ever present in Chinese minds, and the slightest incident may perturb it. So marked is this preoccupation that it colors all personal relations. Historically it has created that peculiarly Chinese phenomenon, the middleman, whose role between two sensitive antagonists takes on in China proportions unknown, I believe, elsewhere.

When both sides are notoriously thin-skinned, an intermediary is indeed indispensable. He makes it possible to proceed by finer degrees of movement than under any tactic of direct attack, which might draw blood at once; and both sides favor him since in an altercation he must carefully allow the vanquished, whoever he may be, to heal his wounds unobserved by the world. No one will then have seen the damaging blow delivered except this one man, whose own face would be lost did he not, in such a delicate matter, observe complete discretion.

So easy is it to wound this Chinese sense of dignity by the merest thoughtless word, the slightest gesture, such as, for example, snapping the fingers—which for some reason to the Chinese is simply infuriating—and so difficult is it for these wounds to heal, that I was much helped in comprehending such phenomena when I invented for this quite special condition the name of an imaginary disease, "spiritual hemophilia."

Hemophilia indeed it is. The patient inherits the tendency at birth; it is a liability engendered after a lengthy process of breeding, and it is a constitutional lack. No secretion can surely staunch such wounds and make them heal. Lesions that might in the West be only a momentary scratch of slight annoyance, in China are not healed even after the passage of months. The bleeding may be internal, but it is none the less deadly; and the foreigner who does not know what is happening, may only irritate a condition that at times approaches the morbid.

Fortunately the disease is not always so intense as this. Sensitive good humor rapidly applied is often of salutary effect. Yet in the use of language itself, the greatest precautions have been devised to safeguard personal dignity, to stress what is agreeable, and to avoid at any cost what is unpleasant.

Death is never mentioned, for example, in phrases of formal politeness—although commonly enough in daily gossip. One simply states "when one hundred years have passed, then . . ." A friend's father is, or used to be, invariably and somewhat pompously, his "stern prince"; his mother, obliquely, his "revered hall," where presumably she dwelt. Such varieties of euphemism are familiar, to be sure, in all tongues. Yet to the average Westerner they seem carried to remarkable lengths in China even in the ordinary exchanges of daily life. For instance, one may meet a friend who has grown stout; and wish to remark on it. How can one express this simple thought? A compliment is made: "Elder Born So-and-So has put forth happiness!" So of course, the implication follows, it is now visible in this most satisfactory way. Examples of such circumlocutions, often quite elaborate, surprised me from my first day in the Orient until the last; and new examples still turn up constantly.

There is further a convention of humility, which continues to be observed even in our "democratic" present. It makes one exception: the primary assumption, as we have seen, that China herself is central to all. Aside from this, everything that is one's own—one's possessions, one's abilities, even one's name—must be expressed as less in value than that of the person one has addressed. "What is your precious name; your lofty age?" The answers, to be learned simply as a formula, are "My humble name; my lowly age," invariably. There are even several gradations of expression, conferring lesser or greater honor, from which one selects that appropriate for the presumed "loftiness" of the age considered.

A formal invitation to a party becomes a request to "lend brilliance" —by one's presence. There is no end to the number of opposite pairs: "your deep palace" versus "my grass hall"; "your excellent food" as against "there is no food"—that is to be mentioned as even worthy of the name, one must infer, even at a banquet one has just been served. These set phrases for high and low, for thine and mine, run unerringly, or used so to run, through every form of polite discourse.

In writing it is even more complex. Every time the person written to, or his qualities, or his possessions, were mentioned in the old-style letter, and often even today, a new line must be begun. A polite epistle finally resembles a fringe of hanging willow fronds; one must repeatedly go up to the top of the paper—since Chinese writing is vertical—to descend again.

This process is known as "elevation." For any mention concerning the Emperor, in the past one had solemnly to elevate a space of several characters outside and above the normal margin. The characters for his forebears, if there were need to refer to them,—the writing of their actual names was of course severely proscribed—were raised even higher still. Official documents with much mention of sovereigns thus had ruled top borders looking somewhat like a fantastic crenelation; yet no one of education could afford to be in doubt about what number of these units of elevation was considered properly respectful.

One might from this description acquire a totally false impression, imagining rigid and severe formulae prescribing all the details of Chinese social life, a set code with no room for human grace. This would be far from the truth. Spontaneity, and a saving appreciation of humor, are far too ingrained in Chinese nature—especially in contrast with Japanese—to permit this. Ease of conduct, indeed, is almost the criterion. I have seen men prostrate themselves in the kowtow so lithely, so naturally, that one was left wondering how it could be that this deepest of genuflexions was being performed with apparently less bother, and in not much more time, than we should use merely for a very slow formal bow.

Under the old system this whole code of etiquette was so ingrained that it was observed with a minimum of conscious thought. "Politeness of position" as one might describe it, known to everyone, maintained assurance for all. Where it has been abolished, as in present-day China, manners—or rather the lack of them—can become very bad indeed. In his halting attempts to fashion even a rudimentary modern code, the Chinese of today seems quite lost, unable to borrow effectively from abroad and coming too late himself for the one system that in the past furnished secure authority.

East and West, finally, direct their considerateness, which is the basis of true courtesy, toward quite different things. Privacy, which we value so highly, does not seem to be among Chinese attainables. Unfeigned curiosity, unsuppressed comment, even simple determination to push forward wherever entrance is not specifically forbidden, are universal traits among the lower classes; and although often innocent enough in intent, they never cease to annoy us, often more than slightly. On the other hand, our lack of a sense of gradation, for use even in common speech, our prompt and ready solutions, above all our active execution of them, breaking down personal safeguards and the saving assurances that the Chinese have so carefully built up about themselves: all these are to them offensive and even alarming behavior.

Such constant tendencies toward mutual divergence are among the realities of any social relation between different peoples. In all nations, also, the Little Men must ever vastly outnumber those whose nurture has been more delicate. We must not in this world ask for too much; and remain grateful for what we have. The Princely Man, who knows this, accepts it with wisdom and cheer. In China, it is he who can best be our tranquil-hearted guide.

CHAPTER IX *Grandeur and Gentleness*

THE preceding chapter attempted to define certain traits in individual behavior, which make the Chinese man Chinese. There
are also, however, certain abstract qualities that help to give Chinese
life its particular character. Enveloping disparities, suffusing life in
general, there brooded over Peking a proud consciousness of human
achievement, of civilization attained, difficult indeed to define, but so
pervasive that every passing visitor felt its spell.

This atmosphere of an old court town did not, of course, represent
the nation as a whole, even if it did preserve the best of the traditional
China so rapidly vanishing. Part of the effect, further, was created by
the surrounding region. Here one was in North China, with its high
skies and broad prospects, with an ever-present suggestion of remote
High Tartary beyond its wind-swept stretches. The impressions made
by the landscape were intensified by effects of sharp light, occasionally
of incredible brilliance. All this was completely lost as one moved
toward the more humid South.

The prime fact about the human geography of the region was that
Peking had been one of China's chief capitals for centuries. This made
differences in the most casual transactions of daily life. Even the unlettered coolie could always "open-open eye" as the everyday idiom had
it, and see about him myriad examples of mundane pleasure unrealiz-
able in a provincial setting.

The background for the actors in these public scenes was superb;
doubtless man had chosen this place for its natural superiorities even
before he had begun to transform it. The city was not on any impor-

tant river; large waterways were lacking. It merely lay in pleasant fertile open country, adjacent to the hills. In the past the advantages of this site had been vital. Peking had been near enough to the Great Wall—writhing powerfully across the mountains, to the north—so that when the central government was strong, it constituted an ideal assembly point for military forces. From its almost impregnable walls they could promptly reach the scene of any irruption, and yet the city itself was not in the hills.

Enhancing the site, as we have already seen, was the noble man-made scenery of its fortifications, and also the architectural treasure heaped within. The perspectives of rose and yellow, the wings and backdrops formed by countless walls and spirit screens, gave a theatrical effect to any action played against them. I believe that even the ordinary inhabitant had a feeling for this. Leave Peking, and one would never find such riches the length and breadth of China. Although the prodigality could be overwhelming, a gift of imperial largeness, it was not easy to bring to clarity the feelings it roused. Finally I chose for myself to describe them the pair of words that heads this chapter.

These two qualities—grandeur and gentleness—seldom occur in combination in the Western world. When we are grand we usually wish to be forceful, to display our grandeur; when we are gentle we become humble. Our willful energetic architecture, in the Gothic age a creation of almost pure thrust and counter-thrust, is a perfect expression of this tendency. It contrasts revealingly in this old capital with the art governing the arrangement of the largest, most splendid palaces, which far from overawing, only the more spaciously displayed the grand balance that was their essence. Grandeur in Peking was not a display of tamed forces, but gentle—much as a tranquil and dignified aged Chinese himself might be. Conversely, gentleness had about it a breadth and humanity that made the quality one of deep wisdom. Within a field made ever vital by this double polarity moved the daily life of the city. Where the West sought domination, the East had achieved harmony.

Chinese grandeur, though, assumes a very different form from nobility of the Western stamp. A story is told of a Chinese sage who was begged to impart his wisdom in dealing with others. "The answer is indeed simple," said he. He thereupon called for ink and a brush, and also a large sheet of paper. These were brought, and he then began to cover the paper with Chinese characters. Only the characters were all the same, repetitions of a single one. The suppliant looked, and read: "Bear [with what is inevitable]; bear; bear!"

This is conduct as preached by the sages, in the Chinese grand style. It implies long-lasting problems, a need for magnanimity and breadth of vision, for a workable philosophy. It is Eastern rather than Western in that it seeks freedom by internal liberation rather than by physical triumph. To a Chinese it has the stamp of true grandeur. One fits oneself inside situations, and ends by harmonizing rather than by ever attempting to crush.

Chinese grandeur differed in many ways from that of Europe. The French thought of it typically—it seemed to me—in baroque terms, as a self-conscious and almost bellicose gesture, a demonstration. Enveloped in it a mortal might go upon his journey through life like some *roi soleil* down his garden perspectives. English "common sense" did not trust this. For the English, grandeur seemed more related to qualities of developed character, to the nobility of the solitary struggling individual.

Neither of these forms, however, included the natural good cheer, the relaxed and smiling acceptance of the humor of life, that in China are not incompatible with the grandest of living. Nor did the ordinary coolie ever need to fear that he might be debarred from sharing in these feelings by his place in the economic scheme. He was not handicapped by a sense of false shame. He well knew how weak he was— as were finally, all men—in any ability to withstand, still less to oppose, the larger dispensations of fate. Yet his humor came partly from the fact that he realized not only how tiny but also how active a creature he was! It is the Chinese, we must remember, who of all peoples of high culture, have seen and depicted insects most sympathetically. Their fellow-feeling for such very small creatures as the cricket, to take an example, is indeed a native touch! It sings while it may, and when the season grows cold the typical Chinese will shelter it in a cage, even in the folds of his clothing.

Yet small and cheerful though man is, above all he has one splendid dignity, which has raised him above all other creatures on the earth. This is the possibility of a glowing, indeed a radiant, moral nature. Chinese history, Chinese philosophy, abound with anecdotes concerning the nobility of minuscule man in spite of all his handicaps and inadequacies. He is little, yet he is able to smile with composure at the monstrous strength of brute nature.

Another trait of the Chinese also removed them from the present-day world: they were a variety of man, except for the thinnest dilution of the newly-educated, completely without science. Even in the past this was not so in Europe. In the civilization from which we spring, from early times, from the speculations of Roger Bacon through the experimenting of Galileo or of Leonardo da Vinci, and thence onward to a whole range of dignified figures such as Newton, we have always been passionately absorbed in a great probing of nature. This is something that to the traditional Chinese seems little less than a profanation.

Man with science, it must be admitted, has failed to attain the dignity and repose of man without it. Perhaps a Chinese legend will serve as an allegory. Once upon a time the great Lord Buddha was discussing this world with the very clever monkey who appears constantly in familiar tales of wonder. "At least," said the monkey—somewhat irrelevantly—"I can run extremely well, faster and nimbler by far, I am certain, than yourself." To prove his words he straightway darted off, and ran away as rapidly as he could.

Looking back he saw that he must surely have outdistanced his rival, who was not even in sight; but yet, for good measure, he kept on running. At last sheer lack of breath forced him to a halt. So he sat down monkey-fashion, panting, waiting for the Lord Buddha to catch up. There still was no sign of him.

A slight haze about the monkey now began to lift; and as it did to his astonishment he saw that he was perched at the end of a finger-tip of a gigantic hand, the size of a mountain—that of the Lord Buddha himself, effulgent in majesty.

So appear certain agile Western efforts in the tranquil sight of Oriental grandeur. Man is always in danger of being too curious, of being more impetuous than wise. "With all these abominable inventions serving restless man," the Chinese philosopher seems to reflect, "how can all *not* end ill?" And indeed who can say finally whether the immanent wisdom of Asia may not yet transcend the machine.

Yet in the West the airplane was early imagined. Our aerial navies battled in the central blue, in prophetic verses, before they were actually created. Even today in the West, contrasted with contemporary Asia, we are making the transcendent changes imperative in fitting ourselves to a new science with far more awareness of its implications than we ourselves may realize.

All such wresting of powerful unknown forces from the visible world, all our production of boundless transferable energy, simply do not appear as exciting activities to the average Chinese. What he cares about in nature is what he sees of it, obviously surrounding him; and even here he amuses himself by improvising his own conception of its laws. No natural urge toward practical experiment exists. It is so much pleasanter merely to invent explanations.

My servant Hsü Jung once reassuringly told me, when we were discussing the symptoms of head colds: "The whole space under the human skull is hollow, but it is conveniently connected with tubes leading both to the nose and ears." He chose for the moment to disregard certain facts that he himself must have known—even if only from slaughtered animals—in order to indulge in a much more appealing use of his imagination.

Thus it seems almost always to have been in matters scientific. The Chinese are an ingenious people; but this trait is different from scientific inventiveness. They enjoy contriving an original method of using the already known. Yet if a modicum of comfort for some minor need has been secured by such ingenuity, the search is over. The comfort itself is forthwith cheerfully enjoyed by those who can command it; and there is a minimum of curiosity to carry experimentation further. The great problems of motion, of light, or heat, have never been attacked on any grand scale in China. Donkeys, candles, and braziers still do all there that the common people ask of them.

Consider the laws of perspective. For the Chinese the actual look of objects is different! Observe the drawing of the foreshortened rim of a vase in any traditional Chinese scroll. It is as imagined, rather than as actually seen. Anatomy? After all these centuries the human heart, in theory, remains for simple Chinese where they place it in familiar gesture, in the center of the chest. It distresses them to think of it as being actually to one side; so they prefer not to observe the anomaly too closely.

The Westerner, therefore, often indeed almost laughs outright from sheer and obvious superiority of knowledge. Yet in our distracted present, when science blocks our view, it was illuminating to watch the life of a great people who inwardly did not possess even its rudiments, who had no feeling for it; and who continued to live, therefore, much as our own forebears had lived in all the long stretch of the centuries before modernity. Imagination was free; and it was fantasy that provided escape from the everyday.

Under these circumstances life was, of course, much more stable and uncomplicated. Indeed one of the beauties of Peking from a purely artistic point of view, lay in the fact that nearly all labor was still being performed with the muscles of men or beasts. There the human body still retained what it had lost in the West, the meaning of itself as the primary symbol of humanity. The world became an unending frieze of it, composed in all its attitudes and poses; no rival disputed its power. The ensuing simplicity of life had wonderful charm.

There were, of course, many lighter touches. They occurred constantly in the little events of daily living. I shall give a single example. One day some friends installed at the Temple of the Sleeping Buddha invited there for tea a Manchu of high rank, who was also an artist of repute, together with his family. They were to come from their own summer dwelling, also in the hills, by motor car. All of us were aware of the "modern" aspect of transportation by such means for such people.

We waited for quite a while that afternoon before a servant from the gate ran in to announce that our guests' "vapor chariot" had finally arrived. As we then hastened to meet them, a curious sight met my eyes. The family was indeed descending; but not at all as if from a modern automobile. Somehow it was even difficult to see *that*! Wrapped fittingly for the hazards of a journey in this self-moving vehicle, with even a certain excess of clothing—I fancied—if it were to run wild, the Prince and his wife, the elder and younger daughters, and also two small sons, obviously the idols of the family, as well as a female servant or two bearing still further clothing on their arms, all were climbing cautiously out of the car, not unlike voyagers descending from some interplanetary rocket. They had ridden before, even perhaps frequently, and of course they would ride again; yet each time it must have been as in a contrivance that did transport them long distances with great speed, but that remained itself completely alien.

Except for the seats and windows of the vehicle, there seemed nothing about it that they actually recognized. Even the seats were to them foreign upholstered sofas upon which they could sit while being conveniently moved by a foreign mechanism. It was the business of a chauffeur, sitting in front, to make the collection of metal parts in the concealed machinery produce this motion. Their sofa and chairs would then also move, hopefully without too much jostling. It would never occur to any of them, I felt sure, even to glance under the hood.

We have above reached almost a caricature—I hope not unkind—which shows what can happen when the products of an alien system are introduced into the blood stream, so to speak, of a people wholly unprepared by temperament to take an understanding interest in them. The general Chinese ineffectiveness in handling such Western innovations only made it further obvious that in adjusting themselves to these new powers, they remained what they truly were—gentle animals.

One had only to observe them. They moved about the world in slippers; they gave way to others out of a set conviction that fighting, all fighting, brought loss; and they could yield the field to violence without the least suffering of pride. If only face were preserved, everyone agreed that all things could best be settled, not by the victory of one of the two competing parties, but by yielding and compromise. Chinese proverbs, surrounding them from cradle to grave, perpetually exhorted them to avoid conflict rather than to attempt to conquer. The knights of medieval chivalry were surely the complete opposites of these men with an unashamed desire to avoid being hurt, who wished always to be able to flee from conflict, almost at any cost.

In Asia, however, this softness did not appear ridiculous. With the great numbers of the population, with life generally insecure, there was actually less possibility of heroic individuality. Small man therefore sought, and found, other pleasures.

Perhaps I can illustrate this. One cold day I took a friend, a quick and intelligent Englishwoman, to a half-deserted and only seldom visited temple north of the city walls. Part of the land within its enclosure had been plowed to make a kitchen garden, which was in charge of an aged caretaker. He was a smiling figure, as if out of a Chinese folk tale.

We wandered about the temple buildings for some time, but it was a raw winter's day, and the wind was so blustery that when he offered us the shelter of his warmed little lodge for a few moments before the long and frozen ride by ricksha to within the city walls again, we consented with no demur.

He was proud to be host; and to have us as guests within his tiny room. The little place with its low ceiling and its white-papered walls was exceptionally attractive, cozy as a ship's cabin. As we sat warming ourselves on the *k'ang,* I began to read his *tui-tzŭ* or antithetical couplets. He was almost incredulous that to me also the characters made secure sense:

> Of what importance if the roof be low,
>   when beneath it flower plum-blossoms?

> What matter if one's destiny be humble,
>   when within it is fragrant friendship?

Such a sentiment, here in this humble shelter, touched us; and for a few moments our two worlds fused.

They split fairly soon again; for once he saw our obvious friendliness, and that I could read his own language without impediment, he began to be polite after his own fashion.

"How great is the lofty age of your honorable companion?" he asked.

I translated this into English for my friend, who mused for a moment.

"Tell him that I won't answer!"

So I translated back again, although not quite literally: "The Very-Very [a polite title for ladies] wishes me to state that in our humble country it is not the common wind [ordinary custom] for women thus to respond to age-counting. The Very-Very much hopes, nevertheless, that this will be clear white [understandable] to you. We much thank you for your warm-heartedness!" I could do no less.

He was still courteous, but somewhat puzzled. Why had we responded incompletely? As we left, soon after, I remember looking back into that little room with longing. Poverty here was fragrant; simple gentleness a consolation. Perhaps we too should be happier if we were free of separating independence and of compulsive audacity. Perhaps Occidental pride isolated men, while Oriental humility brought them together.

The long centuries of Buddhism in China have also worked for peaceableness, teaching men of an ineffable calm, attainable through contemplation, which lay as an ultimate base under human consciousness. Further, since so much activity in China must of necessity be communal, with privacy so often a physical impossibility, there was in general far less self-consciousness in the public display of many feelings that in the West we attempt to hide. Sensitive pleasure did not have to be private. Cultivated toughness as a defense I found completely absent; although in Japan, by contrast, it could become almost an obsession. So where we should feel shame if we did not fight, the Chinese were ready to make adjustments; and they were at no pains to conceal their feeling that putting up with each other, being gentle, was much more prudent, and therefore for them more natural.

In this group society, however, there were quite special ways of showing personal sympathy. When all is well between yourself and another Chinese, a slow, soft, smile will usually inform you of the fact. I have seen total strangers on the road, whom I liked or who liked me; and perhaps after the exchange of a word or two we should come to feel that between us was the quality of *yüan*, or "affinity" as the dictionaries have it—a very poor word for something that we are not used to experimenting with. "Sensitive feeling," I submit, would be a better translation. If we become aware of this, we quite often barbarously hide or suppress it; but not so the Chinese.

I remember sitting at the wayside during a long walk one day, upon a rock, with a Buddhist priest who was quite silent until he suddenly made such a discovery, and broke into speech to announce to me simply and solemnly that between us there was *yüan*. The gates of his glance flew wide open, spontaneously. When this happens, in China, the light from within can be so beautiful, and life suddenly becomes so rich of itself, that even bitter affliction or poverty seem unimportant.

If they had the slightest imaginativeness, all Westerners in some part or other of their sojourn in China have fallen a little under this spell. If they are uninstructed, unskilled, or mutes in the matter of communicability, their pleasures are those of signaling only; not much more is possible. When speech can help, however—and with simple folk even a few words are often enough—one is soon in magic lands far from the asperities of life. Tenderness and sensitiveness can then make whatever happens turn well. It may be because the Chinese live by preference so much in this happy state that they constantly neglect the upkeep of their physical surroundings. The lowest—not the highest—standard of living, to give them leisure, seems literally what they choose. "Since the labor necessary for existence is perpetually irksome," they might phrase it, "once existence is assured, even if poorly, what then happily employs the mind becomes the only thing that really matters."

Once alight, this imagination can indeed become a powerful force. The Chinese consider themselves pre-eminently a literary people, moreover, simply because they know that they are able to use their writing and characters, skillfully unlocking latent forces of symbolism within them, to stimulate this sensitiveness. In the old order, the scholar gently read his way through life, ever refining upon such sensations. Almost every gate that one entered, every threshold that one crossed, bore some literary message on its name tablet or on the pairs of vertical boards placed on either side of the door frame, with symmetrically contrived inscriptions upon them. The mind and spirit were thus ever being played upon, subtly and powerfully; and it was a point of pride for a Chinese in the old tradition to be able to seize promptly any impression or mood, even if surrounded with complex allusion, thus evoked. So intent was he, under such circumstances, in using his imagination, that the real surroundings could become almost a matter of indifference.

I remember, in the early months of my sojourn in Peking, and before I could read, how one evening I was taken to a Mongolian mutton restaurant, in the South City, where we were to have a small party, grilling platefuls of this meat, sliced thin, and served with wheaten cakes, over an open fire. We were soon standing about tables set in a large and slatternly courtyard. The place was remarkably untidy; glaring electric bulbs shed a harsh light over worn benches, upon lengths of rusty stovepipe, upon piles of all manner of discarded objects stacked pell-mell in the corners. I was new to China, and my eyes were still untrained to the trick of disregarding such large amounts of litter.

Over one of the doors of the buildings making the court was a wooden *pien*, or horizontal tablet, shaped like a curving scroll and painted an unlovely pink, upon which were carved four large Chinese characters, the usual number for this type of inscription. For some reason these took my eye; and since I could construe only a little, I asked a friend to read the whole for me.

"That," he said offhandedly, "Oh, that!" "It says 'Abundance of flowers, drunk with moonlight!'"

For a Chinese such a sentence was enough. With this to stimulate him, actuality became unimportant.

This sensitiveness to the written word seems to run through all Chinese culture. Characters are recognized and esteemed as personalities. Each represents indeed a whole group of related thoughts, in general with a meaning more ample than that of the single word we usually employ to translate it. They have, so to speak, both a larger area and more indefinite boundaries. To write the characters with their brush strokes in a given order is important; and when they are applied to objects or people, this conferring is taken seriously.

Personal names follow a quite different system from ours in the

West. In a family, the *hsing* or common surname is placed not last, as with us, but first. By Chinese logic one always progresses from the general to the individual; what else would be fitting? This *hsing* is most frequently of a single character. The given name follows; but all men among the educated classes use several, for different purposes, not one alone. They are formed with unfailing imaginativeness; and generally—although by no means always—with a pair of characters. Women, too, are given fanciful names. Thus we may name a little girl Mary Smith, while the Chinese would name her, if she were of the Wang family, let us say, a surname as common as Smith, Wang Yü-Shuang, or Wang Jade Frost. Jade Frost she then would be at all moments of her existence, a circumstance that naturally to a sensitive person influences imagination profoundly. Little boys are given names to develop their will, their courage or magnificence; for little girls names are chosen that bring to mind the grace or elegance of birds, the delicacy of flowers, the purity of gems.

For a man, there is a whole series of these personal names that he may normally assume during the course of his life, progressing from one to another. When he is born he is given an impermanent name, a secret one, his "milk name," which is to be used only by his parents. This is a name bestowed in pure affection. Then when he first goes to school, or did in the old days, his Confucian teacher, upon the boy's presentation, is requested to confer upon him a "book name" that will spur him to learning and accomplishment. At the age of fifteen or sixteen, he adopts his *ming-tzŭ* or "official name," which is used at law and also before the world.

Naming, however, does not stop here. As facets of his character develop through life, he can always acquire new names for each. Any man of culture or of literary inclination, in the old system, might have several additional names; and these *tzŭ* and *hao*, or courtesy appellations usually given by friends, were used with satisfaction to everyone in all developed social relations. Today this causes much complicated searching in dictionaries of biography, since often one man is named historically, it seems to us, as if he were several. Yet the refreshment and spiritual significance of these further literary names was not to be forgone because of any minor detail such as this!

A man, moreover, could also make use of the name of his library, or of his *chai*, which is his studio, or of any room in which he cultivated his personality. Taking a title for himself, he thus became the "Master of the Book Room of the Pine Torrent," or of the "Study of the Tranquil Clouds." Or, if he were a poor devil living in a shabby little den —as did a friend of my teacher—his friends might affectionately address him as the "Master of the Blue Hole-in-the-Wall." Here were imagination and humor, forever at work. No one was too poor for this.

My own progress was typical. The American Legation gave me my first name. For identification, it was made to fit the sound of my surname in English, three characters—one for a *hsing* and two for a *ming-tzŭ*—being combined to reproduce this in so far as Chinese sounds could manage.

My *hao* or additional literary name was not acquired until the familiar Dr. Ferguson, dean of our small colony of American Sinologists, and a mature man extremely wise in his knowledge of how the Chinese felt in such matters, suddenly observed to me after the passage of some time that I lacked one. He thereupon consulted with the scholar who was his secretary; and it was duly decided and I was so informed, that henceforth I should also be called, besides "Thoughts of Power," my original *ming-tzŭ*, the "Philosopher-Student Who Cherishes." This *hao* had been chosen for me because of my obvious love for China; and in due course a second and smaller pair of characters was added to my name on my calling cards. With the new name, of course, I also began to develop a further personality, permanently amplifying the first, as time had brought it into existence.

It was quite a while later that I acquired a third name, my appellation of courtesy. One day I happened to mention to my teacher my admiration for a poem by Verlaine, reproducing with great skill the effect of scudding dry autumn leaves, driven by a wind along the ground. The lines seemed to me somewhat allegorical of my fate in China, in a progressively more difficult, colder, age. A Chinese analogue had brought this to mind; and we discussed the symbolism of the whole idea. Suddenly Mr. Wang decided that it was now fit for me to assume a further title, to be used whenever I wished, the

"Master of the Study of Autumn Leaves." The workroom in my rear court could thus also have a name conferred upon it. Gifts soon began to come to me bearing this new designation. A pen tray was inscribed with it; it was written on a fan.

Incidentally Chinese imagination never shows itself in brighter dress than in the poems inscribed on fans. One that I was given, for the warmest weather, had written upon it by Mr. Wang in stubby characters a "cold" poem. Its short lines described a boat, moored in snow and mist beneath the dark walls of an ancient city, on a freezing winter's midnight. The rooks were cawing; in the distance could be heard the cracked bell of an old temple. Would not these images, in old verses, cool me pleasantly in feverish weather?

There were many complexities of formal naming beyond those in my own simple collection. Priests, who usually had two characters only for their names in religion, drew upon the whole range of Buddhism. For princes, for members of the imperial family, and finally for the Emperor himself, grandeurs were arrived at too complicated to be described here in detail. Various periods in the reign of an Emperor—whose personal name, for the very reason that it could not be used, had to be learned privately—were given auspicious appellations, changeable at will. He could then be referred to openly, if obliquely, by these. If the coming of any New Year were to be marked publicly with a change of heart, the name of the reign date could thus always be changed to correspond.

There was also, in personal names, a chain that went through the generations, linking all members of a family together. Perhaps a moral sentence or short motto was chosen, as it was by one Emperor of the Manchu dynasty. Then each generation of his descendants had the first character of their *ming-tzŭ*, or personal names, made up of successive characters from this. The second character could be chosen for the child individually, to fit his own destiny. Or one "radical"— that is only part of a character, such as wood, or jade, or fire or water —would be chosen as a component of the first character for each member of the same generation. Variations were numberless; yet it was not uncommon to have someone identify a distant relative and place him at once in his proper sequence by some such effective system, adopted by that family for its own use. "He was my grandfather's first cousin," someone might say; "every member of that generation has the sign of the boat in the first character of his name."

The names of the *chai,* too, of many famous men, poets, calligraphers or artists, were well known to educated Chinese. It is not easy to translate this small word *chai*. The term "studio" often used is far too bohemian. Painting may indeed be done in a *chai,* but it is properly a room set apart for privacy and study, for intellectual accomplishment. It is that room where, surrounded by the objects of his choice, his books and scrolls—with a sympathetic view if possible—a man may develop his personality to maturity in tranquil and cultivated leisure. So the names of such rooms were never bestowed lightly; nor to the Chinese did they seem fanciful. The power of names was obvious and important; this was a matter of simple and complete belief.

This same simple belief touched matters affecting human dignity. Everyone had a name; through it everyone had a right to his established personality. I sometimes think of China as above all others the land where every single man is by right an individualist, concerned with enjoying human pleasure as he himself desires, and not according to the dictates of others. Indeed, in this sense China has been perhaps the truest democracy on the globe; and I doubt whether any revolution, military, political, or economic, can ever much change this.

Strangely enough, though, it is also a country where, contrary to a general Western misconception, there is almost no feeling whatever for aristocracy by birth—although the superiority conferred by education is universally respected. Man is man; and although the advantages of wealth and power are obvious enough, it never occurs to him to be ashamed of any condition in which destiny has placed him. So in China one never finds, for instance, the embarrassed class consciousness that so often makes for mutual awkwardness in the West. Social false shame is simply unheard of, unknown; and it is a great relief to be done with it.

Those who know the country only superficially can quite misread the character of the ordinary coolie, ascribing to him prodigies of sustained effort, or even a romantic depth of resignation. On the contrary his labor is simple, practical and cheerful; much more intermittent, it may be observed, when he is working for Chinese than when he is bound to foreigners. That it may be his fate to earn his living with "bitter toil"—which is what *ku li*, "coolie," literally means—rather than not to have to work at all (the obvious ideal), never for an instant makes him feel inferior in personal dignity.

It used to be amusing to listen to conversations between the puller and the pulled, when a Pekingese ricksha boy had a local Chinese fare. There was not the least self-consciousness on either side, never the handicapping distinction of class. The world was the world; and to exchange comment about it passed time reasonably for both parties.

The puller, for instance: "So you bought the cabbages cheaper in the country?"

The pulled: "Well, who would not go to buy them there, when they are as fresh as the ones you are pulling?"

It was the Westerner who through ignorance might falsify the relation; and in Chinese eyes become extremely uncivilized. Even then the Chinese still kept his personal dignity; that could never be rooted out! It is this great innocence of the very thought of congenital inferiority that gives certain Asiatic faces, I believe, their purity in repose; so that the head of an unlettered peasant may occasionally resemble a bronze image of one of the immortal gods.

Yet special techniques were necessary to maintain personality intact in so numerous and often so clamorous a society. There could be so little privacy, especially in the poorer dwelling quarters. Here one might exist in company from the beginning of one's life until its end. Indeed even in the families of the well-to-do, group life was so normal that to withdraw, to lock a door, to seek to be much alone, would have been regarded as a social offense. One has only to read Chinese novels with chapters of lament, delivered by unhappy daughters-in-law imprisoned for life in complex and unsympathetic families, to find how irksome circumstances could become.

How, then, did these individualists behave? They were, above all, it always seemed to me, a "rubbed" people; so many corners had long ago been worn away, so many surfaces had been smoothed, polished even, by immemorial convention, to make for ease and deliberately to avoid the heat of friction. It had been necessary to do this. How else, for example, in a large family could the wives of various sons ever get on with each other at all? It was the general duty of everyone to see to it that there were no rasping edges to speech or manners. Outspokenness, at any rate among the young, in the old order would have been suicidal folly.

People had to be very careful; especially if they were forced to lead whole lifetimes with others whom they disliked. They had to numb their revulsion, or at least take good care not to show it. Yet one often saw the technique so developed that it had become second nature. In the midst of crowds, with a group of companions, or in family court-yards, one might catch glimpses of faces showing clearly that their owners, physically present, were yet safely, in their own thoughts, leagues away—still individualists. These were the only secret places possible in a group society; and long training had taught the Chinese to enjoy them.

There is more to the matter, however, than this. I believe that the underlying philosophy of Chinese life bears with it a conviction that simple cheerfulness is—by all odds and under all circumstances—the most sensible and the wisest attitude for anything that may befall. The smile of good humor, though, must really come from within. Why be haughty, or arrogant, or tense or morose, when everything in the world runs so much better if one will only take it easily and in good part, and then enjoy the amusement and cheer? This lesson has been well learned. Laughter springs up of itself; at times the gaiety is infectious. Nowhere better than in China can a man outwit his destiny by the simple expedient of finding something simple with which to divert himself, within it.

In such a good-humored conspiracy to cheat life of at least some of its asperities, to turn it into something more congenial, less thankless and unprofitable than it would be of itself, there are many devices. A great number can be grouped together under the Chinese name of *fa-tzŭ*, a pair of characters difficult to translate, but meaning literally a little plan, or small method. Two Chinese take counsel in a given situation: "What is to be done?" The answer is invariably the same: "We must think of a good *fa-tzŭ*!"

Perhaps a few homely examples will illustrate how such arrangements work. In my time there was a young girl, quite poor, employed in the American hospital in Peking, who suddenly developed symptoms of tuberculosis. She therefore found herself in a critical situation, overnight, and unexpectedly falling into peril of destitution—or so it might have been in the West. Further, her parents depended upon her; some *fa-tzŭ* had to be invented without delay.

Now it so happened that someone who knew her was acquainted also with a wealthy Chinese banker, recently widowed, who urgently needed a well-trained person to act as a substitute mother for his young children, but who also did not wish to acquire another wife in thus providing for them.

The *fa-tzŭ* was promptly devised: "No perfect solution is now possible. She can, however, become a secondary wife or concubine." So off she went to a sanatorium, as soon as arrangements had been made; the banker was willing to take a risk. Her parents were also supported by the new agreement. Since her tuberculosis was only incipient, once anxiety had been removed and she was given proper care, she did soon become better again. The problem of her future husband, who wanted not so much full marriage as care and training for his children, and her own, were thus both solved together. This most un-Western arrangement is a typical *fa-tzŭ*.

I knew of another similar case. Three extremely dashing and attractive young married women in Tientsin had a widowed father who pined alone after they had all left home to make fashionable marriages. He felt indeed solitary. What could be done? They had an inspiration: "Why not all club together and buy papa, for his birthday, a really excellent concubine!" She must be both nurse and charming companion, to care for, cajole, and distract him. This was arranged, doubtless by the choice of someone of proper qualification, for whom it became in its turn also a good *fa-tzŭ*. The West would find it difficult, I believe, to cope so easily with similar situations.

These two cases may perhaps be thought a little garish; but they illustrate their principle. *Fa-tzŭ*, however, are also applied to find solutions for minor matters. I remember so well, when we found ourselves at a temporary loss in some small household difficulty—changing to a new sewing woman; or even having an old suit altered at the tailor's—how my servants would come to announce that a *fa-tzŭ* was going to be necessary, and then go back to the kitchen to "think-arise-arrive" it. This might take a while; but a smiling face usually appeared at my door in due course, a solution was propounded, and some ingenious dovetailing of matters, impossible to reconcile completely, but better thus resolved than if allowed to run their course, would finally bring content to all concerned.

Perhaps the childlike pleasure that all Chinese seem to take in familiar plays at the theater is really in part their appreciation of just such a sharpening of the wits, pointed up by clever acting. They can vicariously participate in marvelous solutions to complicated problems; during a few hours of bliss they may even feel what it is to achieve triumph in matters of state. The *fa-tzŭ* of the hero are invariably magnificent; and he never fails to execute them superbly.

In their judgment of human destiny, there was one aspect on which I found Chinese and Westerners stood at opposite poles. That is what each of them thinks about old age. I had come to China with the value of youth—its preciousness and glory—duly impressed upon me, as it is upon every young man during his university years. This attitude had been re-enforced by humble admiration given to it in the West from those who had passed beyond that light-filled region. Westerners often seemed to feel almost guilty about their gradual decline of vigor, and the passing of perfect physical cleanliness. Indeed when youth is past, the road of life in our world lies ever downward. Although certain rewards of the maturer years may philosophically be conceded—"Grow old along with me," one repeats—they are not actually much believed in. When old age comes, it is very nearly apologized for, its inadequacies made the subject for shambling excuse.

To my surprise I found that in China the grand lines of life ran literally in the opposite direction. The Chinese had created a veritable cult of longevity, as a high and proud goal at the end of the human journey. This, they serenely pointed out, was indeed the core of their civilization. For of what use was human wit, if one were to end life on the level of the beasts? They, therefore, had long ago fashioned another system, a chivalry of age, which commanded the enthusiasm of millions. To them it was a grand thing to explore reaches of time beyond the mediocre stretch of the middle years; to be able to say to those still young and therefore immature: "I have crossed more bridges than you have crossed streets!" The ascent ennobled; the very arduousness of the journey stimulated the voyager.

So no excess sympathy was given to youth, which was to know that it was not really at the height of life because it was callow, and was to behave itself properly in consequence. The grandeur of old age, on the contrary, was majestic, at last completely sure of itself. He who cultivated it successfully was rewarded by universal regard. I have seen old men so superb, so dignified as they climbed the last, the hardest, and the most wonderful slopes of their lives, that the very sight of them sent a shiver down my spine. These white-bearded giants of the years were indeed on the ultimate peaks, from which the view, although somber, was broadest. If the temperature in that elevated region was always cold, and sometimes even freezing, such was the human price of the journey. This was in China a conviction, a respect, commonly shared by high and low, by old and young alike. Those who were not yet old might even yearn, almost romantically, for the stature that could only come with the years.

One day, meditating upon such matters during a long country walk, I was overtaken by a rainstorm and sought refuge in a tiny hut, at the edge of some rice paddies in the region of the country temple where at the time I was living. In this small shelter several peasants could sleep in bunks along the wall, and thus take turns guarding their ripening crops at night. I had often seen the little place before; and now I was made welcome by the one young farmer there at the time.

The rain continued longer than I had expected. After greeting me he continued to lie comfortably on one bunk; and I accepted the hospitality of another. So we fell into a good conversation, both of us superbly at ease.

"Why is it," I asked, "that in China you seem actually to enjoy growing old? In the Western countries we dislike it so intensely."

I had, of course, no explanation to make to him, who earned his living with the well-known "bitter toil," of the obvious drawbacks to old age. He knew these far better than I. When almost a man's sole capital is in his frame and his muscles, he is aware of how calamity may fall unannounced; and of how in the end the best that he can ever hope for is slow decline in earning power, to final defeat.

Yet with all this clear, though unspoken, between us, he did have to consider for a while, meditatively, before finding an answer to a question as obvious as mine.

Finally he had it: "One might as well *try* another year!" That is, he implied, anyone with the least enterprise, anyone who loved life at all, yearly took on living almost as a dare, merely to see what it would bring with it. Why not find out how to test in further use what one had acquired?

"Of course it is a good thing!" he concluded.

Yet to "try another" is not something attempted alone in China, but ever in a great company. My farmer could thus always learn what happened to him personally while in a larger pattern. Life might be good, or might become very bitter. Yet one was not solitary, what one had learned was precious; and in another round of the same game, in another cycle of the eternal seasons, it could be put to use, with anticipation, and also—since there never is a last word to life—with hope.

Consequently, as the years passed, there was not for the individual, in this system, any creeping alone into the shadows, or pride reduced against the will to ashes. The respect of a man's friends, indeed of the world at large, could be assumed. Even women whose beauty had once been the passport to their fortunes, did not feel that to exchange it for such dignity and authority as came with esteemed years was too outrageous a bargain. To be called *lao*, or old, is in China a compliment appreciated by both sexes.

At anniversary birthday parties, such as the very important sixtieth, celebrating the completion of a full cycle, I often saw as a gift to be suspended on that festive day, a pair of antithetical couplets, commonly enough presented as scrolls.

> May your Longevity be as the never-aging pines
> on the Southern Mountains.

> May your Happiness be as the ever-flowing waters
> of the Eastern Seas.

This was the expanded and sunlit landscape of the later years, which we in the West grimly could take no pleasure in. The Chinese, by contrast, had smilingly conferred upon themselves no less than a minor variety of immortality. Here was indeed grandeur; yet it was specifically reserved for the old and the wise, who now had also become the very gentle. They, in Chinese minds, had gone the journey; and having seen what life could offer, were pleased, cheerful even, with the sights that fate had vouchsafed them.

"Five Generations in One Hall," the maximum stretch that humanity can know: it was so fine an ideal that silversmiths frequently engraved it upon simulated padlocks, made of thin beaten metal, presented as a first gift to little babies. These charms were symbolically to fasten them down to the earth, where it was hoped that finally at the end of their journey, now only beginning, this ultimate reward and dignity might also be theirs.

CHAPTER X *The Imperial Lakes*

I CANNOT too highly commend leisurely residence in an ancient capital. Gently decaying palaces offer charming possibilities for re-arrangement and simpler dwelling; manners are markedly more sensitive and refined; and the simplest acts of daily living are performed more agreeably in such surroundings. Time is used elegantly, in courtly fashion, with a quite special knowledge that its luxury abides when others have departed.

This was true of Peking; and by good fortune I had been able to make mine, if not a palace, at least a small house that in unspoiled simplicity and advantage of situation had in my eyes few rivals in the whole city. It was indeed unpretentious, although the effect of its ancient tree in the outermost of my three courtyards used often to remind me of scenery for the opera, where a single silhouette, a trunk of great girth and almost horizontal branchings, is made to spread from the wings across the whole stage. Indoor space I had in abundance.

Further, only a few minutes by bicycle, or a very modest walk on foot, and I could be at one of the entrances to what remain the most completely preserved traditional pleasure grounds in all China: the three imperial lakes to the west of the Forbidden City.

Once, perhaps a millennium ago, there may have been marsh land on this site. Or it may merely have been low-lying ground to which water from the Jade Fountain, behind the present "new" Summer Palace, was early diverted. Whatever their misty origin in the distant past, we know that long ago these lakes were so extended and enlarged that by far the greater part of their area is now undoubtedly the work, not of nature, but of man.

This fact always had about it for me something of the incredible. Until one had examined levels and shore lines very carefully, they seemed nature itself. Strung out so that one could always progress the longest possible distance by barge—since this was undoubtedly the chief pleasure they provided for the court—they extended along the whole west side of the Forbidden City, from a line even with its outermost southern gates to farther north than the stately buildings to the rear of Coal Hill. There was a prolongation of them beyond the palace grounds, the so-called Hou Hai or Rear Lakes, almost to the northwest corner of the city wall.

Had nature created them as they are, these lovely mirrors of water— surrounded by old trees and set about with many buildings for different pleasures, for worship and repose—would have been the perfect accompaniment and contrast, in their irregular grace, to the majesty of the rectangular plan of the palace. Man, however, here conceived of a nonexistent amenity, and then provided it by his own effort. We wonder at this today; but Marco Polo, describing his sojourn in Peking in the last quarter of the thirteenth century, when mentioning the Pei Hai or "North Sea" and the palace-crowned artificial island rising out of its waters, felt and recorded the same wonder at substantially the same sights.

. . . On the north side of the Palace [he wrote] . . . there is a hill which has been made by art [from the earth dug out of the lake]; it is a good hundred paces in height and a mile in compass. This hill is entirely covered with trees that never lose their leaves, but remain ever green. And I assure you that wherever a beautiful tree may exist, and the Emperor gets news of it, he sends for it and has it transported bodily with all its roots and the earth attached to them, and planted on that hill of his. No matter how big the tree may be, he gets it carried by his elephants; and in this way he has got together the most beautiful collection of trees in all the world. And he has also caused the whole hill to be covered with ore of azure, which is very green. And thus not only are the trees all green, but the hill itself is all green likewise; and there is nothing to be seen on it that is not green; and hence it is called the Green Mount; and in good sooth 'tis named well.

On the top of the hill again there is a fine big palace which is all green inside and out; and thus the hill, and the trees, and the palace form together a charming spectacle; and it is marvellous to see their uniformity of colour! Everybody who sees them is delighted. And the Great Kaan has caused this beautiful prospect to be formed for the comfort and solace and delectation of his heart.

The North Lake was thus the setting for the pleasures of a magnificent although barbaric court, that of the Mongol Emperor Kublai Khan, the founder of the Yüan dynasty. We are told of certain of these festivities in some detail; they seem both to have fascinated and horrified the decorous Chinese men of letters who describe them in moral poems. Here pomp and splendor were unbridled at a time when—on the same globe—the gothic Middle Ages in small and remote Europe were still near their beginning, distant in thought and removed in intent as if they existed on another planet.

As the seasons rolled by, these lakes became by singular good fortune virtually my own to roam in, by day or night, for pleasure and repose but also for work. I had early learned that if the Chinese language would not yield to intense assault of an impatient Western variety, I could successfully attack it quietly, even peripatetically. It was not necessary to exhaust the mind; only more gentle efforts must be unremitting. What, then, could be better than to take along my current packet of character cards and with them to wander beside tranquil waters, beside abandoned pavilions, under overhanging trees?

This habit began early and naturally; but it was the lakes themselves that lured me to develop it. There were times when I veritably lived within the spacious enclosure, not even returning to my nearby house for meals; for within the grounds there were well-run restaurants and tea houses here and there, each offering some combination of good cooking together with its own landscape.

At the beginning I had the surprises of the first cold winter, when in fur cap and gloves I skated by the hour over their surface—then covered with good thick ice. There followed boating in summer, in weather so lush that I still think of it primarily in terms of deep green lotus leaves with large rose flowers on graceful stalks rising between them. Year after year, as I grew to know the site better, my pleasures became something to be anticipated in advance, a gift of imperial lavishness.

In winter, for example, there were glassed-in, heated pavilions by the lakeside, excellent places for hot tea and steaming stuffed dumplings after skating, and genial talk with Chinese friends. When the heat of summer was at its sultriest, the days not unlike those at home, I learned where the shady places were, and which were the coolest. There the long hours glided by as insects filled the air with alternating orchestras, to celebrate their profound content. At sunset I might cross by ferry to one of the larger eating places at the water's edge, busy at that hour with much clatter and voluble conversation, its lighted Western carbon lamps suspended under high stretches of slanting matshed. I would then give myself the luxury of a good Chinese supper, breaking with gusto a mood of withdrawal that perhaps had lasted for the whole day. With succulent food such as diced morsels of hot spiced chicken prepared with green peppers, its sauce enriching heaping bowls of good rice with a flavor that one cannot find in the West, I confidently planned further.

Finally the site became almost my own garden, at least in the sense that I now knew beforehand where the feeble sun would be warmest through the thin willows in spring, or in the dog days which were the ravines where the sultry moonrise of midsummer was most mysterious; to what hillock to go for an open view with a breeze off the water; or where to shield myself on a cold day, as the year waned, if I still wanted to work in the open. For I lived much out-of-doors, these years, here.

One close summer's night, after some time had gone by, out of the blanketing darkness the guard at one of the rear gates unexpectedly called out to me *not* to buy an entrance ticket! They cost only a few coppers. "You are now," he addressed me comfortably, "a familiar man." This casual sentence—merely five Chinese syllables—made me flush with pleasure: it informed me that my love of the place had become a passport to it.

It was the high rocky island in the northernmost lake that I liked best. For the first year or so I saw it chiefly using only my own eyes to enjoy its effects, or with a little dubious knowledge derived from superficial guide books, either in English, or later—almost worse—in Chinese. Gradually I became aware that these slight accounts were very inaccurate; and I would have fact. So my teacher was one day a little startled to have me suggest that we plunge into rather extensive literary investigation. Our reward was great; and finally he caught my enthusiasm. In all his years of routine, this kind of reading—for pleasure but also about pleasure, long since vanished—was new to him. We made our plan, though, soberly enough. He would copy out in his neat hand passages that we selected in the local histories; and then with his help I put my own translations between his even rows of Chinese characters, which we therefore ran horizontally instead of vertically in notebooks we arranged for this purpose.

Gradually there loomed before us, like some high vision glistening in the mists, a twelfth-century island that became my delight. It was new to both of us. So many details, completely forgotten, were now by our curiosity being brought back to memory again.

Parts of the story, of course, were familiar.[1] Long ago the great conqueror, Genghis Khan, who had never himself come to Peking, here installed a holy Taoist priest whom he had first summoned all the way across Asia to the slopes of the Hindu Kush, a journey consuming some three years, because he desired the pleasure of a few conversations with him. An attachment so real had thus begun, however, that upon the sage's return to China the island in the Pei Hai was conveyed as a gift from the "Lord of All under the Sky" to the holy man, to do with as he would. Here he subsequently came to live, rambling about its slopes, composing gentle poems, which my teacher

[1] The interested reader is referred, for the tale that follows, to a book of great charm: Arthur Waley's *The Travels of an Alchemist*, etc., in the Broadway Travellers Series, published by George Routledge and Sons in London (although undated) in 1931.

and I now read together; here, having transcended the vicissitudes of life, sorrowfully yet calmly, we are told, at the end he died.

We then became absorbed with Genghis's magnificent grandson who reigned in the latter part of our thirteenth century, Kublai, one of those dazzling figures who from time to time come into history and monopolize the stage when they appear splendidly upon it. Everywhere he went Kublai had planned for himself regal pleasure on a scale that makes the reader rub his eyes.

Yet he was specially fond of this island. Crowning it was a splendid palace—as we have seen—named after one in the moon. From it he could survey his rich new capital. Here played his mechanical fountains, their water raised from the lake by contrivances probably borrowed from the Near East, since the whole was in charge of a Mohammedan as chief architect. Here he had his halls for steam bathing—a luxury probably also imitated from the Mohammedans—with warm and perfumed waters spouting from a coiled dragon's jaws, and marble channels for it to flow in from apartment to apartment. Mongol Peking, in these bathing halls, is thus even related to the Alhambra, where strikingly similar baths still remain. We know that in his hours of repose Kublai liked to be diverted in this place by recitals of long journeys. Here would be summoned the hardy voyager who had returned after seeing distant marvels, to describe them and to be questioned at leisure by his sovereign.

At the Mongol court, in this respect completely un-Chinese, women were customarily present at feastings and merrymaking. One contemporary poem that my teacher and I unearthed described, for instance, how as day ended the concubines could often be seen slowly riding their white horses from the palace to this place. (My teacher's shock of surprise at the word "riding" was illuminating.) There was even arranged for them here—we read further—a "Rouging and Powder Pavilion."

Mongol pleasures constantly reflected the violent temper of the race. Yet these conquering nomads were not unaware that their strength had come from their old habit of life on the grassy uplands of their native Mongolia. One emperor even commanded that this grass be planted in open spaces within the Forbidden City itself, constantly to remind his descendants of their origins.

In these gardens they were at ease, yet still boisterous—only temporarily sated. To divert guests, one Chinese author informs us, there were kept here a variety of wild beasts in cages. The cages were on wheels, and could be rolled one next to another. They then enjoyed watching how certain animals dominated others, even though bars intervened. Strange beasts, brought from great distances, interested them specially.

Revelry must often have been both violent and drunken. Marco Polo gives extraordinary details about the feastings in the palace itself. "The Hall of the Palace is so large—" he tells us—"that it could easily dine 6000 people." Here banqueted the Horde, cross-legged upon cushions and mats. Sets of platforms were arranged, their heights varying with rank; and women had their own side of the room. The Emperor's throne, placed on a dais against the rear wall, was so high that he could overlook the full assembly.

In the lakes, and especially at the "Green Mount," the enjoyments seem to have been more private, the guests fewer and especially privileged. The degenerate last Emperor who came to the throne in 1333 (it was a very short-lived dynasty), introduced here an esoteric variety of dancing, making Lamaist Buddhism a flimsy pretext for other quite unholy varieties of pleasure. Selected young dancing girls, costumed in luxurious brocades with a profusion of jewels, were dressed to represent minor religious deities; and as such they gave elaborate performances of which we still have descriptions. They went by the extraordinary name of the "Fourteen Heavenly Devils"; and as they danced they made their own music, marking the rhythm with conch-shell rattles.

There were also evening boating parties upon the lake, with female musicians seated high upon silk-bedecked towers built out over the water, and barges with extravagant trappings. There was even devised a kind of water ballet, the chief female dancers singing laudatory verses upon a floating platform. This was repellent to the Chinese of course; they were both conquered and critical. Yet while their power lasted, here as in Europe, the Mongols were implacable. Their pleasures might conform—irregularly—to certain aspects of Chinese traditions, yet at bottom they reflected undisciplined will and native desires.

As usual, a time of troubles came with the overthrow of this unstable dynasty; and the last weak Emperor died ignominiously in the desert, of dysentery, a coward forced to flee from the soft delights of his capital. We have, placed in his mouth, a poetic lament for bygone pleasures he had enjoyed in these lakes that is indirectly a poem of sweetest praise for Peking.

When the Ming line began in 1368, one of the new Emperor's first acts was to order the demolition of everything possible in the capital of his now fugitive enemies, including the Forbidden City itself. There even exists a unique description of the Mongol palace drawn by the surveyors the year before this great destruction was carried out. Nanking was to become the capital, and Central China the heart of a new empire.

Yet the lure of Peking was too great! Only a generation later we find the Emperor Yung Lê (1403-1424) deserting the lesser city; and there begins again a rebuilding. With it came renewed prosperity for the "Northern Capital"—the literal meaning of Peking's old Chinese name. Even the ruin of the great palace had not reduced its attraction. So all was done again, with interesting variants (which by this time my teacher and I were tracing with the satisfaction of initiates).

The Ming emperors had little taste for travel. Like most Chinese, who do not enjoy displacement, once installed in the broad area of Peking, they took their ease without much moving, even during the summer months, when their Mongol predecessors had gone away upon great hunting parties in the uplands of Xanadu. But the Ming sovereigns, by contrast, remained almost motionless within the walls of Peking, enjoying the pleasures of boating upon these lakes. From Yung Lê's return, during the rest of their tenure they built extensively here, although nearly all of these works have also disappeared. Yet we could reconstruct a little from brief mentions that we stumbled on in forgotten books.

Here, we read, were celebrated such high days as the Fifteenth of the Seventh Moon, a late summer festival, when at dusk—the banks crowded with onlookers—lotus lanterns were set afloat by hundreds upon the moonlit waters. For it is always full moon on the fifteenth day of any month in the Chinese lunar calendar—an elementary piece of knowledge in Chinese eyes. At this time, and by this light, the souls of the dead who have perished by drowning are invited back to the human world again. With much music and chanting by priests, food is also dropped to their watery graves, where a civilized people, one is told, has never forgotten them.

Not overmuch of its origins subsists in this holiday as it finally has developed. Even a few years ago in Peking it was made rather into a great occasion for boating parties, especially on one canal to the east of the city. In these Westerners often joined, hiring barges for the evening almost as if for boat races on the Isis or the Thames. Crowds began to assemble by late afternoon; later the frail lanterns were set out to float on the water, as they had been for centuries, guttering as dusk turned to night. Finally a great model of a spirit boat, made with paper on a frame of reeds, was set ablaze, as vestmented priests beat gongs and intoned sutras.

Then in 1644 came the Manchu or Ch'ing dynasty, the last of all, ruling until 1912. The record now became so abundant that compilation was difficult. Two remarkable emperors, grandfather and grandson, both extremely able men though of very different characters, each held the throne for sixty years. The periods of their respective reigns are titled K'ang Hsi (1662-1722) and Ch'ien Lung (1736-1795), which in English have now become virtual equivalents for their personal names. The K'ang Hsi and Ch'ien Lung emperors were the great monarchs of modern Chinese history. Each fills this lake, still, with story and legend.

K'ang Hsi, for instance, who enjoyed simplicity, commanded that the common people be admitted to this most forbidden enclosure at the time of the Chinese New Year, to see the fireworks customarily set off during that holiday. They were allowed to group themselves along the ice on one shore, while opposite sat the Emperor, clothed in sables, surrounded by his full court.

Ch'ien Lung's traces were literally everywhere. At times in the lakes one progressed only a few yards from inscription to inscription. Here was a writing Emperor, a consciously literary one; and his formal descriptions of the new halls he ordered to be built in the lakes, including detailed reasons for their building, and poems celebrating their virtues, were methodically carved into stone or white marble.

Every small pavilion, of course, also had its gilt-framed name tablet above the entrance. The Chinese do not have unnamed structures in such a place; to finish a building one must title it properly and imaginatively. One that always amused me was called the Hall of the "Prompt Snow." The story about it was simple enough. Not long after it had been completed, Ch'ien Lung one day arrived, wishing to make a winter poem. To aid in his composition he wished that there might be snow about him—and as he made this wish, wonderfully enough, snowflakes did begin to fall. So he conferred this name upon the place.

As the eighteenth century gave way to the nineteenth, these glories faded; the nineteenth century became a time of prolonged—and finally for the old China, tragic—difficulties. Taste, declining perhaps even because of its past virtuosity and elaboration, became deplorably, irremediably poor. A period of dullness ensued. Yet during the reigns of the succeeding emperors, and all phases of the regency and other compromises arranged to prolong the reign of the last Empress Dowager, the lakes continued to play their customary role.

The Empress, indeed, was markedly fond of them. One could see where she had arranged her theatricals about a rectangular courtyard in a group of buildings poetically named "Spring Rain in the Forest Grove." This had a flooring of water, which was said to improve the timbre of falsetto voices. Her attendants grouped themselves about her under a central porch, or along galleries at the sides; while the actors performed under a somewhat smaller shelter opposite, across the water.

Or one would hear about the "dragon" who cavorted for her on ice, made up of a number of skaters crouched caterpillar-like under a yellow covering. Its huge head of decorated papier-mâché had out of respect always to face the Empress herself. This was not so difficult;

it was the tail man, one was told, who in crack-the-whip maneuvers had to be the clever fellow.

So, from nomadic conquerors down to the present century, the rich record was spread before us. The literary vestiges became my teacher's preoccupation; we daily stumbled upon further discoveries. Poems celebrating this or that occasion took on new meaning when we could easily walk to the settings described in them. Perplexing allusions became simple on the spot; and we made human sense again of matters long since forgotten.

The point should perhaps be made that one can attempt a proper comparison between these pleasure grounds and the lesser ones of Europe only if one imagines that continent not with a number of capitals, but merely a single one. In China, the history of an area much vaster than small Europe, and very much more populous, had developed through more than six centuries practically from this single center. As one dynasty had yielded to another, these gardens, their site unchanged, had been only further embellished. Here Chinese scale and a Chinese sense of fitness had created a sylvan region not at some distance from the capital, but literally at its heart. Yet so broadly conceived was the plan that in no way did this seem illogical. One knew that a million and a half souls lived beyond these high walls; and yet from the waters of the lakes one saw only the distant hills, and the sun could set behind them as if in the open country.

How was this done? It was done in the traditional scheme of Chinese garden planning. The word "garden" means very different things in different parts of the globe. We think of our own gardens in terms of growing things, of flowers blooming in beds, and well-kept lawns. The Chinese, on the contrary, have comparatively few flowers in a garden; and these are most often potted, brought from cold-frames by the gardeners to be put on display in various garden houses only when they are at their best. There are no lawns. To a Chinese, besides the natural contours of the land and of course shade-giving trees, the charms of a garden are chiefly those of water and rockery. Water mirrors the sky, and its sparkle animates a landscape; while well-shaped rock—masses of· it, often brought from long

distances with much labor—moves the Chinese by its constant suggestion of the strength of nature, of what is permanent, enduring,
and imperishable.

There have been characters in Chinese history who have cultivated
this taste for simple rock with an assiduity and a passion hard for
us to evoke. In days of prosperity, wealthy amateurs made a pastime
of collecting strange stones for their gardens. This was carried to such
extremes that the last Northern Sung Emperor is said finally to have
lost his throne by neglecting the business of government, while he
absorbed himself in an attempt to create one transcendent and wholly
artificial site. The exactions of his eunuchs and the outrageous expense
created the wave of popular disapproval that overwhelmed the state.
My teacher, quite converted now, even enthusiastic, painted for me a
map of this remarkable garden as reconstructed by him after much
reading of old texts.

To begin any Chinese garden, whether large or small, the procedure
is almost always the same—and simple enough. It is compelling as
child's play. One scoops out a hollow; and then heaps up the earth
one has removed. Into the artificial depression is run water, whether
a few feet only, or as in the imperial lakes, enough to float a whole
court upon splendid barges. So long as boats can be poled about, so
long as lush lotus in summer will grow from the shallow bottom,
spreading its great flat leaves over the surface, further depth is of no
concern. The water must flow easily, of course; and the channels for
inlet and outlet often take the form of pretty brooks or small ravines,
"naturally" bordered with set stones.

The excavated earth is then made into a hill; and the hill is if
possible made into an island; for islands give one an opportunity to
leave the mainland, and thus to use bridges. The landscape is then
complete.

Rockery is introduced, in a plan like this, to make the whole seem
finally not the work of man, but of nature. A margin of stones is
always used, for example, to imitate a shore line. Simulated outcrop-
pings also come to the very sills of the garden buildings, the irregular
meeting the polished in a contrast that seems perennially to delight
Chinese imagination. Caves are also created, to give similar pleasures.

The more they suggest landscapes not of this earth, but rather in fantastic regions inhabited by the immortals, the more they are appreciated.

On this island in the Pei Hai there were several chains of such caverns, one cave leading into another. Their passageways meandered up and down, first underground and then suddenly back into the light again, or even tunneled to oddly planned buildings, equipped with staircases to allow the wanderer to change levels. One such tunnel, by an unexpected climb in the dark, led steeply upward into a fan-shaped garden house. The rocky steps debouched unexpectedly in the middle of a polished marble floor, with an effect of utter fantasy. To wander thus was to enter a land of genii and immortals!

Another familiar Chinese artifice was also at its best in the Pei Hai: the rimming chain of hills that concealed the world outside. These were made simply of earth raised to a height sufficient to mask the enclosing walls. They were often only sparsely planted, but their contours simulated those of real hills. This device was further used to conceal buildings, either for privacy or for service.

All this was not nature, but came near to it. The plan was never regular and could therefore always include or conceal further isolated structures. It made possible all the picturesque arrangements that spring to Chinese minds when they think of a great garden. Our lawns and flower beds, our concentration on growing flowers and clipped greenery, do not really interest them. They find the imaginativeness of their own scheme much more satisfactory. For a Chinese to make a garden is no less than to fashion a world as he would like it.

The Pei Hai, as the oldest of the three lakes, held for me by far the most interest. It was the largest, and it also had the finest building. There were better surprises. Its chief gate, beyond the northwest corner of the Forbidden City, was placed so that one could look back to a particularly glittering perspective of tiled pavilions and palace walls.

Nearby, like a small detached fort outside the enclosure, was the so-called Round City. It was not really round but shaped like a skull; and some said that this proved a Mongol origin and was a concession to Lamaist superstition. Broad military-looking staircases, open to the

sky, curved gently upward within its battlemented walls, and a venerable white-barked pine tree, so ancient that in the eighteenth century
Ch'ien Lung had commanded that it be formally ennobled, giving
to it the title and dignities of a Chinese earl, spread its limbs across
the paving on the terrace.

Nearby was an irregular basin, hollowed from a single mammoth
block of mottled gray-green jade, and so large that it was housed
under an open pavilion of its own. Carved in relief upon it were
horses and sea monsters cavorting among jade waves. At imperial
banquets in Mongol times this was said to have been a vat for wine.
Since then it had had a long history. At one time it had disappeared;
and Ch'ien Lung himself had rescued it from the monastery where it
was rediscovered, in use as a tub for pickled vegetables. When it was
restored to the palace once more, he ordered a full account of its
long history, which he drew up, to be inscribed within it.

Leaning over the ramparts crowning the thick walls of the Round
City, one could look down upon the urban traffic flowing about its
base, or crossing the long arched marble bridge that spanned the nearby
waters to the west. By convention this bridge divided the northern
from the central lake; although the two were really one. In Yüan times
—my teacher and I discovered—there had been a removable central
draw, taken away for security by imperial regulation whenever the
Emperor was absent, thus automatically imprisoning the palace concubines.

Once inside the entrance to the lake, one was quite near the central
island, which rose high across a broad and ancient zigzag bridge of
stone. As one climbed the prospect broadened. Archaeologicially one
was on rich soil; although Chinese building being the comparatively
perishable thing it is, there was not much from a time older than
Ch'ing that still met the eye. The Mongol palace had long ago vanished, of course, and on the summit it once had crowned was now
a religious monument of strange shape, the great white Dagoba, a
Buddhist stupa. This to the Chinese was doubly exotic, as an importation from India.

First by a path winding among rocks, and finally by a short

flight of steep marble steps, one could mount to a small building in front of its base, covered with brightest glazed tiles. Here one looked out not only far to the south over all the lakes, but eastward to the Forbidden City as well. It was one of the best views in the capital. Generally, for this very reason, it was not long without visitors; yet one could have it all to oneself, like the high deck of a superbly decorated galleon, on days of storm and rain.

Behind it facing north, and thus gratefully in the shade of the towering stupa during long summer days, was a pavilion called the Hall to Seize the Verdure, facing toward the back of the lake. This had been turned into a small restaurant where—if one knew about it—an ex-imperial cook would prepare a special variety of large round bun, covered with sesamum seed, which he split open and filled with delicately spiced hot chopped meat. It was a fine invention. To accommodate the visitors who became numerous in summer, an additional platform had been built as if on stilts over the side of the hill, which here descended sharply to the lake. One could thus dine high among the trees.

Later in the year, when the weather grew colder and the place became deserted, bundled up in extra clothing I could still have steaming fragrant tea and these delectable stuffed *shao-ping* to go with it, here by myself. As the darkening colors of the evening slowly faded, it was a wonderful place. Far below a barge laden with water grasses might crawl across the lake (even what grew beneath the surface, here in China, was useful to someone); and on the north shore one could look off toward the Little Western Heaven, a Buddhist temple within the grounds; as well as toward several groups of secular buildings, including the ever-charming Five Dragon Pavilions, set into the lake like so many jeweled reliquaries, and connected by small stone bridges over the water.

Completing the perspective in the northwest corner was an imposing group of rose-walled buildings, foursquare and set within their own moat, with an archway of colored tile in the center of each wall. These led to a sculptured Buddhist pantheon, modeled life-size and in full relief, representing a hierarchy of gods upon a Chinese magic mountain. It was called the Great Western Heaven. The sun would

186 THE YEARS THAT WERE FATTHE YEARS THAT WERE FAT

go down in clear ruby light over the wrinkled water, now dark aquamarine with its lotus shriveled and gone, as these buildings first sharpened and then died away along the horizon.

The northern shore of the island had been arranged as a single curving rotunda, with marble balustrading on two levels, not unlike a large segment of tiered wedding cake. A two-storied covered gallery—also curving—bordered the highest level; and along its top one could pass through the upper floors of several lakeside pavilions. The Hall of Tranquil Ripples was one; that of Distant Sails another.

Behind them had been made romantic glens of rockery, steep declivities planted with white pines. Here were also various deserted cabinets or book rooms—their doors wide open, the books and furnishings of course long gone—or porches and studies for retreat. They bore strange names and contrived odd surprises. Some were reached by vertiginous open staircases, intentionally made to curve as in a dream. One came upon others hidden from the world, with miniature internal courts of the greatest privacy. Each suggested a different adventure.

At times it seemed an impossibility that the whole island with its rockery could all be thus completely artificial, within a lake itself dug by man. Time, however, had lent itself kindly to the scheme. In the autumn, when the great winds blew, the tall trees shed their leaves to cover a landscape that in the course of centuries seemed finally to have earned for itself a right to its entity.

The Chung Hai or Central Lake was a region of quite contrasting pleasures. A year or two before my arrival, a stretch of its west shore had been made the site for one of Peking's most successful concessions to modernity, a good swimming pool. With tables set under its bordering matsheds, this place was animated all summer long. Young Chinese at leisure had taken to the novelty readily, liking its combination of not over-strenuous exercise with so much gregariousness.

Arriving in the cool of the morning, I could dally here beside the water's edge, usually with some task of memorizing to occupy me intermittently, passing here a good part of the day. There was always a savory dish for lunch, often fried rice with fresh vegetables, topped with tea and pastries copied from the local French bakery, at a table near the pool; and leisurely conversations with Chinese friends to pass the long hours. The better part of the afternoon would have slipped away before I thought of returning home.

The pool was south of a group of abandoned buildings set in a grove of spindly trees, with the façade of their main hall fronting upon the broad marble terrace. It was named the Hall of Purple Effulgence; and the enclosure formerly had been dedicated to the military glories of the empire. Before this Hall of Purple Effulgence the emperors traditionally had watched military maneuvers; and here also, a typically Chinese arrangement, were set the physical exercises, the riding and archery, that were part of an examination for a military "Ph.D." to parallel the literary one.

In my time these halls were completely deserted. The system that continued to produce only archers and to put its faith in bows and arrows in a time of modern weapons, maintaining in idleness banner-men pensioners of no ability whatever, had brought China to a sorry pass. The locked and abandoned buildings told their own tale. One had no need to enter and puzzle out long inscriptions praising vanished heroes, set into now dusty walls.

Across the lake toward the palace from this place was a large temple group, its buildings roofed with shining plain black tile. These were set about with ginkgo trees, the most stately that I had ever seen. In Peking, in the autumn, the days become crystal clear, as under a burning glass when the sun is hot, although the main body of the air has already cooled. Here was the place for such weather, with sunny walled courts, shadowy halls of worship, and quiet terraces overlooking the water. Then, finally the snows of winter would cover the branches of the old trees, and drift high on the broad platforms before the closed temple doors until they obliterated the marble steps.

Off the shore, now connected by a rickety wooden bridge, was one of the most appealing structures in all the lakes, the small Pavilion in the Heart of the Waters. It possessed one of the formal "Eight Famous Views of Peking," and from it one saw at their best the long marble bridge with the stupa-crowned island of the North Lake beyond. Even today the eye here can discover almost nothing that is not sheer perfection. Ch'ien Lung, as usual, had ordered a large stone tablet, with an imperial inscription in his own hand.

Going toward the South Lake from this place, interest waned. There were the usual groupings of small buildings hidden behind artificial hills, and also willow-planted walks along the water's edge; yet after the arrangements in the North Lake they roused only minor interest. Finally one came to a lock, over which the quiet water poured to a level a mere few feet below. Here began the last of the three "seas."

Almost immediately, also, the late architecture became much more elaborate. One saw too much carved brick; an ineffective straining for effect was everywhere obvious. Scale also had become pretentious. This was inferior work, either over-ornate "Ch'ien Lung," or made for the last Empress Dowager. An artificial island had been created off these shores also; and looking toward the south this did offer a broad and imposing view, especially from a well-placed ample open building set over the water in front of it. Facing sunward, this had been named the Pavilion to Welcome the Southern Fragrance.

Yet to such connoisseurs as my teacher and I now had become, the whole island seemed overbuilt. We conceded to it only minor novelties, its flying galleries or its clusters of rapier rock. The tiling was too elaborate, and too much had everywhere been attempted at once.

The site remained to us interesting chiefly for incidents that had occurred here as the Ch'ing dynasty had waned. It was on this island that the Empress Dowager had held captive her own son, the Emperor Kuang Hsü. A drawbridge, and eunuchs to guard it, had assured her plans. One could even wander freely into the now abandoned Emperor-prisoner's former bedchamber, and see where two cupboard-like partitions had been built into the walls, one at either end of the imperial *k'ang*. Each, it was said, was contrived to permit a eunuch to stand concealed within, during the night watches. His duty in this uncomfortable position was to inscribe in a register whatever transpired in the imperial alcove. Each of these was brought to the Empress

Dowager every morning; and by tallying them she was able to keep watch over the poor captive who was her own son.

Another unfortunate, a woman, had also left traces of her passage through the South Lake. Not Chinese but from Aksu, far to the west, and a Mohammedan, she was known as the Fragrant Concubine. According to tales told and retold without too much historical foundation, her great beauty had led to her capture as part of the spoils of war in one of Ch'ien Lung's Central Asiatic campaigns. The Emperor is supposed subsequently to have become romantically infatuated with her.

As his nominal mistress she still determined at any cost to remain faithful to the memory of her own husband; and at the last she could end only by suicide a situation that had become impossible. In spite of her lack of interest in him, Ch'ien Lung apparently wished to grant her more than any of his other favorites; and since the chief mosque of Peking, in the Mohammedan quarter, was merely over the wall of this south lake, he is said to have ordered that an upper room in the main gate tower be arranged for her from which she could look out and see her own people in lanes busy with Mohammedan traffic. This large entrance, probably much rearranged, still exists; and so does even the minaret of the mosque, across what is now an intervening boulevard. Yet in between, clanging trams and honking automobiles go by, making unreal the unhappiness of long ago.

CHAPTER XI *A Garden in the Mind*

CHINA has suffered one outrageous loss at the hands of Westerners a deed of vandalism that by a single blow robbed her—and the world—of many great treasures from her past. This was the deplorable sack and burning, by British and French troops in 1860, of the great Summer Palace, the now vanished old one. The "new" Summer Palace, which exists today, was already in being at that time, so that in one sense it is not new; but it was a subsidiary creation, not originally intended for residence. Many of its buildings were also destroyed, never to be rebuilt; and the grounds of the old Summer Palace were so systematically laid waste that the blow proved fatal.

The details of this incident do not here concern us; it formed the climax to a situation that had become progressively more involved during a military campaign. The ill-advised burning was deliberately ordered to make the Emperor himself, rather than his subjects, suffer for acts of treachery, and for the inexcusable torture of European hostages in violation of a flag of truce. Alas, the Emperor's residence contained much that was irreplaceable, part of the riches of the nation. The objects taken by French and British troops as plunder, or souvenirs of the campaign, were tawdry trifles compared with such rarities as scrolls by great artists, Chou dynasty bronzes or Sung porcelains. These were scarcely noticed by the looters, for our modern appreciation of Chinese art was as yet unborn. The fires lasted for days; and in them perished beauty never to be replaced. So this is in part a chapter about a palace in the countryside not far from Peking that no longer exists.

The name of the great enclosure was the Garden of Perfect Brightness, the Yüan Ming Yüan. To Chinese minds in a dwelling like this, palace and garden are one; for the buildings—no matter how grand in scale—were always set apart and among rocks and trees. It had been the favorite, and finally had become the principal residence of the great Ch'ien Lung. Toward the end of his life he preferred to dwell here even during the winter months, going to the main palace in Peking only for formal celebrations at the time of the New Year.

One can consequently imagine what treasure had been heaped together in this place during an age of great prosperity, to perish only three generations later, when the hazards of war forced another Emperor, his great grandson, to abandon it all and flee to Jehol. Here he was struck and killed by lightning. His flight and death, in 1860 and 1861, were symbolical of the time of calamity for China that the nineteenth century had become.

So soldiers plundered a defenseless palace; and afterward peasants carted off everything they could use. Strewn with heaps of rubble, the site reverted to primitive farming. The buildings of course had vanished; and except for a few old pines in the imperial family shrine, literally every tree had been cut down. Topography alone survived. It was only by frequent and prolonged visits, armed with precious maps, that the original plan could be reconstructed, and palace halls be made to rise once more in the imagination. I found a Western friend, a professor in the neighboring Western-style university, Yenching, with whom I set about doing this; and what we found together on long walks, over several years, I shall recount below.

The artificial lakes and various water courses did in general remain, and most of the man-made hills were also traceable; although these, completely denuded, were slowly slipping back to level earth again, and the local farmers had everywhere constructed crude terracing to suit their simple needs. Overturned rockeries, and here and there rubble-covered foundations, sometimes a little more, had to represent for us—map in hand—once handsome groups of buildings. After less than three generations the reversion was so complete, and had become so striking a symbol of all things mortal, that at sunset, across deserted and reed-covered ponds where imperial barges once had idled in splendor, the view brought with it, by its very evocation of extremes, a new poetry. So deserted were these vast grounds, except for an occasional burrowing peasant, that this place, also, gradually became "ours."

As finally completed, the Garden of Perfect Brightness is said to have had a circumference of some twelve miles. The character for "perfect" also signifies "whole" or "round"; and round was indeed the approximate shape of the lake in the first great section laid out by command of Ch'ien Lung. Later this original plan was much amplified by the excavation of an even larger lake, its shores studded with whole groups of handsome structures. Then, finally, two other already existing and very considerable gardens belonging to princes of the imperial house were also incorporated. Yet the first lake always remained the nucleus, and upon the largest island in it—there were nine so-called "continents" in all—lived the Emperor.

The road to the main entrance branched off from a highway leading westward from Peking about eight miles from the city gates. As one came near to the walls, one first passed a bannermen's garrison for the palace guard, named the Village of Suspended Armor. One then turned between two triangular ponds in the shape of fans, the Fan Lakes, dug to bring freshness to the site in warm weather. They had been made by peasants in a time of famine, the Emperor granting survival in return for this labor. Beyond stretched the walls of the great garden itself, round the circuit of which, at night, went companies of Manchu bannermen passing the tallies that secured the watch.

Inside the main gate, flanked by symmetrical rows of waiting rooms, the main hall of audience lay straight ahead, placed near the entrance. In 1793, toward the end of Ch'ien Lung's reign, Sir George Stanton, Secretary of Lord Macartney's mission from George III to the Chinese Emperor, visited this building; and we have a description of it—even including a floor plan, slightly erroneous—in his subsequently published report.

For many years not only this Emperor but also his grandfather before him, had employed a band of able Jesuits, chosen for many varied skills, to serve the court exclusively. Ch'ien Lung, indeed, had installed certain of them in a kind of studio within this very garden, not far from the entrance and off to one side. (My archaeological friend, who had a special interest in the doings of the Jesuits, traced its site with particular satisfaction.) Father Castiglione, an artist of charm and capability who headed this group, was even granted the unheard-of privilege of riding, mounted on a donkey, anywhere within the Summer Palace—so many were the tasks that the Emperor assigned him.

The main throne hall, of which we could just trace the foundation, must in its day have been quite similar to many still standing within the Forbidden City. It served for business of state and was therefore placed before the garden proper. Behind it was a high spreading screen of rockery making a barrier of separation completely in the Chinese taste, through which one passed inward obliquely.

Then the lake opened out, with its nine islands forming a circle upon the waters, each at no great distance from the shore. The largest of them, nearest the entrance, was built over with courtyards. Here dwelt the Emperor himself and also the members of his intimate family. On old maps it looks curiously like a hive, with many cells. Here were the courts for wives and concubines, for imperial children and grandchildren, a numerous group: the first in the empire, of course, but living communally as a Chinese family nonetheless.

The other islands, connected by picturesque bridges, made a circuit of the lake. Each had been planned, with undulating hills thrown up, either to afford privacy or grant a view, to surprise with one novel effect or to soothe with another. One, for example, was given wholly to rockery and peonies; another simulated a rustic farm. A third housed a temple; a fourth an elegant secluded library. Here was every charm and refinement in an elaborate age that could be drawn from virtually limitless resources.

Armies of the lower grades of eunuchs must have been necessary to care for the site. Once one could stroll at will along curving pathways, or else go about in light skiffs. There were numerous bridges set zigzag over the water; and at a certain place there was even a long marble one, arched over its own pond, placed there solely for its reflection. We knew the intent of such sites from poems composed to describe them—all illustrated and printed by imperial command.

Man had here imagined a whole region, quite unreal, and of great perfection, corresponding with his most refined tastes. In its time of glory it must have been an incredible place. The Yüan Ming Yüan is what the Chinese dream of when they think of a perfect garden: a collection of many different and surprising buildings, each in its own setting among trees, rocks, and flowing water, at the edge of the shores of a lake, and under the open sky.

So imperious was the desire to have here not what nature had created, but instead what would please man, that during certain final demolitions in my time it was discovered that parts of the original site had actually been a swamp. Hills had first been made, and then upon them had been set buildings; but for some of these it had been necessary to lay deep foundations several times their height, with piles driven into wet mud and clay. The moisture had actually preserved these timbers—of I know not what wood—and so I watched peasants come, two centuries later, to secure them by their labor, since they still were of value.

Several zones to the rear of the nine islands bordering the round lake had first been added to the original garden. Far toward the northwest was an ancestor temple that in majesty yielded to none in Peking. About it once rose stately evergreens within high walls; here all had been silence and dignity. Until a comparatively few years ago vestiges were still standing, enough to make interesting photographs that we still have. Since then almost everything had disappeared.

In the extreme northwest corner, behind, was a mountain of piled rock called the Cold Hill, which the Emperor ascended by ancient custom once a year, on the feast of the ninth day of the ninth moon. At this time it was fitting for him to climb to a height and look afar—as did that evening all his subjects. Only the Emperor's hill had been created for him.

Behind the original lake and islands were rice fields, laid out to simulate open country. In a great garden such as this, emperors often sought to have interspersed with imperial magnificence something to remind them of the humble destinies of the "Hundred Old Surnames" —the masses of the people. Their residence thus became a microcosm of the empire. The air blowing from these rice paddies, irrigated with clear running water, was also considered healthful.

In this region there had stood a notable building of two stories that had housed a great library. It had been copied from a famous example in the South, in Ningpo, and stood within its own lakelet. (We wandered much here, tracing the vistas from within.) On the shelves had been deposited one of the four copies in the empire of a great compendium, including all that imperial command had been able to assemble, of the whole body of Chinese literature. This, titled *The Complete Books of the Four Treasuries,* had been too enormous, finally, to print, and so it was copied out in manuscript. It, too, had vanished in the flames of 1860.

Thus, building after building was now present in our minds only. Yet occasionally one still came across some fragment of carved marble balustrade, or other trifle, which had escaped being carted to the local kilns for its lime. There was also one towering rock from Lake T'ai, cut with a number of inscriptions, lying prone before the library's vanished entrance. The pond surrounding it was dry. Upon it Ch'ien Lung had recounted grandiloquently how he had come to order this building, copied from its famous prototype halfway across the empire.

There were other sites to explore. One was a racecourse, used for military exercises as well. A gallery had once existed alongside this, for the Emperor's use when he wished to be present. This field, too, was on ground probably added to the original plan; by now we could follow, step by step, here under the open sky, how the imperial ambitions had expanded. "Here we are passing under this arch!" "Now we have reached the next wall!" Neither of course existed.

Yet the area occupied by these supplementary buildings was minor compared with the enlargement now begun. To the east was dug out a new and greater lake, which became the central one. This was roughly square in shape, and almost half a mile long on each side. It was given the name of Happy Sea. At its center rose a group of three small islands called after fairy ones off the North China coast. Two had architecture simulating that in paintings of this legendary region by a celebrated T'ang dynasty artist; the third was more rustic, a retreat here in the heart of the waters. All were connected by bridges.

Set at intervals along the shores of the Happy Sea were other marvelous constructions; and behind rimming hills to the north, screened from the lake but near, were placed boathouses necessary for a whole fleet of barges. Novelty followed novelty: one group of double-storied buildings, placed on a high foundation, was connected with its symmetrical outlying pavilions by flying bridges on an upper level. Or a water gate was pierced through a section of simulated city wall. One could pass under this by boat, to land in a sequestered region between two further bodies of water. The place was curiously named There Is a Further Recess of Heaven: one had entered another world.

Nearby was a group called The Double Mirror and the Sound of the Lute. The name came from a celebrated verse describing a place here imitated, which appeared as if afloat, all brightness and reflection. The poem had mentioned the sound of a waterfall nearby; so upon the top of one of the bounding hills a reservoir was dug; and water was hoisted bucket by bucket to this height from a deep well. (One day we scrambled up the hill, to discover that the old lock which had controlled the flow was still in place.) It must have taken hours of toil to produce only the briefest effect, timed so that the waterfall might play as the Emperor passed.

Thus we wandered about, resurrecting one vanished setting after another. On the west shore of the Happy Sea we traced a section of walled Indian town, a replica, our texts said, of Sravasti, where had occurred many miraculous events in the life of Sakyamuni Buddha. A paved granite causeway led south from its main gate, once bordered with shops and houses such as might be found in an ordinary Chinese city. Here in the New Year season the eunuchs customarily put on a lively show—with farces—reproducing for the court the brisk traffic of a market town. This was also the site of an annual fair.

A Jesuit priest was once admitted, and he has left a record. It constitutes that rarity, a description of intimate scenes of court life recorded by a European eyewitness. We are told that the wares displayed on this street were transferred from the best shops in Peking.

The Emperor also customarily arrived with his daughters to join in the fun, jesting at their efforts to drive good bargains; for on this one occasion, imitating ordinary mortals, they attempted real shopping.

Farther south again—beyond the lake with the marble bridge created solely for its reflection—were the imperial schoolrooms. Here the young princes, sons and grandsons of the Emperor, were placed under the best instructors; and it is related that Ch'ien Lung himself often visited the classes, to make sure that their studies were being pursued with diligence.

Yet all this was still not enough. The Emperor was seized with a rage for enlargement. He now further incorporated the pair of detached gardens already completed for imperial princes. Their walls, though, were not dismantled, merely pierced to allow for the passage of barges. Near the shores of a body of water in a far corner, finally, was set the largest piling of strange rock in the palace enclosure. This was an imitation of the Lion Grove in Soochow, one of the famous gardens in Chinese history. Such copyings were apparently far from literal: what was wanted was chiefly something to stimulate the imagination.

On a long and narrow strip of land now added behind these enlargements, there was finally begun that late and extraordinary folly of the period of Ch'ien Lung—an extensive group of structures of special interest to ourselves—the so-called Foreign Buildings. Since nearly all these were constructed with cut stone, rather than of wood with brick, Chinese fashion, more of the ruins still existed. (Many had enough substructure still in place to afford us, with the help of contemporary engravings and old photographs, the excitement of putting the whole quite acceptably back into place in the imagination. We were now, my learned friend and I, "garden stalking," as experts.)

The scale had been majestic, the materials of the solidest. Although their baroque architecture, as designed by the Italian priest Castiglione, seems quite to have lacked subtlety in proportioning—as was perhaps inevitable with work executed by Chinese artisans—the general effect must have been striking. A number of concessions had been made to Chinese taste. There was, for example, so much glazed tile—no doubt

used to add color essential in Chinese eyes—that not only were European roofs and chimneys built up of it, but even classical pilasters and
entablatures, applied to the various façades, as well. There were many
details of carved stone—some curiously misunderstood by the local
stoneworkers—although no use of the human figure whatever. Effects
were hybrid throughout. In all the history of the transfer of architectural styles I had never come across any more intriguing singular-
ity than this experiment in "Europ*éenerie*" (if one may coin such a
word) which here in the tranquil countryside beyond Peking constituted an eighteenth-century Chinese counterpart to the *chinoiserie*
at this very time flourishing exuberantly in all the courts of Europe.

First there had been erected, apparently somewhat as a trial, a single
building with a hemicycle of curving, glass-paned galleries—a novelty
to the Chinese—which served as an orangery. At the back were two
smaller buildings, one to house the waterworks for some small fountains in its pools—these a complete innovation in the Chinese tradition—and the other a *volière* or peacock cage, an idea also foreign.
(All this had been swept away, but in our minds, helped by the engravings which kept revealing to us one detail after another, as we
learned to interpret them, we now could see it clearly.)

Behind had been laid out a boxwood maze, altogether like familiar
ones then the rage in Europe. (We had a very convincing engraving
of this.) The plan, however, also included a small raised pavilion,
from which it is said that that Emperor used to amuse himself watching the court ladies vainly endeavoring to find their way through
blind turnings and passages. The Jesuits, it was apparent, had racked
their brains for every device that would amuse.

Then, presumably stimulated by this first experiment, the Emperor's
imagination seems really to have been roused. A new axis was made
at right angles to the first group; and although the further strip of
land was narrow, it was very long. Here one new arrangement after
another was called into existence; the Western folly began to take on
imperial scale. (Our own pursuit also became exciting. We discovered
further documents in the library of the Catholic fathers in the cathedral
within the city walls.)

First there was a foreign canal winding about a rectangular building of imaginative baroque architecture, called A Look Abroad. The latter word was applied, though, in Chinese minds to anything exotic; so for some reason this gave on to a series of open pavilions constructed entirely of bamboo.

There followed a much larger and grander group, set across the new axis, the Hall of Peaceful Seas. On either side of double external staircases in high baroque style, cascades descended in runnels, the water splashing along as it glided downward, finally to fall into a pool before the entrance. Grouped symmetrically about this pool were statues, not of half-clothed gods or goddesses—in Confucian China that would have been impossible—but of the twelve beasts of the Chinese horary cycle. These were conceived as half human, and also half horse, or pig, or serpent, and so on; very strange inventions. Each was also a symbol for a length of time the exact equivalent of two of our Western hours. These figures were made to spout jets of water, each in its turn, so this fountain also served as a clock. (We were almost able to overhear the Jesuits, in imaginary conversations, as they must have conferred while planning such effects.)

It had become hazardous for priests, whose knowledge of hydraulic engineering was self-acquired, to satisfy the Emperor's growing interest in fountains. They were aware of the unthinkable peril of an accident in the calculations for their tanks. So in planning the next and finally grandest arrangement, behind the Hall of Peaceful Seas, they apparently resolved to run no risks. The retaining walls (fragments of which still stood) were of extraordinary thickness. To make more sightly this vast bastion, designed also to house a pumping machine within, upon its flat top they further contrived a shallow pool under a grape arbor. Italianate staircases led up to this, a Chinese "hanging garden," set above a great pile of vigorous baroque architecture.

They now planned an imperial throne of marble set at a place from which the fountains could be seen at their finest. The throne was backed by a high screen of marble decorated with sculptured trophies. (These we simply found, one day, lying abandoned in a grassy corner in the nearby garden of Prince Ts'ai T'ao. We knew at once, from our engravings, what we had discovered!)

To realize the innovation of all the new waterworks, one must remember that to the traditional Chinese, a fountain is a dubious interference with nature. Water might run downward, as in a water-fall, still in harmony with the laws of the world—even if coolies had to sweat for hours to produce a few moments of surprise and diversion. Yet to make water spurt upward: this was extremely daring! Only an Emperor might experiment with such things brought from abroad, which the sages moreover long ago had specifically condemned as unnatural.

Backing the perspective of the fountains was the most imposing building of all, set on a high base to which one acceded by ramps. Here were columns of the most elaborate stone carving. European furniture, European mirrors, clocks and tapestries, presumably had also once made rich its interior. (We learned, my friend and I, that a whole set of tapestries had been presented by Louis XV to Ch'ien Lung—and quite a few survived, in widely separated places. We also went to see one painting in the Bishop's parlor beside the cathedral, presumably a perspective view of the chief interior in this very place.) Yet except for overturned stones, this grandest of all the Foreign Buildings existed no longer.

When all had still been erect, though, one next progressed through a triumphal arch in high baroque style to a completely circular mound, known as the Hill of the Perspective. Looking off from the summit one saw still another gate, opening on the farther side. Through this the visitor came finally to perhaps the most fanciful arrangement in the whole region: a place where a large oblong waterpiece had been dug in front of an outdoor theater. The brick wings on the sloping stage, using diminishing perspective, imitated houses of Western architecture. Here at the end of this region given over to elaborate, indeed fantastic, experiment, one came upon paned windows and high projecting chimneys.

Nothing actually remained but a few crumbled fragments of rubble wall. Like the whole garden this place too was chimerical. Yet looking backward I can half believe that, somewhere and somehow, my friend and I must have glimpsed it in its heyday—perhaps when the Jesuit Dom Pedrini was playing European music for the Chinese court, and, surrounded by his womenfolk, the Emperor had arrived for novel theatricals, after watching a display at the fountains.

CHAPTER XII   *Summer Palaces*

W E HAVE wandered through the strange ruins of a garden that
dissolved into a wraith of the imagination. Let us turn from it
to one that still exists—at the new Summer Palace. Beyond doubt the
largest of such arrangements still kept up in China, for the tourist this
was the Summer Palace! The other he scarcely heard of, and would
almost surely never go to visit, lying as it did off the direct motor
road from Peking. Yet this newer collection of buildings—either fronting an artificial lake or built into the recesses of a steep and isolated
natural hill rising behind it—was inferior, even though in its arrangement and scale it was still imperial.

As we see the buildings today, they are in general a restoration of
what was demolished in 1860; although here the intentional destruction
seems to have been less complete, and a rebuilding was undertaken
after the Garden of Perfect Brightness had been rendered uninhabitable.
The Empress Dowager also conceived for this place a special affection;
and as a result most of the architecture bears the dubious stamp of
her time.

Its history goes back, as usual, to the Emperor Ch'ien Lung. Even
when his great palace nearby was virtually complete, he could not
restrain himself from further building. The new site, the Mount of
Longevity, takes its name from the picturesque hill—a sudden final
outcropping, standing apart, of the range descending from the Western
Hills to the Peking plain—that would have been a temptation to any-

one. Its nearness to the Jade Fountain made new watercourses easy; and the Emperor apparently could not resist adding still more places to the magic acres where the imperial barges could float on their gliding journeys.

So a dam was made to contain still further waters, and the lake thus formed became extremely handsome and open. Of all the gardens that I know in China, this is the only one where the details seem to have been planned to produce a single all-embracing effect, centered about the shores of this large lake. Thus even to its plan the new Summer Palace is a late creation.

After the new works had been ordered, the Emperor seems to have felt perturbed in conscience. He had already put himself on record in stone that with a single palace, his Garden of Perfect Brightness, he would be content. Yet in a further inscription, on a tablet now erected here, he explains that he has never used this new garden as a place of residence, for which there was indeed no excuse, but only for excursions to secure repose when free from the burdens and responsibilities of state. In this curious detailed justification, he states that he has never spent a single night within the enclosure.

The plan does reflect this. There are dwelling courts by the lake-side, to be sure, arranged both for the Empress Dowager and for her son, the Emperor Kuang Hsü; but they are of later date. These nineteenth-century living apartments, further, are comparatively simple in extent and obviously supplementary. Even the hall used for audi-ences, near the main gate, where the Empress received her reports from court functionaries when she was in residence, is not large, although it is a dignified building.

The charm of the new Summer Palace lies in the sweep of its open views over the broad waters of the lake, backed toward the sunset by the amethyst Western Hills. One breathes, there, good air, and one can see long distances. In the center of the lake was a large artificial island, with temple buildings and halls for repose, and terraces of marble balustrading overlooking the water. On stormy days it became a special pleasure for me to promenade on them above its rock-bound shores, watching the plashing of small dark waves under a wind-swept sky.

Here in my time was also a restaurant, generally deserted, run as an accommodation for a tourist "industry" that never developed. I even spent several nights in certain glittering palace rooms of an adjoining courtyard, during one brief period when they were opened as a part of this plan. The scheme met with no success, though: wealthy Chinese could not be regimented and made to travel. Yet the island, with its paved courts, its gold-decorated vermilion buildings, their beam painting brilliant with color, all splendid under trees now grown sturdy and tall, did achieve a palatial effect and from its courts one looked out upon quite ideal scenery.

Access to it by land was across a long curving bridge of no less than seventeen arches, leading from a causeway crowning the dam. Across the lake to the north, opposite, a bastion of cut stone, broad and high, projected boldly in front of the Mount. At the center of its flat terrace, placed like a reliquary upon a pedestal, stood a pagoda-like structure of many stories with elaborate eaves of colored tile. Those of us who knew the history of this place knew though that it was a lower re-building of what had originally been a much taller and prouder tower. So it never gave much satisfaction, being so much less than the pinnacle Ch'ien Lung had once ordered to crown the whole.

Mammoth slabs of jagged ornamental rock, which must have entailed extravagant amounts of labor to transport, covered much of this hill "naturally." On either side of the projecting bastion there were also descending courtyards, balancing each other symmetrically. Many of the further arrangements were novel. There were towers with great Tibetan prayer wheels; there was one aedicule upon a peak made altogether of weighty bronze, even to the tiles of its roof and its simulated latticework. On one axis was also a great memorial tablet, a monolith of giant size, bearing the imperial inscription for the entire site. Yet all these effects were obvious, duller and more conventional—in some way—than the earlier work.

Below and almost level with the lake, yet still centered on the bastion, was propped a broad quintuple *p'ai-lou*. Here a covered gallery, stretching in both directions for nearly a quarter of a mile beside the lake, gave way to a large forecourt in front of the main yellow-tiled halls. This gallery, which was celebrated, also achieved too obvious an effect. In my time it was constantly being photographed by visitors, tempted by its long vistas of diminishing perspective. One could walk along it the whole way from near the outer entrance even as far as the Empress's marble barge.

This as modernized architecturally was quite dreadful. It had an enclosure of jigsaw carpentry serving as an upper deck, laughably reminiscent of a nineteenth-century steamboat. Its windows were made hideous by foreign glass, with panes of intense color; and its carved woodwork reeked of Western vulgarity. Yet the fantasy of a stone boat, which does not move, had been long familiar to the Chinese, who enjoy sitting comfortably upon it and jesting about journeys that they are making in their imaginations. At least its location here, at the end of a long covered walk, had originally been well planned.

High above, edging the square bastion, was another and diminished variant of this same type of gallery. I remember climbing the steep stone steps along the raking faces of the bastion, one winter's morning, to look back on the lake from this vantage point. The landscape at that moment was surprisingly like a gold and white screen, picked out with the silver of ice on the lake and of snows stretching to the horizon. Mist caught by the sun made it a vision of another world, in which the palace buildings in glittering color represented perfectly the dwellings of the immortals. At that hour, as I loitered high in these charmed expanses of silence and space, gratefully sipping hot tea at a small table set out in the narrow passage aloft in the sky, by some wonder the world of Chinese imagination transformed itself into reality.

There were also country walks about the irregular curving walls bounding the lake to the south; and other broad ones upon flat causeways going across the water. These last were provided with high camel-back bridges, which allowed for the passage of barges. Weeping willows grew luxuriantly upon them, leaning toward the water on either side. On a windy autumn day, as their small dry saber-shaped leaves flew through the air, this was an exhilarating place in which to take better exercise—a Western need that I never outgrew—than was usual in palaces.

At the back of the new Summer Palace, over the crest of its hill, was a completely other region. This slope was nearly always in shadow since it faced north, and it had of course no views of the lake. From its heights, though, one could look down on peaceful farming country just over the palace wall. The destructions of 1860 were very apparent on this side, and much had been left untouched since that time. The later effort had been to create a show over the top of the hill, overlooking the lake. One temple in tolerable repair still crowned this back slope; it had no doubt survived because it was of mortar and brick rather than of wood. Its walls were made with rows of external green glazed niches, each filled with a small Buddha—an obvious architectural tour de force. A number of ruined stupas, also of glazed tile, were on the terraced heights, and rose-colored walls still begrimed from the fires of long ago bordered the deserted upper walks.

On the way toward these steep regions there was a much brighter paved and rectangular open place, provided with stone benches. High trees, set within a courtyard long since vanished, here caught the sun aloft; and the ruins against the hillside were tranquil and smiling. This small piazza always reminded me, in its classical dignity, of canvases by Hubert Robert. It was pleasant to come to it and walk upon the even stones, savoring its pleasant blend of architectural ruin with the charms of nature.

At the foot of the rear slope of the hill was a winding gorge, which once must have been the most ambitious piece of artificial topography in the whole region. Ch'ien Lung's mother was a southerner; and it was said she at times longed to see her native hills again. So with filial piety on an imperial scale, the Emperor had ordered made for her this section of waterway, in which the hills, planted with all things suitable for such a landscape, imitated those of her native province. Here, during the festival of the New Year, another street fair was held much like that in the old Summer Palace. Only here it was old Soochow, the famous city of Central China, that was imitated. The scheme was elaborate, but it served for pleasures simple-hearted enough.

The winding stream in this gorge, coming from the Jade Fountain, finally reached the one place in the grounds where it changed levels. The fall was of a few feet only; yet every possible effect had been drawn from it. First there was a miniature rapid, then a small water-fall. A large slab of rock nearby was inscribed with two characters reading "Wisteria Moon"; and nearby there had indeed been arranged an arbor overgrown with this vine. The whole was planned to be seen from a small rustic bridge, placed at just the right distance away.

Passing along a winding road, one soon entered a separate en-closure completely walled in, a palace reproduction of a well-known southern garden. Here were engaging pavilions over the water, and from low seats between their columns one could look down at fish swimming among waving grasses. One could progress irregularly, in part on land, and in part on tiny causeways built across the inlets of a small central lake. There were various houses for repose, and a lofty sunny hall to be used as a library. Either in sun or rain, every-where one could also walk under roofed galleries, always with a continuous view and changing perspectives. Ch'ien Lung, as was to be expected, had lavished a series of his own poems upon the place; and as one wandered one could read comment after comment in the imperial hand, incised upon marble or carved on wood. In winter the enclosure became ideal to enjoy the enchantments of frost and snow, with the little pond at its heart changed to shining ice.

There were other detached villas, smaller places, in corners near the rear palace wall. In my time they had been rented out by the authorities and were silently inhabited by what must have been families of the greatest discretion, for although one might find windows open, and odd objects hanging here or there, one never saw any other indication of life. This was always a withdrawn region. Nearby, how-ever, one could reach the back wall itself, and from the top of hills thrown up intentionally to overlook it, see peasants cheerfully traveling the dusty open road below, in carts or on foot, laughing and talking as they went; or else working silently in the nearby fields. Merely thus to look out was said once to have been a pastime much valued by court ladies. Their lives were so confined and artificial that to see free human creatures, moving about as in another world, excited their curiosity.

Once restored from the disasters of 1860, the Mount of Longevity became the chief summer residence of the Empress Dowager. Even in remote corners it bore her stamp. Annually she would progress to it by barge along the canal from Peking, playing cards with her ladies-in-waiting (and she always had to win) on the short but slow journey. Starting from the city walls, only one change was necessary. This was at a lock in front of the temple of Wan Shou Ssŭ, where there was a small traveling palace, the shell of which still exists. Here she would customarily descend to rest, before changing to a somewhat smaller boat on the higher level, which took her finally through the palace walls by a water gate broad enough to allow for barges, and then across the lake directly to a jetty in front of her own courts.

Within the palace enclosure were her embroiderers, whose workshop she would often visit, to see what progress was being made with projects in hand—particularly for her high Manchu slippered clogs, which she wished always to have fresh and elegant. Manchu women, of course, did not have bound feet as did the Chinese, but to be well shod was a point of pride. Here, too, were the courtyards where were bred her little Pekingese dogs; of these she was especially fond. She walked about much and often, always followed by a small retinue bearing a whole collection of assorted objects that she might suddenly require—a small stool, a cushion, or perhaps her fan or water pipe. The new Summer Palace was her garden, her estate.

Something of this vanished life would come back to the lake-front on the rare days when the civic authorities of the moment gave large receptions, with formal cards of invitation, as was occasionally done. Then the palace was in gala dress, all the halls open, and the refreshments superb. At such times the state barges would be out on the lake, manned by their crews of oarsmen; and all were free to mount and ride. The old men in charge still remembered how it had once been done, so there was quite an air of ceremony to these unhurried excursions. The largest of the barges was of two stories, with sloping Chinese roofs of wood imitating imperial yellow tile; and its main cabin was furnished like a small Chinese drawing room. Through its wide open windows, beyond the low, pretty, furniture set against the papered walls, the landscapes of the lake swung about as the boat went here and there.

I once heard a story of how, during the season of the lotus, the Empress had her tea perfumed in this place. The large rose flowers, when first they come to bloom, close their petals each night, to open them the next morning. At dusk, therefore, ladies-in-waiting, from shallow skiffs that could make headway through the thick round leaves, deftly placed within them little packages of tea wrapped in soft paper. These were left during the night in the hearts of the flowers, to be gathered when they opened at dawn again. They then would be delicately perfumed with that scent so difficult to describe, and yet so fragrant that it almost may be said to represent by itself the dignity and beauty of the Chinese ideal of life.

Round about this region of the two summer palaces, old and new, were many smaller and yet ample gardens that in Manchu times had belonged to various princes. Since the court was often here for a large portion of the year, it was natural enough that the Emperor's mother, his many brothers and kinsmen, should also have residences nearby. There had been large properties of this kind for some time before the advent of the Manchus. Here a certain Marquis Li, whose daughter became a consort of one of the Ming emperors, possessed a garden famous in all China. It was specially renowned for its handsome tall trees; and vestiges of it—without the trees—could still be traced in what had become part of the grounds of the present Yenching University. The site still kept its old name, the Ladle Garden, presumably from the winding shape of its former lake.

It required four or five years of patience, waiting for occasions when one could appropriately be allowed to visit—and also be free to explore —to reconstruct something of the former appearance of this collection of minor gardens. The aged Prince Ts'ai T'ao still lived in the best of them, poetically named the Garden of Moonlit Fertility; and although one could wander at will through the grounds, his own courtyards were always kept closed. Adjoining were several once imposing but now abandoned sites, in deplorable yet picturesque disorder; and certain outlying ones had gone even further back into the soil, their land farmed by the local peasants.

All of these places had small lakes imaginatively arranged; although the buildings were in general completely in ruins. Like so much of the old China everything in them seemed now to have tumbled down.

The name of one of these abandoned structures, seen at its best across an idyllic body of quiet water, I always remember with pleasure; it was called the Tower of the Floating Mirror. There were many hills and caves, of course, always artificial; and everywhere quantities of old rockery. This last might still remain intact even though the buildings long ago had been plundered for more immediately useful materials. Among these ruins also, the human insect, antlike, everywhere had been at work.

One or two gardens were in better state than this, in particular a large one kept in good repair as the property of a rich old woman, Yüeh Lao T'ai T'ai, the matriarch of a family of prosperous Chinese druggists. Such latter and bourgeois splendors, though, were invariably in poor and degenerated taste; abandon was really more agreeable.

The impression finally formed that in its heyday this region had concentrated a sizeable part of the riches of the imperial house and of families related to it. The nearby village of Hai Tien had been the marketplace supplying local needs; and it was said that the palace eunuchs spent large sums there daily. Peculation was so outrageous, however, that when a commodity reached its final destination, in one palace or another, it no longer bore any relation to its original price. The chief eunuchs in consequence grew enormously rich.

The Emperor K'ang Hsi in his day had no stomach for such extravagance. Then there had been much more simplicity; and it is recounted that he liked to go about the countryside incognito and almost unaccompanied, mounted on a black donkey. Ch'ien Lung's mother later had a garden of size and consequence across from that formerly used by K'ang Hsi; although both of these, except for a few slight traces, had by my time gone back to the soil. This last Empress had so much enjoyed the ringing from the forges in nearby Hai Tien, where the local armorers also worked, that they were commanded to keep their hammers going, even when there was no particular work to do, merely to give her the pleasure of this sound. The story reminds one of that Empress of Chinese antiquity whose ears were similarly ravished by the sound of tearing silk. Rain on banana leaves, or on the dried leaves of the lotus in the autumn, were also known to be specially pleasure-giving. It was in discussing such enjoyments as these with my Elder Born that I learned peculiarities of the Chinese spirit.

As time went on, we have seen, Ch'ien Lung's projects swallowed a number of the minor gardens, even though for some the walls had been left intact. It was the duty of the imperial guard to make the round of the whole enclosure, especially during the watches of the night, which were carefully set. Their numerous garrison villages were common features of the surrounding region; as were also a number of simulated Tibetan watchtowers, and odd sections of fortification with no particular beginning or end—for use in military exercises. Centuries of construction, in a region blessed with good water, had finally metamorphosed a whole section of the plain beyond the capital. When one passed beyond it, one always became aware that history and embellishment ceased simultaneously; and then began again the dusty, timeless, North Chinese countryside.

From the existence of these so ample palaces for residence in summer, only a comparatively few miles from the walls of Peking, one must not deduce that the court never went on journeys to more distant regions during the warm weather. In Ming times, once the capital had been transferred from Nanking, the emperors on the whole did travel comparatively little. There was never a Ming summer palace at this place. They were a true Chinese dynasty, in contrast both with their Yüan predecessors and their Manchu followers, and for generation after generation they seem to have led a quite sedentary existence, much of it within the walls of the capital.

Their Ch'ing successors, however, had come from the North; and Mukden was always regarded by them as their original and true home. Even the last Empress Dowager carefully maintained these memories. Manchu as a language was indeed given up—the Manchus took special pride in the purity of their Chinese speech—except for a preliminary formula or two retained at court ceremonies. Yet the tombs of the first rulers of the imperial house were in Mukden, and within that city another, although much smaller, palace was maintained.

There existed, however, a still further northern site much more suitable for the summer sojourns of the Ch'ing court than any urban palace, one high in the uplands and healthful, fitted by every advantage of site to be what it became for years, a summer capital. This was Jehol—as the West has decided to spell it—a name derived from two Chinese words, Jê Ho, meaning simply Warm River. Hot springs, indeed, combined with excellent hunting grounds, made the attractions of the site. Here K'ang Hsi customarily came in summer to enjoy a freer life than was possible merely in gardens outside Peking. Here when the plain was baked by summer heat, was cool weather.

We have one vivid and detailed European account of how the court passed the warm days in this place, a description by the seventeenth-century Jesuit, Father Ripa, who enjoyed K'ang Hsi's special favor. Father Ripa tells us how the Emperor courteously insisted that he precede the entire retinue when the court moved up from Peking. This was a great honor; but the dust and clamor raised by the great train were known to be extremely wearying, and the Emperor had wished to spare him these.

The gardens as described by Father Ripa seem in K'ang Hsi's time to have been brought to great perfection, as was possible since the site, although in a dry region, nevertheless had abundant water. Even today its springs make green broad stretches of park land, altogether a rarity in China. On a happy journey there, one summer, it was pleasant to ramble about fresh meadows and observe how little the nibbling deer feared the visitor.

Father Ripa's account gives us an intimate view of K'ang Hsi at ease in this summer retreat, either arranging pleasures for his aging mother, or amusing himself heartily during excursions on the water with the palace concubines. It must be remembered that except for a rare and quite formal boat ride conferred upon specially deserving ministers—who thereupon generally felt stirred, by tradition, to record their praises in verse—there was literally no society here such as we of the West might expect. These charming bodies of water, these rustic islands and bosky groves were never used as a setting for guests, for mixed company, or for any general gatherings. Such was the adamant requirement of Chinese decorum, which had been adopted in its entirety by the Manchus. All here was for the One Man, or for his numerous family, alone. To many of its lesser members, especially to concubines past their brief day of favor, the rigidity of the system must have entailed lifelong confinement and hopeless ennui.

It was in the long reign of Ch'ien Lung that Jehol reached its apogee. The court, then, was brilliant; and the Emperor deliberately made use of his great hunting parties, or elaborate religious ceremonies also held here, to gain far-reaching political ends. For although this place was created wholly for imperial sojourns, and included only a very small town outside the walls of the palace enclosure, its situation was far enough north to make it a natural place of assembly, annually, both for the nomadic Mongol nobles and their religious leaders. On the pretext of sport or worship, they could be summoned to visit an Emperor to whom they owed an uneasy allegiance. Here they could incidentally be surveyed and in part controlled.

Ch'ien Lung seems to have used these visits to impress upon the border princelings a crushing sense of his own grandeur. The architecture itself reflects this. One great building, among a succession of splendid structures set in a valley beyond his hunting park, was no less than a reproduction of the Potala itself, in Lhassa. Here, within the space made by four surrounding curtain walls, was hidden a majestic temple, free-standing in the open and roofed literally with gilded tiles.

My first sight of this marvel was after a long climb up a spacious stairway of honor, tunneled between enclosing walls, and finally from the vantage point of a lofty corner pavilion rising asymmetrically above the roofs. Looking off from this fine height one saw the bare wrinkled hills; and that day shadows cast by the luminous clouds were roving constantly over them. Below was this noble building, completely concealed from the world as if the better to guard its preciousness. Its curving golden roof shone dazzlingly under the bright sky, regally covering a hidden shrine.

The air in this region was keen upland air; the country barren and empty except where the imperial will had arbitrarily summoned into being some glazed and glittering temple on an otherwise completely waste site. Here the land of China, peopled with docile timid farmers, had already yielded to something freer and bolder. Although neither the infrequent inhabitants, nor the poor priests whom one saw in one deserted court after another in this valley of temples, seemed formidable, one was already in a borderland. The breeze that blew was a northern breeze, the waters and waving grasses moved under other skies. For a Westerner this was exhilaration, a release from the downward drag of too much culture, too much civilization.

Jehol thus reflected earlier customs at a distance, in a rich but quite artificial late variant. Ch'ien Lung seems here only to have maintained a gorgeous shell. The very proportioning of the excessively rich temple architecture, high and unsteady, lacked conviction; everything was for splendid show only.

Nowhere in North China, though, more clearly than in these deserted palaces and temples, arbitrarily set in a wilderness, could one sense why China had long felt herself to be at the center of the civilized world. By contrast, all about was wild and empty country. Here, where literally the desert met the town, one could also understand how when the inhabitants of High Tartary came down to mingle with such enfeebled and luxury-loving latecomers, there could only have been sentiments of mutual contempt. For the nomads despised the too elegant rulers of a people who never moved for a whole lifetime from the soil they tilled—agriculture for them was a poor-spirited, dishonorable, occupation—while the Chinese looking out from their imported palaces and gardens, artificially planted in this waste, must have regarded these descendants of former conquerors as roving outsiders, once powerful but fortunately no longer to be held in awe, ignorant of every amenity of life as they knew it for the rest of the year, back in the capital, in Peking.

CHAPTER XIII *The Hills and Temples*

PEKING, in Chinese minds, is a northern city. Its climate may not be so severe as Mukden, which is for them the remote stronghold from which Manchu conquerors descended, some three hundred years ago, to rule a fertile empire to the south. Manchuria is the Scotland of China. Yet to those millions of Central Chinese, of smaller bones and slighter stature, who come from cities such as Soochow, with its reputation for learning and elegance, or from Hangchow beside its marvelous lake, and to all the further millions of delicate Southerners, who need their native rice and cannot eat wheaten cakes, Peking represents the North.

The Westerner generally welcomes the familiar extremes of climate in North China, the blustery winter and the hot summer. Here men are taller, and many of them have rosy complexions. Their manners are franker, their actions more forthright. The women, too, seem larger in stature and in character also. There can be something in their warm welcome to a guest, or in their mirthful comment on the course of life generally, that not only impresses one as Northern, but is even reminiscent—amusingly enough—at times of Ireland. I have seen many North Chinese women who would make wonderful "biddies"!

These are all true children of their soil; they cannot bear to emigrate. So, in the West, we have formed our general impression of a "China-man" (a term, by the way, for some reason near to opprobrium in the ears of educated Chinese) largely from Cantonese or from other

Southerners, who are as little like North Chinese as are—let us say—
citizens of Seville like those of Edinburgh.

What is true of the people is also true of the land. It is broad open
country, swept by every wind of heaven, under a boundless sky, its
blue often so pure as to be truly celestial; but also occasionally streaked
with dust storms that completely obscure the sun, tearing dragonlike
toward the walls of the capital from the deserts of Central Asia. Man
fits well into this land. Blue-clothed figures are ever at work in the
fields, the unbroken succession of the simple crops harmonizes with
the cycle of the year; and agrarian China, leviathan, deeply good,
touchingly simple, is indeed the true China.

The broad stretches of good North Chinese earth are only part of
the charm of the Peking plain. Beyond it, visible from the top
of the city wall, and even from vantage points within it, are the
familiar Western Hills. They are molded like the hills in Chinese
paintings, purple as thistles or the vivid color of bluebells in the shifting light. Although to the countryfolk who inhabit them they must
seem only poor land from which wresting a living demands even more
toil than on the plain below, to the sophisticated inhabitant of the
capital, Chinese or Western, this region promises all the delights of
picturesque nature, withdrawal, and repose near at hand. In truth
some of the temples there, veritable citadels enlarged through the
centuries, grant even better than this; and finally make their Buddhist
gift of perfect and utter tranquillity.

The most familiar of these nearby refuges is Chieh T'ai Ssŭ, the
Temple of the Ordination Platform, so-called because it includes one
housed in a separate building, used for the elaborate ceremonies held
when neophytes are admitted to the priesthood. Chieh T'ai Ssŭ seems
a far journey across the sun-baked summer plain from Peking, for
it is set broadly halfway up a long and gradual slope, across a small
river flowing through sandy soil, in a region almost deserted. It is,
however, only several hours away, these days, if one travels first by
motor car and then by donkey. It lies apart in the hills, a majestic
retreat for the spirit.

The morning of my first visit to spend a few days there, the stimulation of the site was so powerful that I was up and wandering about with the dawn. What was my surprise when having turned hastily down a path or two, I suddenly found myself on a hillock, looking off toward the rising sun still low in an aquamarine mist through which—precisely as if it were a picture finely painted—far away could be seen the feudal walls of Peking itself, rising erect from the smoky plain!

Once one's bedding roll had been settled in a guest court, pacing the long terraces of Chieh T'ai Ssŭ was not unlike touring the decks of some large, if stationary, liner, a motionless hull upon which one was temporarily permitted a journey through the ineffable calms of Buddhist time and space. All but the most callous Westerner felt this. Conversation would always become gentler during the long shaded afternoons as we sat together in reclining chairs; the ladies in our party would invariably make the points of their conversation better; and we were readier to accept them. Life, completely suspended, took on passionate interest—in no matter what aspect of it we felt at the moment absorbed.

The sight of this temple was a wonderful old tree, the "nine dragon white pine," so-called because of the shape of its trunk. It was a giant of great girth, with slanting limbs spread so broadly at the edge of a high terrace that one or two quite overhung it, stretching out horizontally beyond the balustrading. The scales of its shaded bark turned in the rain from dazzling white to palest gray-green or mauve; its clean pine needles were glossy and long. There was a sense that its tree nature had been intimately understood by the monks who now had cherished and protected it through centuries. An impression of its slow power as it had thrust upward the girth of its spreading trunk, or run its bulging roots for long distances under the tumbled brickwork of the uneven paving—this must remain with thousands who have come to see it.

At times, in summer, a sudden shower might send us scurrying to the rooms we occupied on this or that level, with different views across the plain. The rooms were usually in a litter, sponge-bags and miscellaneous gear scattered about as on a camping trip. We might then sit and talk on our cots. Or we would go off to take long deeply refreshing naps; to awaken with an almost numbed sense of complete removal from the problems that even recently had been preoccupying us in the world below.

The black-robed monks knew how all this felt, of course; they knew much better, and with much greater clarity than we, the causes and effects. I remember well the first time that I was allowed to glance into one of their Halls of Meditation, a cavernous building included in many temples of this size. One is politely asked not to go in: glazed porcelain placards, set low on wooden stands beside the door, request those at leisure to "avoid entering." Yet the prescription was waived for me on one occasion, and I found myself within a deep and shadowy empty hall, its walls compartmented and separated by partitions making each recess a broad shallow niche. Upon low platforms filling these were placed felt mats. Here one could install oneself, almost unaware of others and set apart from them; here one might sit cross-legged—which for the Chinese puts the body at peace—to meditate free of interruption for as long as necessity or desire might suggest. The urge to do so, the promise that here one could at last face every intimate problem, every internal reality, and wrest from them finally a solution and peace, this urge has never left me since. In those sanctified shadows many and many a Chinese soul must have found an issue to some of the riddles of life.

A little of this peace of withdrawal was always about us in the courts reserved for our use in Chieh T'ai Ssŭ. To those who have not done these things, elaborate week-end parties in temples may perplex the imagination, their worldly pleasures threatening impiety; but in reality the proceeding is altogether simple. Only part of a large temple is devoted exclusively to religious services; and except for the abbot's and monks' own quarters, there are no places where one cannot wander freely. Even to these more private courts, if one knows the custom of the country, one is usually in the course of time invited. The halls of worship are nearly always open.

There are no strained religious prohibitions; one is quite free to come and go during the services; and there are no peremptory rules. The kindly monks do prefer it if one does not bring animal food to eat within the enclosure, since to take life is to them a sin. If one has become a friend, however, in return for this one request they may offer veritable banquets of their own preparing, with mock meats and game so marvelously contrived—even to simulated laquered duck skin—that one is left with the sense of taste bewildered.

To live in a temple one need not even know the abbot; he can be, and often is, much occupied, a learned and somewhat aloof personage. The *Kuan-chia-ti*, however, the Administrator of the Household, is the best man with whom to make arrangements, avoiding intermediary servants if one speaks the language. The courtyards in a large establishment are many and varied; with tact one usually secures what one wishes. Upon leaving, it is simply sensed what present to the monastery would be fitting for the hospitality received, besides money to the temple cook and other servants, for hot water and similar necessaries, and other small fees for errands and messages.

A preliminary gift of good tea to the *Kuan-chia-ti* upon a first and formal call, is the best introduction of all. Everything consists in proportioning, and also in proper timing; and if the heart is in it, and kindliness too, all cannot but go well. So many generations have come and gone, in these places, so many have been grateful and donated one gift or another (perhaps even to the building of a new courtyard), that somewhere there is generally the very spot, perhaps with a quiet window and a maplike view of the world below, that one feels predestined for one's own use.

I remember one small building set apart, in a quiet temple on P'an Shan, a half-deserted mountain to the east of the capital, that was all this, and more, to me. It was named the Tower of the Sleeping Clouds, and on its broad *k'ang* platform I could lie comfortably by the hour, never tiring there of reflecting and planning. For in that place all thought seemed to come to me, in solitude, with justness and truth.

In Chieh T'ai Ssŭ the best accommodation had been given over for many years to Prince Kung, who had been in charge of the government at various times during the reign of the last Empress Dowager. Here he had retired, when no longer in favor, to occupy himself with literary pursuits. Here were his private courts, rich with silken peonies in the spring. His portrait, showing him in a simple gown, a Chinese gentleman seated among rocks in a typical Chinese landscape, still hung in the central chamber of his former suite of rooms.

T'an Chê Ssŭ, the second of the two great temples in this region, I came in time to know even better. Its Chinese name signified—vaguely—that it was a temple near pools and scrub oak, both of which did exist; but it could also be approached through a steep tree-filled ravine, almost a small forest, which in those comparatively bare hills was a rarity. The way to its main entrance, up from the plain, was like the approach to a medieval castle; but there was exceptionally also a small postern gate opening toward the mountain side.

In its courts grew soaring ginkgo trees. On clear autumn days, their yellow-green foliage towering unbelievably high in the crystal air, these were the trees of a Buddhist fairyland. Their huge trunks seemed grown for immortals, not for the little creatures who stepped this way and that the better to look at them. The ginkgo, of course, is not only one of the oldest trees in the world, but also one of the most slow-growing. Among other names the Chinese call it the "grandfather-grandson tree"; for if it is planted by the former, the latter will be the first to enjoy it.

In T'an Chê Ssŭ I finally became so familiarly known that I could arrive whenever I wished, with only the scantiest of personal belongings. Even the temple bedding, including quilts of excellent wadded silk, the pious donation of some wealthy Chinese, was put at my disposal. Foreigners, it should be said, invariably brought their own sheets and blankets; and not liking the hard native *k'ang*, unfolded Western cots and pulled out feather pillows. My simpler methods brought other rewards. In this temple I was often asked into the mammoth kitchen—in any land a mark of favor—to taste delicacies that the monks might slowly be preparing somewhere in its spacious recesses for anticipated guests of the abbot. I also spent long hours in the private rooms of the *Kuan-chia-ti*, where we used to enjoy conversation with much tea.

This temple had walls and terraces like feudal bastions. It must once have accommodated hosts of pilgrims. The cauldrons to cook for them, still in place from the old days, were so large that the gruel had been stirred from trestles with veritable oars. I had there, whenever I could, a distant courtyard to myself, on a narrow terrace of almost dizzy height. It was ideally secluded, wonderfully quiet, and in it grew four tall pine trees, perfectly straight and completely symmetrical. Through my sleep, I could hear their branches soughing softly in the night wind; and if I came at midnight to my door, to sense in the darkness their perfect arrangement, the stars above them sparkled as if they were ornaments on a Christmas tree.

A withered old priest seemed to have charge of this single court as his only duty. Here he ate his gruel from a cracked bowl, with a few pickled vegetables. He silently swept the ground under the four great trees with a besom such as might have come from a fairy tale, never making more of the task than necessary, as if unwilling to add any action further to a life now completed, except for a little dim contemplation, before it would flicker away. He dwelt in a small watchman's cubicle somewhere near the double red doors that barred the entrance.

It was curious to find how far apart one could grow from fellow Westerners when one looked down upon them from such a fastness. I remember one spring evening being sought out by the *Kuan-chia-ti*. By this time he had long ago told me all about how he had made his decision to become a monk as a lonely widower, and had shown me photographs of his only daughter, now married and far away in Shanghai. We were fast friends.

"A large party of foreigners has just arrived below," he said. "Should we not together go to greet them?"

We went quietly, he leading me literally by the hand—so great was his simplicity—and irrupted upon a chattering group from my own embassy. Its members, well-known to me, immediately and completely misinterpreted the scene. They had come here, with cocktails and crested china, napkins and ice, all the appurtenances of a traditional legation picnic; and white-robed servants were even at that moment laying a feast in a handsome yellow-tiled open pavilion, heavy with trailing festoons of lavender wisteria. It was a brilliant little picture, yet strikingly irrelevant.

Soon my monk and I drifted away. There was nothing at the

moment to hold me; and the temple was quite large enough for me to think only intermittently of my foreign friends that evening, as I supped far away on another terrace, nearer the kitchen, in rich evening light. This was a place fragrant with rare *la-mi hua*, a small flower with delicate and translucent waxen bells, at that season in perfect bloom. I was being nourished with Buddhist food, in more senses than one. Finally I went up to my high courtyard of the four great trees, the doors were bolted, and slumber came early and was sweet.

Several hours later, I became conscious of a strange combination of sounds: a solemn mass was being intoned by many voices, with the rich dissonances, so difficult to describe, that make the effect of Buddhist chanting. It must have been droning on for some time. Intermingled with it, although from another quarter, came a roistering and lusty, very lusty, Pilgrims' Chorus, from *Tannhäuser*. I turned over and went to sleep again.

My slumber was not to last for the rest of the night. After an interval, I became aware that my compatriots from the embassy were indulging in a prolonged celebration. Perhaps the voices were fewer, though by this time they were buoyant and happy, familiarly invoking Daisy, to give them her "promise true," all quite delighted at the mere thought of a bicycle built for two. The unremitting Buddhist clappers were still pounding away, the incantation, a little more rapid, going on endlessly. The priests, too, were apparently quite content. Surely the two worlds were not destined to meet that evening.

It must have been hours later that I roused myself to consciousness for a last time. Even the priests by now were mute; and the night must have been far spent. Yet the singers were still vocal. This time from another direction, they were informing each other, although irregularly, that when life in temples should be past, they wished merely to have their bones pickled in "al-co-hol." I preferred my own courtyard.

There were other Buddhist temples, many of them, all about this region. I had two favorites, Wo Fo Ssŭ or the Temple of the Sleeping Buddha, beyond the Jade Fountain; and, more distant—to be reached

by a steep highland walk over the bare hills—Ta Chüeh Ssŭ or the
Temple of the Great Consciousness.

Wo Fo Ssŭ was a familiar enough place. The Chinese YMCA had
sometime before taken part of it over from the monks, who now
were obviously too few to fill it; and there they had opened a hostel
that did have the advantage of prepared, if simple, Chinese food. As
a temple, Wo Fo Ssŭ thus suffered occasionally from spells of student
popularity, when it milled with activity. Yet there were other times
when one could enjoy it quite undisturbed.

There was one broad court near the entrance, imaginatively named
that of the Sky-Clearing Moon, where iron bedsteads could be dragged
from the empty rooms and set up under the porches of the side-houses.
Here one could sleep out-of-doors in summer, under crazily strung-
up mosquito nets, below the monarch-like spreading trees which rose
high above the roofs.

There was a charming eyrie, high and remote, at the back of the
whole enclosure. It had yellow-glazed tiles on its double roof—so that
it had been an imperial gift—and was known as the Tower of Kuan
Yin, who is, of course, the Goddess of Mercy. Up steep twin flights
of steps made of uncut rock, here one could sleep either indoors or
out. This was a fine place in which to install oneself perhaps late in
the autumn, or else in the chilly days of the new spring; for there
was a small iron stove in its single papered room, on which water
could be heated night and morning, so that one could wash or shave in
comfort.

Missionary friends had another large and quite separate section,
which once had been an elaborate traveling palace used by the Emperor Ch'ien Lung. Here as everywhere he had set his obvious stamp;
the architecture loudly proclaimed the man. There were several spacious
courts, all embellished with highly carved woodwork, although the
main building—having burnt down accidentally—was now lacking.
Grass had also been planted to make a most un-Chinese lawn in front
of its *kuo-t'ang* or entrance passageway; and this had further been
walled in and pierced with Western windows. It made a cozy but
not beautiful guest house.

By the kindness of its host, a genial retired missionary, I used to have for my own here, however, a marvelous rickety nest across the lawn, halfway up in a great tree, made of unsteady flooring and roofed with very worn matting. This overhung the temple's outer wall, so that one looked directly down onto wheat fields and the public road below. It was a remarkably cheerful corner. Here I could perch—with a large bed, a wobbly wash-hand-stand, and even a writing table—between a number of worlds, which only could have come together in such a place.

From time to time, there came here such figures as the grave old Swedish missionary, tall and very lean Mr. Söderbom, whose Sunday prayers had a particularly gentle and old-world quality. We used to sit about on the grass lawn—to remind us of "home"—conscious of our clean clothes, to hear there prayers and then to sing hymns, in lieu of church services on the sabbath.

One bright calm Sunday, after a while I drifted away from the hymn-singing; and wandering to the Chinese part of the temple, out of curiosity I poked my head into the monks' dark brick-floored kitchen. I found the cook also in beatific mood—outdoors the weather was magnificent. He, too, was resting from his ordinary labors, only reclining at his ease, smoking a pipe of opium. Outside the hymns soared onward: "I know not, oh! I know not, what joys await me there. . . ." I could not tell the missionaries where I had been.

The Temple of the Great Consciousness was reached after a more enterprising journey, over the high bald hills. The shade of its fine evergreens was consequently the more grateful; and there was a limpid silvery pool behind the main halls into which we invariably dipped our handkerchiefs in warm weather, to cool our faces after the long walk. Here, backed by a small house all latticework, now faded to dull red, the gray rocks and trees, and a single lichen-covered stupa—the grave of some old abbot—made a setting of absolute peace. The air was pure with the scent of pines.

At the front gate there were nearly always a few gossiping eunuchs, leaning on their staffs; for they owned a farm property of some sort not far away, in which to spend their last years. They would hobble over to Ta Chüeh Ssǔ to taste a little of the world on the warm quiet afternoons when one could almost hear the wheat ripening, growing taller and blonder hourly in the neighboring fields. Many rural scenes like this, with only slight change, might well have been set in the rich and nourishing countryside of provincial France.

If we were living at Wo Fo Ssŭ, we could never tarry too long at this place, for it was considered unsafe to be out on the heights, in back country, after dark. Once when we were overtaken by inky night-fall, and went on, stumbling horribly along stony pathways, with no habitation to guide us for miles, we reached Wo Fo Ssŭ to find ourselves being urgently searched for, with lanterns on the roads, everyone unquiet at our late return. We were given supper though; and there had been no bandits, not at least that night.

In the course of time I acquired another friend, one of the priests in Ta Chüeh Ssŭ, who invited me to spend winter days there. Then I used to go round by the highway, a circuitous journey, to reach the temple by bicycle. This friendly priest treated me spontaneously almost as a lay brother, insisting upon my sharing the large *k'ang* in his inner room. The first night I went to sleep with the not quite comfortable feeling that I might almost thus be qualifying to become a novice. My good priest, however, had only taken my complete acceptance of his own way of life for granted; he had in simplicity offered me what he had.

The next morning, after his private prayers, for which he beat time with a small mallet upon his own "wooden fish," and while I was still shaving in leisurely fashion, I became aware of something of unusual interest. He had begun to practice calligraphy. His hand was known to be good; it was he who wrote the yellow paper inscriptions, either in large single characters or else in pairs of symmetrically planned sentences, pasted on every door or door-frame for the New Year. He was attacking this task intently, little by little gaining speed, for all the world like a fancy skater perfecting his form. Ever faster sped his brush, his energies concentrating themselves to wrest from flying movement, at the right instant, that ultimate imprint which is a good Chinese character.

Finally his whole being had been channeled into the poised tip of his well-inked brush. Then, but not until then, did he trace on good paper the characters already chosen. He who has not seen a serious calligrapher at such a task does not know what stores of intent energy can passionately be released and transferred to fragile paper. Nothing is of more value in Chinese eyes than just such a sheet; providing of course that the spirit behind it has been so eloquent, and so able to express itself, that the result can pass muster with the connoisseurs.

There were other more vaguely Buddhist places to go in the Peking plain and the nearby hills. The religious side never obtruded, the priests somehow in charge never pestered one for money, the services were most irregular; and there was always a feeling that the casual visitor was welcome. The underlying humanity was unfailing.

One of my favorites in this vaguer category was the Black Dragon Pool. At a place where isolated hills were already beginning to crop out of the western rim of the Peking plain, there was one, not particularly high, with unpretentious temple buildings covering only part of it, that long had been remarkable for a spring of very clear water. Here had been made an irregular pool that we used for swimming. It was enclosed by a high raised walk bounded by stretches of curving wall, which was irregularly pierced with small windows of fanciful shape, no two alike. Through them one could look out as from a raised gallery upon the farms and fields below. At each few windows the view would be quite different. Within, the color of the pool, refracted through the clear water, was a vivid glassy light blue-green.

The glory of this place in the spring was the oldest, the largest, and the most writhing wisteria vine that I had ever beheld. A stout framework, so extended as to cover part of the pool, supported it; and when the flowers were in bloom, and the air alive with the urgent sound of bees, one might swim below this trellis as lavender blossoms dropped onto the green water. China gave, neither measuring nor caring, so many pleasures like these!

One missionary friend for many years had rented her own courtyard, high in another craggy part of the hills, in what was known as the Monastery of the Golden Immortal. Here the well-built halls were unusually lofty. (I have heard since that all this is now gone, bombed in the war.) In her part of the temple were tile-bordered beds of magnolia trees, and there was always one short season in the spring when the place achieved perfection. Then we would go there, tended only by her dignified old manservant, appropriately named Autumn Orchard; and at the end of day we often sat out in the late sharp mountain light, watching the petals drip one by one, like some magic of white blood. A sense of the brevity of existence, and the keenness of its beauty, would almost overwhelm us, waiting in the quiet hills for the oncoming of the night. Later as we sat reading silently within, by the light of a kerosene lamp, it would be as after a *Nunc Dimittis*.

From this place there was a most tempting walk, very uneven, skirting round the prongs of the mountains as they descended to the plain below, and then inward past walled houses in the recesses of the hills, houses so still, under their trees, that they seemed deserted. This led finally to a quite magnificent group of buildings, the Tomb of the Seventh Prince. The grave itself, in a lovely upland grove, I remember only as usually dappled with sunlight; and all was so impersonal and quiet there that death itself seemed robbed of regret.

Our curiosity was not about it, though, but with the arrangements made there for the living—a set of still half-furnished chambers used by an intriguing son of this Seventh Prince, we were told, when he fell dangerously out of favor at court. At this stage of his fortunes he had decided to disappear from the scene, and departed to "guard the tomb of his parents"—as the phrase went—in other words to save his skin. In pairs of antithetical couplets on wooden tablets suspended to the columns of his porches or to his door-frames, he ostentatiously announced to the world how little interest he now had concerning it. His "head was in the clouds alone" he stated; or his "feet trod only mountain ways."

Yet we could never quite believe this, because of one strange house in the garden that he had ordered built—most unusually in such a place—beyond the residence courtyards. This small building was carefully isolated, even hidden within a large basin of elaborate rockery; and there were elevated vantage points upon it, pinnacles from which the approach of any visitor could be spied from quite a distance. Then, even if one succeeded in entering the little house, the very sliding door that one had pushed back to get in, by a curious trick closed off a further entrance down a short corridor and round a turn, until one had slid it back again—and thus shut oneself in! What could have been its use?

At the Tomb of the Seventh Prince there was also a children's garden, unique to my knowledge. It was only a little place, conveniently near the main buildings; and there really was not much to see. Yet all the garden furniture, the little stone tables, the little benches, the seats and stools, were uniformly of miniature size, arranged with great dignity. This was another facet to the puzzling character of the Seventh Prince's son.

We wandered often, these years, among Buddhist temples and tombs; and I do not think that there can be much question that most religious building in China is Buddhist. There are, however, two other quite equally accepted faiths, Taoism and Confucianism. Many Chinese, further, have no difficulty in participating vaguely in all three. Each is good, they will tell you, and each appeals to a different side of our human nature. My Elder Born once exhorted me, when I was passing through a period of enthusiasm for the technique of Buddhist controlled meditation, not to "use up Buddhism." This was a religion, he said, for old age, and for peace. It was most valuable for the time when disenchantment with the world would naturally arrive. "Why not save such special studies, then, for when they will be more useful?"

Taoism is resurgently popular, generation after generation, because it appeals, I think, to a streak of nihilism present in average human nature. Its upper reaches have about them a subtle quality of almost mocking skepticism; they contrive paradox after paradox to put to shame the unthinking. As an everyday faith, however, it has taken on much grosser forms; and the popular version of the present quite degenerated creed is so riddled with superstition that the ordinary wandering Taoist priests have become not unlike the gypsies of Chinese society.

Historically, though, Taoism was once a very different system, showing man the futility of a great part of his planning, and the uselessness of almost all his action; nursing him finally to freedom through cosmic humor in the contemplation of human vicissitude and its basic absurdities. In return for illusions cast away, it promised him the next best thing to immortality attainable in this world, absolute well-being, provided only he exercised and dieted carefully, and kept himself not only physically clean but also mentally unworried. Amateur Taoists, even today, are living examples of what such a regime can do to the human frame. Indeed, they age remarkably, with a fire to their glance that proves how much this system has done for them. It is all very appealing; one can only regret that much of the high style is now so far lost in the past.

One often sees Taoist priests wandering about in town or country, bearded and with their long hair caught up in topknots through curious hollow-ringed hats, dressed in coats of many patches of black and blue, often in tatters. They have an air of forever passing freely through this world rather than of being enmeshed in it; and to the best of them this gives a striking appearance of liberty. These are dignified men, with a wonderful glowing expression; and in their old age they are, as Walt Whitman might have described them, truly "large, expanded, free."

As an organized religion, however, Taoism is definitely poorer than Buddhism. It draws fewer of the rich donating faithful, perhaps because it offers less opportunity to join in conventional religious observances. The very imaginativeness of its highest flights must have worked against it with any established order. Yet its followers are not few; and outside Peking, a short distance from the west wall, there was one large and handsome, generously built and well-maintained establishment, Po Yün Kuan, the Taoist Monastery of the White Clouds, which represented this faith at its contemporary best.

Even the Chinese name for Taoist foundations is unlike that for similar Buddhist ones. They are called not "temples" but "palaces." At Po Yün Kuan the abbot and priests were men of urbanity, moving at ease with the great of the land. The reception rooms were almost regal in scale and arrangement, the ceremonial invariably dignified, and when occasion required it, splendid. In one of the side-buildings, upstairs, there was perhaps the largest and best-maintained Taoist library in China.

At Po Yün Kuan interest centered on the great holiday fair held in the opening days of the Chinese New Year. Then visitors arrived by hundreds, in fresh cotton clothing, young men with old-fashioned garters tying in their wadded trousers at the ankles, young girls with neat knots of sleek black hair, and perhaps a bang in front. They came in droves, making family parties; by cart, by ricksha, by bicycle. Or within the city, they walked to a gate in the wall, and made the last stretch on careening minuscule donkeys. Everywhere was the merriment of a holiday of the touchingly simple. It has surely antedated and will no doubt postdate the perennial "crises" of our times.

At the fair there were sweetmeats, toys, games of ring-toss—with the cheapest of prizes, but very popular—and also a kind of wishing well, where one tried to hit a target in a pit under a bridge, with copper coins. There was also fortune-telling, at this beginning of a New Year, which was taken quite seriously.

During the holiday time there were also flat silk lanterns in great numbers, painted with scenes from familiar historical romances, set out upon the rear wall of one of the main buildings. This place would be thronged even when they were unlit, during the day. The painting was not superior, although painstakingly done; yet to offer a Chinese the chance to see anything novel is always to invite the mob. Simple onlooking, in a land where illiteracy is great, is the prime form of education. The good humor of the spectacle, however, the spectators add of themselves.

In the open fields behind an elaborate rear garden, Mongol horse races were also held from time to time during the fair; although these were more accurately horse pacings, to exhibit the animals, without any proper starting post or finish lines as we know them. Nobody seemed to care very much about that phase; it was very puzzling. Yet crowds went to see the intermittent riding, and to deliver judgments upon it.

The chief curiosity of the Monastery of the White Clouds, however, was the collection of very ancient men, all alive, in a smaller side-building, to be seen upon payment of a few extra coppers. Here the good-natured mob milled, crushing into the little rooms, and gaped. The cross-legged veterans, on a long warmed *k'ang*, were indeed old, thoroughly battered by time. It was stated that they spent nearly all their existence in controlled meditation and withdrawal, for such a regime was said to prolong life. At any rate they usually did seem quite comatose; but the crowd marveled and was in no hurry to pass on.

In a land where death comes early, and where for most of the population there is less possibility of survival into advanced old age than for us, these men filled imaginations more excitingly. It was not only respect for those who had weathered the longest storms; it was also curiosity to see what happened physically after, let us say, nearly one hundred years. If there were secrets beyond what met the eye, however, the blinking or shut-lidded ones never revealed them. Such a mass exhibit of advanced senility was not pleasant to contemplate. It was not here that one saw the best of Taoism.

Of the third of the three great religious systems of China, Confucianism, I have already given a few details. It is, as we have seen, quite different from the other two—much more so indeed than they are from each other. Perhaps it would be more accurate not even to call it a religion, for it is actually inimical to faith or fervor, and occupies itself with ethics and morals, from which one can proceed directly to the practical ends of good government. Proper Confucianists regard themselves as superior beings; and those who do not hold with them find their customary attitudes rather sanctimonious. Yet the good Confucianist, basing himself on reason and logic, and attempting to keep himself free of all unworthy emotion, abides too by his own standards. At his door there is often posted a sign reading NO AFFINITY WITH BUDDHIST OR TAOIST PRIESTS. Keep away! Here dwells a man who will think rather than feel his way through the world.

During the years that I was under the tutelage of Mr. Wang I learned much of this temper. His father had been high in the old hierarchy, having attained the second of the nine official ranks. The son had been given a thoroughly Confucian upbringing. With memories of better days behind, he knew that although teachers such as he might be granted a modicum of respect, conditions of life were meager indeed. Only when I once visited him in his cramped and shabby dwelling, during an illness, did I fully realize what fortitude and endurance lay behind his carefully emotionless behavior and unvarying correctness.

One day in earnest conversation he revealed to me some of these springs of action. Life might be hard, very hard; it was so indeed for him. Yet if one conducted oneself always according to the most superior standards, whatever happened was in its purity "like the season of spring." He flushed a little as he said this, repeating the phrase "like the season of spring"; and then tried to make me understand the clarity of utter peace of mind, the moral fragrance of good and wise conduct. We were both not a little moved; for it is a brave thing for any man, knowing his weakness, to stand firm for his principles against a stupid and brutal world.

Yet there was somehow always less to see, or do, in a Confucian temple than at the Buddhists or Taoists. It was usually a gravely quiet and empty building. The plain wooden tablet of the Completed One himself—even in daily conversation Confucius is never referred to by name, but obliquely mentioned as "a certain man"—and also the minor tablets of his chief disciples invariably placed in such halls, avoided all imputation of image worship. They were merely inscribed red-painted, upright slabs, each in the center of a large crimson-and-gilt stall. In front were usually broad and empty sacrificial tables.

Once a year, though, in the great Confucian temple north of the Tartar City in Peking, there was an official ceremony of consequence. This was on the anniversary of the sage's birthday, with the mayor and various ancient dignitaries present, all in their short and formal black "horse jackets," over dark long clothing. The dress of the officiants was consciously archaic. Curious instruments were played, so old that even their use had been almost wholly forgotten; although Confucius himself had stated that with proper music one could rule the state. Young boys were the acolytes. I once asked Mr. Wang why this was so. "Because at that age they are the cleanest of all living creatures," he replied. Confucianism took no chances.

Even the Kuo Tzŭ Chien or Hall for Imperial Instruction, attached

to this temple, had a meliorative and reforming air. The building itself, large, high and square, but quite unadorned, was set in the center
of a circular moat. Four bridges crossed this to four broad doors, one
on each side. Traditionally the Emperor sat upon his raised throne,
within, to hear the wise men of the empire, standing before him, ex-
pound to him the laws of conscience and his duties.

These were founded upon the Classics, which were the repository
of Confucius' wisdom, and thus formed Sacred Books. To make them
accessible to all men, nevertheless, a special arrangement had been
made in this place. A covered cloister bounded the entire enclosure,
and under its long galleries, protected from the weather, were erected
hundreds of stone tablets, each carefully incised with a section of these,
in the official script.

Now every Chinese knows how to take a "rubbing" of such stones.
Dampened paper is first smoothed upon the surface, and a small moist
pad filled with Chinese ink is then gently tapped with equal pressure over the whole of it. Since this blackens all but the incised parts
(the characters themselves), when it is pulled off one has a true and
perfect copy, only with white script on a black ground, all at the mere
cost of thin paper, the ink, and the time required. These stones consequently placed the wisdom of the ancients within the reach of any
who wished to come and seek it: again a moral purpose.

A forecourt to the temple proper contained other rows of more richly
carved marble tablets. Each was covered with successive lists, reign by
reign over centuries, of those candidates who had successfully passed
the highest official examinations. These were held in the capital only,
every few years, and they alone opened the way to a political career;
as if our M.A. and Ph.D. led directly to service in the state, with both
prestige and a good salary as well. There were traditionally three literary degrees. The lowest, corresponding to our bachelor's, was auspi-
ciously named that of Budding Genius; the second made one a Raised
Man; and the third expressed the final result of Formed Completeness.

Many and many a story, still listened to eagerly by Chinese of all
ages, concerns the family sacrifices, the prodigies of diligent study, and
finally the vindicated ability of some determined candidate who went
up to the Dragon Gate—the examinations—and succeeded in enter-

ing it. Finally, if success crowned all, and the long-sought-for highest degree was his at last, the victor, dignified with the title of *Chuang Yüan*, "Robust Perfect One" (a sound veritably enticing to Chinese ears), was granted the privilege of a state return to his native place, seated on a white horse, with all the accompanying regalia of his newly won honors. This was a dream that made young heads positively giddy; and the names of those who had come to Peking, and obtained this degree, were duly inscribed row after row upon these old stones. Thus was the empire ruled traditionally; and these were the men finally given the responsibilities and honors of public life.

Within the temple courts proper there were further towering stelae, the largest monoliths that I ever saw in China, erect on giant tortoises with raised heads. Each was housed within its own yellow-tiled pavilion; each had been presented by one of the emperors of the last dynasty. They honored the sage with gravely laudatory inscriptions, but they were so consciously imposing that I could not but feel they must have served chiefly to gratify the self-esteem of the donors. Confucius, however, was always to be given the best. Everywhere this seemed a basic principle; and in this sense China is a Confucian country.

Inside the main hall of the temple proper I never found much of interest to hold me; so that eventually it was pleasant to come out into the sunlight again, idly to watch the cooing pigeons waddling about on the broad marble terrace. The very purity of Confucianism would perversely put me in good mood to enjoy a really elaborate mass, with great dissonant chantings and all the clappers going, in the next Buddhist temple that I might visit.

On one occasion, however, I was able to come nearer to what must have been the wellspring of this creed, which so carefully avoided the emotional aspects of religion. The spiritual excitement of Confucianism, I had found, came generally at the moment of surmise that one had discovered a superb truth, which occurred unpredictably while reading passages in the Classics. Yet this was another phase.

I was on a journey to climb T'ai Shan, the great sacred mountain in Shantung. Upon descending to the plain, I found that by traveling on a local night train departing from the foot of the mountain, I might reach a certain small station before dawn, and from there hire a donkey and ride across the fields on that same morning to the ancient town of Ch'ü Fu, Confucius' birthplace, which was not on any railway.

This I thereupon did, in the loveliest frail and changeable spring weather, the sky washed to seraphic clearness. As my donkey clipped across the neat fields, the attending boy tagging after, and we passed white-walled farmsteads with pleached fruit trees, generous manure heaps, and well-made pens for domestic animals, the agricultural probity of the region reminded me strikingly—to my surprise—of Normandy or Brittany. This is one of the charms of Shantung.

The cross-country journey was made without event; and I put up my beast in a clean inn on the main street of the town, not far from the palace of the dukes of the family line. It should be said that this palace was more of a country seat intentionally planned for the use of some great family, more perhaps like some property belonging to a member of the old French aristocracy, than any other I ever saw in China. The buildings were sober and handsomely roofed, with a deep and broad court of honor in front of them. Here even bandits apparently paid respect; for otherwise it would have been considered unsafe —without walls—to have been publicly so majestic.

Now titles of nobility were never fixed, forever, in the old China. This was considered unwise; so they were diminished by one degree with each succeeding generation until they came naturally to extinguish themselves—as had most often, by that time, also the native ability that had first established the line. The Chinese are practical. Yet so great was the reverence for the one perfect and completed man, Confucius, that in this single case an exception was made. In each generation, the eldest of his family has remained a duke. In Ch'ü Fu, when I arrived, the young man who was the present incumbent had only recently made a properly successful marriage with a rich banker's daughter from Tientsin. They were living there in retirement; and the townsfolk spoke of them quite as if one were, amusingly enough, in Angoulême or Warwickshire. One exchanged news of "the Duke."

Tranquil good manners, and a social sense like that familiar in the West, were everywhere obvious.

I had proposed this to be a peaceful small journey; and I was indeed enchanted by what I found in the smiling temple courts. It was spring, and the air was unusually gentle there; slender lilacs were blooming from the moss blackened pavement even within the spacious enclosures to the main buildings, shaded by gray-green cypresses. A complete tranquillity brooded over all; yet it was a silence stimulating to the mind, charging it with humane reflection, a vibration more sensitively beautiful than anything Confucian I had known among the gaudy formalities of the capital. This was still another, a very tender and ancient, benevolent China.

A thunderstorm that expanded suddenly to a cloudburst changed my plans. I had fortunately regained my pleasant inn before it broke. There in the covered front passage—such was the local custom—the fresh food for the day was neatly displayed in rows of bowls and dishes, only waiting to be selected and cooked. I also had a comfortable room. The cheerful donkey boy would wait. Everywhere the rain was streaming away, and indeed he could do nothing else. So the downpour continued; and for a night and part of the next day I was shut up, given the society of grooms and ostlers for diversion, much talked to, constantly questioned and questioning, at ease and very well fed.

Everyone in the town, I soon discovered, was apparently named K'ung—Confucius' own surname. Never had there been such a flourishing family; in over twenty-four centuries it had ramified beyond belief. Yet pedigree never ceased to be important. It was carefully explained to me, as various people came in to pay visits, how my interlocutor of the moment might actually be older than the one of half an hour before, although the former was of the seventy-fifth generation, let us say, while the latter was of the seventy-third. Everyone was aware of these relationships; everyone knew his place and took pride in it.

When the storm had finally cleared, I walked through the muddy streets to the great family cemetery, and in the returning sunlight stood reverently before the tomb—so well known to me from photographs—of the great founder. Even certain unfortunate modern embellishments could not ruin its effect. Here was Chinese dignity, ineffable peace. I was in a city of grave mounds, of long-linked generations, all connected by family piety as well as by blood to this holy man, who had died nearly five centuries before our era. Here was the trunk, the great stem, from which all these subsidiary branches had sprung. There seemed miles to the enclosing walls.

A curious thought struck me: this was so different a way of life from that to which the Buddhists exhorted their believers. Perhaps, if the world went through more catastrophe, more centuries of violence and sorrow, with mankind progressively exterminating itself, one dark day the last Buddhist monk, sworn by his vows to celibacy, would encounter the last Buddhist nun, also under the same vows. They might then reconsider the dire situation; knowing that unless they consented to propagate their kind, mankind must vanish from the planet. I felt sure that no matter how earnestly they debated, the end would be renunciation. Then, they would decide, human misery could finally be ended.

Might this happen? It never could, in China, never so long as the Confucian ethic continued, founded on reality rather than on theories that led men astray, based on the simple satisfactions of family life, on the joy of decent marriage, of begetting children and watching them grow, of educating them and guiding them on their way. The proof of this lay about me among these numberless hillocks filled with the dead, in a cemetery that held the orderly graves of centuries, here where men for so long had been faithful to principles that had never betrayed them.

CHAPTER XIV *Celestial Time and Space*

IT WAS midwinter, or rather the frozen end of it; and Hsü Jung was buying large red firecrackers. Spread upon his eager face was a zest in acquisition that I had come to know well. "We must," he said, "fittingly prepare for the New Year!" Wên-Pin by intentional contrast, I fancied, continued to go about his daily work stolidly; although we soon did take counsel together on important matters such as the purchase of the supplies necessary to last us over the long holiday. "Prices of meat are bound to go up; the markets remain closed for so many days. If K'o Venerable Sir [an unexpectedly more formal title than the one for everyday use] indeed wishes us to eat *chiao-tzŭ* [the seasonable meat-filled dumplings], this must soon be planned!"

So I ordered a complete New Year; and the pleasurable activity began. The meat was bought; the sounds of the cleaving knife familiarly pounding on our wooden chopping block kept on for hours. We added a provision of rice wine—to be drunk hot—spiced and pickled vegetables, melon and sunflower seeds, some very good tea, and sweetmeats of the traditional kinds. All went forward by the glow from the kitchen stove as the nights became darker and colder.

Then one night Hsü began exploding his first firecrackers. Squatting low on the frozen ground, his face lighted by a flaming spill, he seemed a gleeful demon in black clothes, symbolizing what by now was going on in every courtyard about us.

"Why," I addressed him idiomatically, "why-for-what do you thus enjoy releasing explosions?"

"It is very necessary," he answered seriously, "first to blast the Old Year away, out of myself, here!" And he pointed to the center of his chest. "It is necessary to release explosions."

The purchase of new clothing, my yearly gift to them, their barbering and also visits to the local bath-house, all these were completed; we had come to New Year's eve. After dark, crackers now going off merrily all about us, a table was set up as a small altar in my outer courtyard. On it were placed the customary sacrifices to our Kitchen God, a popular image of brightly colored and gilded paper, who all year had been glued into a small carved niche over our stove. There were sticky sugared candies for him, to seal his mouth, one was told, when he went aloft on this last moonless night of the year to report in heaven about our courtyard also. There were miniature cut-out paper ladders hanging from the altar table, to help him on his journey; there was even a farthing's worth of some dried sweet grass as forage for his horse.

My servants ran to their sleeping room to put on their long robes; they returned to kowtow; and then they burnt the old paper god in a crackling fire of special brambles lighted on the ground. By the light of the flames their faces were flushed with excitement and cheerful with the good food they had already begun to consume. With great patience the Chinese wait for their long holiday; but when it finally comes everything in life yields to it. Another New Year was to begin again!

All through the dark hours the sound of the crackers was unceasing. On that one night of the year no one ever pulled down the paper shades at the windows, even in the most private courtyards. All lamps were lighted; and everywhere about, in neighbors' courtyards, families sat talking of years past and present, keeping vigil. It was only permissible to steal a short nap before dawn, before a long day of formal calling.

The more enterprising, even at that early hour, first went to a small temple just beyond the city walls, dedicated to the powerful God of Wealth. Here, pressing through the gates, crowds came long before it was light to burn incense. This was the center of the whole city's superstition on that cold morning; for to be here, early on New

Year's Day, was to bring luck upon enterprises in the months to come. For several years I went to see it all—bicycling there and back. Saluting everyone with the traditional greeting, "New joy, new joy! Grow wealthy!"—half frozen yet elated, sleepless and ready for much tea, thus I customarily began a round year as it was celebrated in Peking.

Not until I had returned to the West again did I realize that, while like Jack-in-the-Beanstalk I had been all adventure, certain basic principles had been implanted in me not only about the feasts of the year, but about time in general. Our sense of it, like our consciousness of the air we breathe, is not under ordinary circumstances present. Yet take away what we have become used to and we are instantly aware of the change.

This chapter, then, will describe the luxury of well-arranged Chinese time; and the corresponding luxury of well-arranged space. In Peking I came to observe that these underlay many of the charms the tourist was always anxious to have explained to him. Yet it required the implanting of a number of cardinal principles before all could be made clear.

There is a great practical difference between our calendar and that of the Chinese. Now that I have returned to the West, I no longer have the feeling that our year is as symmetrical as it once seemed. Our weeks of seven days, our modern week-ends; our system of short vacations, when those in cities dash off to see what the country looks like, upon our irregularly placed holidays: these do not grandly complete the four seasons as the Chinese think of them in terms of their own lunar—rather than solar—calendar.

Conversely, of course, the ordinary Chinese peasant still knows almost nothing of our kind of reckoning. So little can he figure out what goes on outside his own "central country," that it was perhaps only typical when one evening in the fields some Chinese Lancelot Gobbo, pointing solemnly to the moon, addressed me: "Do you have that there, also, in your honorable country?" Yet he could probably have explained quite well how the waxings and wanings of this same planet divided his own year with almost perfect evenness. Let us not laugh at him too much; we are guilty of ignorance almost as ludicrous.

Once it seems we were more intelligent. It is quite recently that we have lost a general understanding of matters that before were common knowledge. Both farmers and sailors were more informed about practical astronomy until modern weather reporting made its drastic changes. They still feel the harmony of the seasons as never can a city drudge, who if one adds together all his annual fortnightly vacations in a quarter century, will have spent only one year in the "country"—always at the same season—in a lifetime. So there are many disoriented human animals in all our large cities, living ignorant of nature's grandest rhythms.

To one who has lived close to China, the revolutions of the lunar calendar, making a much more even year than ours, are a subtle and constant force. Today this ancient reckoning of time is supposed no longer to be used; legally it has been ordered out of existence. Yet the Chinese farmer knows only distantly of what has supplanted it, and even the more educated city dweller invariably has a calendar block upon his wall on which both forms appear. At holiday times, to make gifts and to pay formal visits, you may be sure that he consults the lunar calendar. When the Chinese New Year approached my servants always bought a yellow bound paper almanac, and relied on it faithfully to carry them through the next four seasons.

Not until I had begun to think about time in terms other than those set from a Western childhood, did I realize how imperfect, indeed how wasteful of some of the joys of life, was our own system. I had simply taken ours as "the" calendar; never speculating how a year might otherwise be measured.

Above all, I had thought of the moon as an erratic planet giving man chiefly the pleasures of sentiment. It was erratic, I now perceive, only because Western and city-bred I had never used it practically, noticing merely that its quarters came at irregular places in the boxes of our Gregorian calendar.

Of course the waxings and wanings of the moon do not correspond evenly with any subdivision of the time it takes for our earth to complete one journey on its orbit around the sun. Yet the moon, as the

Chinese well know, has another even rhythm of its own. They so trust this flow and ebb of secondary light that they base their permanent subdivisions of the year—which of course still remains a single revolution of the earth about the sun, the center of all—upon the minor planet. Thus they have made the lunar calendar.

Now to live through a Chinese year is a new experience. Time has essentially different qualities when measured this other way; even the beginning and end are set at different places. We accept, good-naturedly and without question, the dispensation by which our own New Year begins somewhere in the middle of winter, one week after the high feast of Christmas. Yet why place a renewal here, when outdoors there is none?

Even the classical world did not proceed this way. September was the old seventh month, as the Latin root of its name makes clear. Then came October, November, and December as the eighth, ninth and tenth, literally. This formerly made January and February the last two of the dozen; with an odd trimming necessary—since the sun and moon never jibe—for the end of February, an irregularity that with no great logic we still keep, to make everything work out at the old termination with approximate evenness. Then, in the antique world, a new year began again in March, much at the same time that it still does in traditional China.

Surely this is wise. Surely the best place to make a fresh start is when nature herself makes it, with the renewal of growing things—with the coming of spring. To start thus is to begin at a true beginning. It is to align oneself with nature at the outset of each cycle, and thus to be correlated with the firmament. The greatest lack in our present system is that such an awareness is no longer in our minds. There are no proper endings nor true recommencements for us in time.

Given the right place to start, how then do the Chinese subdivide their year? Their months also differ from each other by a day or two, certain ones "large" and others "small." Yet each represents a complete lunar cycle. Each goes from the dark nights of the new moon through its waxing on to perfect roundness—and then back to darkness again. Chinese apparently without exception look forward to the one or two evenings in each month when they know in advance that the moonlight will be at its best. If the weather is good, this is a pleasure to be enjoyed—and re-enjoyed. For them this time always comes reassuringly in the center of each month. Time, of course, never ceases flowing, and the waning always follows to its inevitable conclusion; yet as with the year, so with the month: the completed dwindling forever marks the moment of new birth. Optimistically, there is never a complete and lifeless end. The rhythm is eternal.

Superimposed upon the harmony of these lunar months is still another system, unique—I believe—to China. It is based upon the four seasons; and consists of a subdivision of each into six smaller portions, roughly of a fortnight's duration, so that together for the whole year they total twenty-four. These are known as the Twenty-four Spells. Giving time progressive shading, they make a guide both to the weather and the agricultural labors of the cycle. Besides helping the farmer, they enhance even the city dweller's awareness of the passage of time on the land, providing him with a surprisingly accurate description of what is happening in the fields as the year progresses.

The first spell of the year is named, naturally enough, Spring Begins. The three other preliminary spells for the other seasons have similar names, always of two Chinese characters apiece; Summer, Autumn, and Winter also "Begin." In the wintry streets of Peking, as projects for the coming months were discussed, one often used to overhear the phrase: "We shall undertake this when Spring Begins." This meant that the business in hand was to be postponed until after the long holidays, yet got round to as soon as these were over. In the old days even the yamen, or official courts, were sealed for this period, throughout the empire.

The symmetry of the Twenty-four Spells as they developed after this beginning is a lesson in the workings of the Chinese mind. There are careful correspondences even to the forms of the characters, and balance wherever possible. This is what the Chinese mean by celestial harmony.

Soon after the year has begun the cold diminishes. Nature, having created man, not only makes his life possible but provides everything in due season. She now sends The Rains; and this is the second spell. Animal as well as vegetable life are both quick to feel its effects; so the third spell is titled—pleasurably rather than jocularly—Insects Awaken. This to the Chinese culminates the arrival of early spring. Their passionate interest in all insect life, as shown in their painting, makes it for them a happy period. Life now again moves, and crawls and flies! Man, too, becomes more active. At this time of the year, in North China, come the traditional pilgrimages. (That to Miao Fêng Shan, in the Western Hills, annually drew peasants from the whole countryside about Peking.) This was a time to come out into the sun for excursions.

There are, in the spells, a pair for the two equinoxes, and a similar pair for the solstices. Again we find balance, solar counterpoint. As we begin the second half of spring we come to the Vernal Equinox. This is the season—which will not come again until mid-autumn—when the days and nights are of equal length. It is a period of evenness, as opposed to the long days of summer, and the similarly long nights of winter.

The Spring Equinox is followed by a spell particularly loved by the Chinese people. It is the holiday time of Ch'ing Ming, or "Clear and Bright," something like our Easter. We have all lived through spring days when a burden is lifted from the heart, no matter through what griefs we have passed. A warmer wind blows, and with wordless conviction we are led back, trustfully—as children, by the hand—to hope again. In China this is the season when yearly each family sweeps the graves of its ancestors. This is done literally, for the ordinary grave mounds are merely of piled earth, and annually they must be reshaped and weeded. New loam is then swept up to renew the surface; and on top of each is set a piece of paper weighted with a stone to show that the task has been done.

In the region of Peking, on clear spring days, there was always much sweeping among the countless graves about the plain. As one bicycled along any road at that time of the year, one could see small groups about this pious task, especially as one neared the chief feast day itself. When the work was finished there would be the usual kowtowing to the dead, to mark respect; and then, perhaps not too surprisingly, the family in a new surge of good cheer generally made a picnic for the rest of the day.

The sixth and final spell of spring reminds us that man's life is possible only if he labors for his nourishment. It is called the Grain Rain. If rainfall is abundant at this time, the harvest in general will also be plentiful. In the rather dry region of Peking, the Chinese have a special proverb about this season. "Spring rain," they will tell you, "is precious as oil." From this spell onward man becomes absorbed with his labors in the fields.

The names of the summer spells fit very well a climate like that of Western Europe or the eastern part of the United States. They do not apply to tropical lands, nor to places with dry and rainy seasons. We are now to have heat, plenty of it; and later it will be followed by biting cold. Even in the city, gauze screens are fitted to the window frames; *p'êngs* go up in courtyards—now transformed to become outdoor living rooms.

First, of course, Summer Begins. There is an obvious change in the air; pearly masses of slow-moving or almost motionless clouds are throned high in the deep warm sky. Then the Grain Buds. The crops are vital: China lives so near the earth, and is so deeply of it. As the cereals ripen all attention centers upon them. The next spell, Grain in Ear, tells us clearly what is occurring.

There come the dazzling days of high midsummer, all brilliance and heat. The next spell, the Summer Solstice, provides mankind with the longest hours of light precisely when he can use them best.

By the calendar we have now reached the time of the year occupied roughly by our own months of July and August. So what could be more fitting than to find the last two summer spells called first Slight Heat and then Great Heat? These are the *fu t'ien*, or dog days, when master and man both take off as much clothing as possible, and seek the shade, fanning themselves constantly, grateful for a slight breeze. At times, in dusty Peking, even the street dogs would whimper as they curled themselves upon the baked earth in whatever shadow they could find. The sun was now tyrant.

Man exists by hope, though; and nothing lasts forever. A half-dozen spells for spring and as many for summer have passed: the lunar year is half complete. What may we expect of the autumn? In Chinese fashion, first, Autumn Begins. There comes at last the Stopping of Heat; and a grateful spell this is! In recollection I seem aware of many Chinese verses in which one feels clearly the poet's own relief as he describes the delicious first cooling airs, especially if borne to him over moonlit waters. Man now will be civilized again; his skin will dry; he will wear more clothes.

The earth meanwhile keeps turning. Soon there are the White Dews. The Autumn Equinox follows: night and day are again in balance. The face of the earth is further changed; there come on Cold Dews, and as vegetation withers—the crops have long since been gathered in—the Hoar Frost Falls, and autumn ends. Another quarter of the Chinese year is complete.

Winter comes to end the cycle. Like the other three seasons Winter Begins. Then we have Light Snow, which often as not does come whirling through the air during this fortnight. It is followed by the Heavy Snow; the calendar, civilized man's great invention, has long since warned him of it so that from wadded robes he can now change to those lined with fur. (Wên-Pin and Hsü Jung always knew from the almanac when to get these ready for me.)

The Winter Solstice begins the second half of this season as did earlier the summer one, precisely a half-year away. Another "Small" followed by a last "Great" finish the cycle: the Small Cold and—finally—the redoubtable Great Cold. The year ends darkly in the dreariest and chilliest time of all.

Yet spring is even now prepared for. One can begin to see from this bare enumeration how the Chinese conception of time, of death ever followed by life, of an end always leading to a new beginning, reinforces—indeed in no small measure may have helped to create—the strong native trend toward optimism. The round year is a great blessing; and Chinese brought up in the old order have always felt it to be so.

One major adjustment must still be made to keep the measure of the lunar months in harmony with that of the earth's journey about the sun. Nature has for all time created these two so that they cannot be reduced to an exact ratio. The West invented the Leap Year; the Chinese have surmounted the difficulty with the "intercalary month," an extra lunar month that from time to time is simply added—at one place or another—to the normal twelve. This produces an occasional longer year of thirteen months in all, to bring the equinoxes and solstices even once more. When the extra month was to be added was a mystery known to the calendar makers; although they could work it out a number of years in advance. Also it was they who determined at what season it should come.

The Chinese name for this month is merely a "repeated" one; and so there may be a repeated first month, or a repeated seventh month, for example, as has been decided. All documents in the old order were then so dated; and there could be no confusion. Strangely enough—as "old China hands" aware of the system would frequently recount—the weather seems to accommodate itself to this occasional readjustment. So if a month corresponding to our June, for example, were repeated, one often did have a long spring. If this always worked out, it would have become incredible. I can only say from my own experience that it did seem roughly true. The extra months accomplished their various tasks with smoothness, and in tranquil Peking we felt sure that the wagons of our small lives were securely hitched to the stars. All good Chinese, of course, knew how comfortable this was.

So much for the single year, calculated by lunar months and by "spells" based upon the progress of the seasons. The rhythm was majestic, the subdivisions interrelated with repeating harmonies. Yet there were also larger divisions of time; first into groups of twelve years apiece, and beyond this, the largest summation of all, a full Chinese cycle of sixty years.

For one diverting reason the grouping by twelves is much in the minds of simple folk. Each year is commonly designated throughout China by the name of an animal. The horse, the monkey, even the rat and the snake, find a place in the list. The year within which one was born, moreover, was the only one by which age was counted. So the commonest way, especially among illiterates, of asking a person his age, was to ask him, "To what do you count?" The smiling answer usually came, "I count to the rooster!" or, "I count to the pig!" There seemed no aversion to being classified under an unattractive animal.

Thus the approximately five hundred million Chinese alive at any time go through existence in annual classes recurring every twelve years. If someone said, "I count to the year of the horse," and it happened again to be that year, everyone knew immediately that such a man had passed either his twenty-fourth or thirty-sixth, or some similar birthday. If the year belonged to another animal, simple calculation forward or backward in the familiar series, left no room for doubt.

One further custom, dying out in my time, marked these cycles. Each time one's own year in the repeating twelve returned, any man could wear a bright red sash binding the wide pleated waistband of his Chinese trousers. This was a long piece of stuff, normally of some plain color, passing several times about the waist, its ends tucked in securely so that they would not slip. So if one saw a middle-aged man walking along a country road with his long gown off, wearing a sash of crimson—in China a color always emblematic of pleasure or celebration—one knew at once that he was surely in the year of his life following the completion of his forty-eighth, or else his sixtieth. Simple inspection decided between these possibilities. Such public recognition of the larger multiples of the years made the progress through life of ordinary folk decidedly more cheerful, I believe, than anything we know. As in so many other ways, in China one was never solitary.

It was not necessary to be accurate beyond this. One's birthday was never counted from the actual day of one's birth, but from before it. The Chinese are completely logical after their own fashion: a baby does exist before it comes into the world. So it was always first given the complimentary age of one, and then another unit was added for each New Year. At this time, of course, changes of age proceeded on a mammoth scale. Amid the setting off of firecrackers and general jubilation, the whole nation saw the New Year in. With it literally everyone in the empire automatically became one year older. The birthday of the year was also that of the individual. How companionable a system where "All under Heaven" went down through time together!

There remains to discuss the largest division used by the Chinese in counting time. Tennyson's error in "Locksley Hall" is typical of our general ignorance. In that poem he makes his romantic hero cry: "Better fifty years of Europe than a cycle of Cathay!" Surely Tennyson here thought of the Chinese cycle as an age, an aeon, not merely a decade longer than the brief half-century with which he compared it. Counting by hundreds—in general our longest Western unit—has of course no place whatever in the Chinese historical system; indeed it still means nothing there. When one had counted to sixty, one began again. The cycle was also considered a good normal measure for human existence—like our somewhat longer "three score and ten." It covered a life span and linked together grandfather and grandson.

The place of the single year in the succession of sixty was traditionally fixed by an odd system still in use today, when inscribing dates on pictures, for example, or on a fan, or on any article thus formally to be marked. The designation is made by grouping together a pair of "cyclical characters," which indicate that year out of all the sixty. The first is from a repeating set of ten, the second from a similar one of twelve.

These progress, like the clicking of beads on two separate rosaries, each always a step further along in its own unvarying series. When the "ten stems," the first of the pair, have been enumerated, two more will still be left unused from the "twelve branches." Each goes one further, however, and the combinations continue. Now by mathematical law no identical grouping of these pairs can occur again until exactly sixty combinations have been formed. The whole then repeats indefinitely.

Such an arrangement is baffling to us. I never met a Westerner who had any natural feeling—as have learned Chinese—about where in the grouping of the sixty possibilities any given pair might fit. Even the Chinese philosophically accept their system as being essentially vaguer than our own, with its years counted in two series, backward and forward, from the zero beginning our first *Anno Domini*. Yet for them the fact that life has existed from the immeasurable past; that it now is and will go on; but that for the individual it must some-day end: these are the great truths. The rest is subsidiary, relatively unimportant. Of course one needs a temporary system, for individual existence. But exactly where, on a time scale running on forever, such and such an event occurred, seems never for them to have demanded a special arrangement like that which we invented.

History as the final measuring rod was of supreme importance; but as we shall see, historical time was estimated differently. Here the norm was the dynasty, based on family vitality, and in length this was notoriously unpredictable. How the Chinese recorded historical time is shown clearly in the wording of a small text that was the very first piece of memorizing given to a little child in the rigid and old, yet grand, system of traditional education. This was the *San Tzŭ Ching*, or Three Character Classic, explaining in concise lines the Chinese cosmos. It used to be learned by heart, shouted off like a little catechism, by every child beginning his studies.

First, typically enough, came certain universal truths about our human nature: *Men arrive beginnings, Nature roots good; Natures mutually near,* [in] *practice mutually far,* etc. Then the planets are numbered, followed by the living creatures—the world in which man lives.

After this came a most condensed history of the classics, the great Books of Wisdom, then of the successive Chinese dynasties, only a line or two for each. How long were they? One was never told the dates in a series of years, but—typically—how often the throne was transmitted. The supreme power was bequeathed by one ruling house only once, by another following it no less than twenty times, and so on. By then the genius of the family, which originally secured the transcendent reward, had inevitably diminished; and a new dynasty "with the will of Heaven"—so that success was invariably legitimized —would supplant the old. Here was a human measurement of time. It put old wisdom, very early, into young heads.

One peculiarity of the cyclical system, which never failed to annoy the Westerner, was that it never seemed to have occurred to the Chinese to number these cycles. One cannot refer to them in any succession. There was not even a mythical point of commencement, for one began with timeless mythology. A paradox of no little consequence ensues. In dating works of art, one often knows from an inscription exactly where, within a period of sixty years, a painting, let us say, was executed. But which sixty? One must try to judge on grounds of style, which is notoriously tricky terrain. Further, when artistic changes are as slow as in the lethargic currents of late Chinese art, this often can not be stated with any assurance. Here sixty years of "Cathay" may be as nothing to a critical European half-century!

So one learned to live constantly with bland puzzles on "dated" scrolls hanging upon the walls of one's own rooms. For the Westerner, to be thus frustrated—seemingly with such negligence—in the matter of proper placing on one definitive time-scale is a serious matter. A Chinese accepts the situation differently. "Perhaps we only do know," he might retort, "the place within its cycle when such and such an object was made. Perhaps its usefulness and interest were never planned originally to outlast sixty years, which is two generations in any case. This cannot be of great importance! What have mortals to do," he may further muse, "bothering to fix small dates to all eternity?"

Placing historical events was not so vague as this, especially if they had anything to do with a given reign. For in the imperial system, the least small happenings related to an emperor were catalyzed by a current that ran from this one culminating figure through the whole of the social structure beneath him. To relate events to times of reigns was instinctive; and it even became natural to all foreigners who lived long in Peking, where imperial survivals abounded. Elsewhere, especially in today's world, the feeling for a pyramidal social structure has grown faint indeed; but the leaders of our own time never seem to dominate quite as did the old emperors and kings.

Now, as has been mentioned, the use of the Emperor's personal name was completely forbidden to his subjects. He was always to be referred to obliquely as the Superior One, or else as the Son of Heaven; or after his death by his "temple name." Yet to designate his reign, or portions of it, for public use, special pairs of auspicious characters were selected, which were then daily on men's tongues. Combinations were chosen such as "The Road Is Bright," or "Transmitted Brilliance," or in general any similar pair that might bring good fortune.

A feature of these designations was that they could start at will, and that a single Emperor might have several, or even quite a number. Apart from superstition, which must often have been involved, they were made to correspond either with the character of the reign or else with the spiritual progress—or perhaps its reverse—of the Emperor for whom they were selected.

Once chosen, though, this combination of characters dated all official events conveniently from the first, or some following year of a so-called "reign date." And providing one knew the reign dates by heart—or looked them up in a manual—all was well.

The Ming and Ch'ing Emperors, rulers of the last two dynasties, had each only one reign date apiece; and this further simplified the arrangement. So if one arbitrarily learned, as one soon did, that Ch'ien Lung or Virile Eminence was not the true name of an Emperor, but actually the designation of all the years when a certain sovereign, whose actual name was private, had held the throne; and if one knew that the First Year of Ch'ien Lung was our own 1736, further deductions were simple enough. In official inscriptions, and in all official documents, the year of the reign was appended invariably, clearly. That, to a Chinese, was sufficient.

In space as well as in time, I believe that throughout their history the Chinese have been unusually sensitive to the harmonies of nature. The matter is crucial. The place of the sun on its daily course with relation to themselves, to their dwellings, indeed to their whole system of building, even to the planning of walled cities: this was to them a primary consideration.

"How"—they seem to ask a silent question—"can anything be right and proper until a human being has put himself into correct relation with the planet that is the very source of our light and warmth, that gives us the day, our crops, our food and clothing?" The necessity for correct orientation has become so ingrained in the Chinese that they cannot imagine the lack of system by which we habitually live, nor the way in which with far greater mechanical means at our disposal we still lightly ignore what to them are essentials.

The sun, we all know, rises in the east, and travels toward the south in its westward course. To secure the full and continuing effect of its light and heat in our latitudes it is obvious that one must therefore build facing due south: any oblique angle is less effective. Then at noon shadows will be cast directly north, in a line perpendicular to one running east and west. On such a north-south axis, we have seen, was laid out the great plan of Peking. The system goes far deeper than this in arrangements for daily living. In Peking there was not a house of any size, even the humblest, that was not oriented to the cardinal points of the compass.

How much personal comfort such orientation of domestic building achieves is not generally realized. If we take the average domestic courtyard, built up on all four sides, it is obvious that under this system the main house, which is invariably the best, and is always if possible built larger and deeper than the others, will receive the most sunlight. It always faces due south. The west and east side-houses will then have the good light divided between them, the former receiving it in the morning, the latter in the afternoon.

The southern buildings, "reversed foundations" the Chinese call them—since they turn their backs to the light—will receive no sun at all, except perhaps at the very beginning and end of the day in summer, when the sun rises and sets somewhat to the north of east and west. These are in consequence always the least desirable buildings in any Chinese courtyard; and they are used for the humblest purposes. Here may be the kitchens, or storerooms of one variety or another, or waiting rooms for tradesmen.

There is a common proverb in Peking, where the prevailing winds blow from the northwest—I translate it literally:

> Rich men use not east-south rooms:
> Summer not cool; winter not warm.

These are obviously inferior exposures, especially since the outer walls of nearly all courtyard buildings in China are windowless, and light is not received from more than one direction.

In the dull days of winter, when the sun would be most welcome, the "reversed" rooms are even less desirable. At that time, because of the well-calculated angle of the projecting eaves of the roof over the south-facing main hall, the amenity of its orientation is most appreciated. The builders of Peking, in planning these gently curving eaves, apparently learned over the centuries to use exactly the right pitch. Since the sun comes much nearer to the horizon in winter, the eaves then allow it full sweep indoors; in cold weather it streams into the "formal room" of the main house the whole day long. Then, after the spring equinox, as the sun rises daily higher in the sky, its light ample in any event, and as the weather grows always warmer, it is good to exclude its heat. The overhanging eaves now shield walls and windows perfectly; all through the summer the best rooms are in the shade—as was planned, with nothing left to chance.

To the Chinese all the foregoing is simply rational arrangement. How little of it do we know in the West, where in many of our ordinary dwellings, let alone those deliberately picturesque, until quite recently a whole house might be so planned that not a single room received the sunlight really best suited for its use!

There is a further unexpected corollary to this Chinese system. One can tell the time of day in a city such as Peking with bricks and mortar. Every court, every wall, becomes a constantly useful sundial. For if all buildings run either east and west, or north and south, and the paving of their courtyards is regular, then it follows that from the shadow even of a twig along or across any line, one can tell when the magic hour of noon has arrived. Then all shadows run north, and even indoors those cast across the paved floor of a main hall make a regular pattern of its columns, its windows and their tracery. Earlier in the forenoon, with the sun in the east, all shadows slant more or less sharply toward the northwest; in the afternoon the angles are reversed.

So I learned not to be surprised, if I asked my servants what time of day it might be, to see them merely cast a quick glance about, and state categorically: "Perhaps near to eleven" (of our own system, which had come into general use), or "Surely, now, at least half-past four!" And they would be so nearly right, by a Western watch, that with the unhurried tempo of ordinary living in Peking, one could dispense with further calculation.

Surely the reader will have asked himself, though, if all was so perfect on sunny days, what did one do upon those when it rained? The answer is, in China: "Nothing; nothing in so far as possible!" That after all is what the birds and beasts, in their animal wisdom, also do. The Chinese, further, simply hates to get wet; and one must not be too contemptuous of this aversion since his clothes do not protect him as do our modern raincoats or leather shoes. Native out-door clothing, except only perhaps the thatched grass coat of the old-fashioned fisherman, simply invites moisture; and cloth slippers also wear poorly when wet.

So one goes out-of-doors as little as possible, and makes other plans. There ensue the pleasures of an unexpected withdrawal, of another use of time. Teachers fail to arrive; one changes a project to go out to lunch; if it is actually raining that is considered enough of a message for anyone. The joys of a session of recapitulation, with its familiar accompaniment of reminiscence, may follow. It is relaxation like this, rare nowadays, that restores health to the mind and serenity to the spirit.

He who has not passed rainy days in a deserted courtyard, even the familiar street cries abandoned, the rain dripping down from the eaves hour by hour, gurgling as it fills the drains, while perhaps he reads old letters, or is bemused by an out-of-date newspaper, or else indulges in an orgy of rearrangement, to consolidate old possessions and integrate new; such a man does not know a Chinese variety of repose. He has missed one lesson of a philosophy genuinely cheerful in part because it has had time in which to integrate itself.

Many Chinese poems reproduce this mood of respite, granted with the patience of the rain; perhaps in a withdrawn gallery of some solemn mountain monastery; perhaps under the awning of a small boat moored under bending willows beside a famous lake; perhaps looking out from some picturesque tower room, with the rain splashing bucketfuls of water on banana leaves in a little court below—or perhaps merely in the familiar setting, yet changed by the storm and lighted by memory, of home.

Another phase of the Chinese concept of space has already been touched on: the regular placing of any objects formally related to each other. So much do the Chinese assume that all proper arrangement will be symmetrical that they are at a loss if this is not possible. Once I was sent five white oleander bushes, handsome plants, which we had place for only opposite the doorway to my main house on either side of my central lotus tub. Two apiece flanking it went well enough; but what of the fifth? The servants thought it over at length, and then finally came to me with a statement of fact. "We cannot," said they, "use such a surplus plant; there exists no method for this!" So we simply gave it away, to be a central object for someone else; and then enjoyed the others.

Once, also, I happened to show to my Elder Born an illustration from a British magazine, of King Edward VIII, seated at a handsome desk of marquetry placed obliquely in the corner of some palace room. (It was nearing the time of the abdication; and Mr. Wang and I were having long discussions on kingship.) He looked at the picture earnestly and silently; and I felt increasingly what must have been in his eyes the glaring difference between such casual placing of furniture and what would have been the Chinese arrangement. Finally he put the magazine down, incredulous in spite of all his experience with "external country" oddities. He gave me a slightly weary smile: "And he a King!" he sighed.

So I lived on in Peking, among the Chinese, to whom all of the above was too natural to require explanation. I had only to bicycle to the Legation Quarter on a short errand, though, to leave this local world and find myself in another that was quite unaware of much that I had discovered, unsoothed because untouched by these harmonies. For a long while I tried to define to myself the difference, deeply sensed in such moments of transition. Finally I hit upon a pair of words that still seem to me to sum up the Chinese feeling for time and space: "cosmic consciousness" is what makes their attitude different.

The average Chinese still remains close to the eternal fluctuations of nature. He is aware of how they minister to the needs of his life. He is, though, so close to this cosmic play, so much part of it himself, that he is almost unconscious of his riches, using these splendid things freely and happily. The pattern that this imparts to his life is peculiarly Chinese. The whole race apparently possesses millennial balance; so much so that even if all go ill—as mortal affairs are liable to for so much of the time—yet cradled in the universe men can know that this world will at least alternate between darkness and light. The rhythm, like that of the planets themselves, may be so slow as sorely to try small human patience; but it is sure.

During seven years of such living, these feelings ended by becoming very much my own. I could even afford to float buoyantly upon time because of them. To my good fortune only the fewest obligations cut across quiet hours of study in such a way as to break the harmony. During the day the architectural regularity of the city made me ever conscious of the sun; at night the moon became my calendar.

Living near to the Forbidden City and the imperial lakes, I could watch at its stateliest the movement of both planets through the year. As for the moon, in summer and on the lakes, to know in advance what its light would become of a certain practical importance. For the largest sloping-roofed barges, which had belonged to the Empress Dowager and could still be rented for evening parties, were naturally most in demand when the moon was full. One Western landlady of a local hotel, who wished to do well for her visiting tourists, was said to have reserved the best of them regularly for the evening of the sixteenth day in every lunar month during summer weather. She knew that the moon was then at its brightest and roundest, rather than one evening earlier. Thus, Chinese fashion, did we refine upon our pleasures.

My servants, of course, were well trained in these matters. If to test them, some serene evening, I might ask how the month was coming, a mere glance upward and the answer, as in telling time, would come promptly. If we then checked the date with the almanac, always handy in the kitchen, it was remarkably often correct. So we lived tranquilly, within these marvels, "cosmically conscious."

How deeply this had affected me I was not to know until I had returned once more to America. My first few days, even in New York—which, as an island, does happen to face nearly true south, so that many of its streets are from a Chinese point of view properly oriented—made me feel curiously alien, chiefly because of a now familiar sense obviously shared by none about me. There was the glorious sun, almost unused, certainly not in any such pleasant way as I had become accustomed to in China. Better provision was made for catching its light and warmth in the hovels of Peking than here in a metropolis!

There was also the moon, looking cold and lost in the sky, as it still looks to me in the West, even now. No one made any civilized arrangements, calculating them in advance, for the pleasures with which all of us had enjoyed its seemingly brighter disc and pearlier light, in Peking. No one in the great city ever seemed to pay the slightest attention to its progress; its rising and setting, its waxing and waning, were unnoticed. Western senses were apparently impervious to these planetary rhythms.

I remember sitting down somewhat disconsolately to write a letter to a friend still in China, upon one of my first days "home," and dating it with sudden feeling: "From a city that never looks at the moon, beside a river flowing unnoticed to the sea." After gentle Peking, where the soaring moonrise might take hours that were simply and happily given to it, the contrast was grim. No wonder Westerners had never painted such scenes as the Chinese love, with the honey-colored low disc round and large, seen from an open place at the edge of a precipice, while seated tranquilly upon a pine-sheltered height some Chinese philosopher might be found contemplating in it the universe.

CHAPTER XV   *The Welcome While Is Over*

EVEN after the passage of time, to contemplate the end of my adventure is not easy. The hour came when, after all my hopes and plans to make secure my foothold among these marvels, I was unceremoniously put out. For a long while, during the years of the Japanese occupation of Peking, the Westerner there had been untouched and unharmed. Nevertheless he did live more and more like a man who, although physically comfortable, knows that he has a fatal disease, clawing even at that moment in the dark at his vitals. Mutely I began to say farewell to many gentle pleasures, sensing that each time might become the last.

This struck at one side of Chinese life with peculiar effect. The accustomed and constant satisfaction of hunting and buying the most diverse objects for their own sake, in this land where acquisition was one of the recognized pleasures of living, suddenly ceased. If all could now so easily be torn away, or might have to be abandoned peremptorily, carting further purchases back to my own courts began to lose meaning. It was chilling to sit with what was about me, no longer cherishing any desire to add, looking at what might only prove cumbersome to transport halfway round a globe at war.

This was the first prying up of the scales of my armor. After long and blissful freedom from interference, I was being hustled by what I recognized at once as a giant force; and I felt shamefully a pygmy in its presence. My unwillingness to leave had added to it a vexation produced by the behavior of the Chinese about me. They, apparently, long ago had known that all of us were birds of passage; that we came—and then, sooner or later, of course all left. They were aware far better than we, it was obvious, how from now on time would pass for us, and what would happen in it. Plans for the future shrank to nothing. The present was flat without them. Life became dreary, and —what had never happened before—tedious.

Then events changed their tempo. As the year began that was to end with the Japanese attack on Pearl Harbor, it became evident that time was beginning to run for us—comfortably ensconced as we still were within the shell of old Peking—with a different, a Western, speed. The long rich tranquil hours were over; and the seven years that had been ones of such abundance for me had run their course.

The American flag now raised over my courtyards in intermittent days of crisis, and my American passport, hitherto granting proud immunity and effortless extraterritoriality, became symbols of the fundamentally different kind of life (even if I still hoped to remain in China) that I now should have to plan. The underlying facts had always existed, of course, but as the old liberties and privileges began here and there to evaporate, they became coldly visible. American relations with Japan also became worse; American citizens, even in tranquil Peking, were the target of hostile Japanese notice.

We strengthened our ties with the embassy. Indeed as the tension gradually increased, we were requested to appear there personally. Two marines from the embassy guard, cleanly dressed, slow-moving and tall, would arrive mounted on large well-groomed horses at my outer gate. The servants would run to fetch me, and we exchanged a word or two of hurried Chinese as they looked on; then they would hand me one or another official notice and ride slowly away again. In a day or two I would find myself in the office of some Secretary of Embassy, sitting in an American leather upholstered chair, while we talked over the "situation."

Those like myself without vital employment were asked to leave first, so that, if—these "ifs" becoming ever more ominous—things broke badly, there would be fewer fellow citizens left stranded, without ships, in an impossible situation. After such visits, American voices and American reasoning would for some hours drown the clamor of Chinese sights and sounds about me. I went bicycling thoughtfully northward to my quarter of the city, toward home— could it now, I was asking, even remain "home"?—already remote from what was about me.

The feeling of increasing estrangement came to focus one wintry day as I was pedaling a somewhat bumpy way across the marble bridge separating the north and central lakes, in the now doubly forlorn pleasure grounds of the imperial palace. Suddenly I was forcibly struck by something that must have been going on for some-time: the whole effect of the buildings on the shores, even the light on them, had completely changed for me.

This Chinese past was now rejoining itself, collapsing and fore-shortening, becoming hourly more distant; while I, with equal in-evitability, was also rapidly heading—whither? We no longer fitted together. I became more of a stranger to what was about me, in that moment, than I had been seven long years before, when from this same old bridge I had caught my first sight of the magnificent prospect.

So I decided to break the pattern. It was a conscious act of will. Another self now perforce took control; while the Chinese part, help-less, had mutely to watch itself step by step put out of existence. Preliminary visits were made to what before had seemed improbable places—coming from my quiet part of town—to steamship offices, to the packers, to shippers. I returned home to tea without flavor, to survey my once so confidently acquired possessions in terms of cubic feet, all to be disarranged, torn apart, and uprooted. I acted mechani-cally, stiffly, accomplishing what was needed, making decisions the meaning of which I knew I should laboriously have to discover later, in time become colorless.

Then the day came when, like a surgical incision, the first object was carted out into my courtyard, and delivered to a waiting crew of five or six men equipped with lavish supplies of excelsior, wrapping materials, boxes and crates. In no time every room in the house was in confusion. In that courtyard the work went on for the better part of a month; but I had at least determined not to be separated from my possessions—and how very many they seemed now to have become! Overhead the midwinter sky was freezing. All of us drank much tea, in intervals of rest; I had ordered an unusually fine quality of leaves for everyone. Within me a numb mind was struggling to find a clue.

One physical circumstance reinforced my impressions. In these days of emotional uprooting I had also to go to the American hospital (hitherto almost unvisited) for a painful extraction of the first tooth that I had ever lost. This was another end to the old sense of well-being. The symbol went deep; under gray skies I was forced to reflect on how impermanent and transitory were human plans. So I cycled in wind and dust along the frozen lanes, between engagements for surgical dressings and the slow, cumbersome, inevitable packing, as the large wooden cases now began swallowing even my tables and chairs.

At night the kerosene lamps cast their light from different angles upon the walls, which were themselves stripped and becoming alien. The lamps were placed on other pieces of furniture, in other parts of once familiar rooms. My carpets and rugs, my growing plants and flowers, the accustomed piles of books, all the amenities of the way in which I had lived, were gone. Even smells had changed; and a fine gray dust settled perpetually over all surfaces, entering one's nostrils, begriming one's fingernails.

All this while, like a judged prisoner, I was pacing the stone court-yards of my mind, ceaselessly roving backward and forward, seeking at least some cause in my verdict, and to find out if possible how to mitigate it. My general mood had become less one of regret than chagrin.

Finally we reached bare rooms. Coolies carted the largest cases to a godown in the Legation Quarter, a number of straining figures slowly lifting the heavy boxes together, to get them over the high sills. The effect, at such moments, was uncomfortably like a funeral. High crates powdered with snow stood in the court against my inner windows, stark under the wintry sky. As day changed to night they seemed presences. Indoors my bare matting showed straw color where vanished pieces of furniture once had stood; elsewhere it was soiled and worn by feet on familiar errands already in the past.

Little was left to me but a few pieces of simulated Western furniture, of wicker, to be abandoned at the end. Even my bright red and blue wadded cotton quilts, once stitched by a cheerful *amah*, completed with pride and pleasure, were to be given to my servants after my last night in the house, before my train journey to the sea. I read late, alone, now in empty rooms; my heart felt curiously even more hollow.

Accounts had to be put in order; many small hard tasks gone through to make an end. Here a pattern was to be demolished, there some pleasant custom ended. Bills were paid for the last time—for fuel or water, for local provisions. So much had been for simple Chinese living. I drank up my last wine; gave away once precious small hoards of Western supplies. I was shrinking my base by inches—and the future still remained completely featureless.

In moments when the flesh grew weary this became slow agony. Fatigue overwhelmed all of us, the servants as well as myself. Yet we kept plodding slowly through duty after duty. Sleep, when it came, was the only anodyne to relieve what had become a time of sorrow.

Finally the night came that was to be my last in Peking. Farewell visits to friends and acquaintances, exhausting with overmuch talk, and particularly fatiguing when interspersed with hollow assumptions of brightness: these too had been made. Bedtime came. It was a relief to have the lamp extinguished, and to hear the servants' slippered footfalls disappear, to be alone in the dark, in that room, for the last time; still trying with a tired mind to keep thinking, to find out—if it were possible—eventually how to preserve some part of this world now in complete dissolution. It had been (I was already using the past tense) so kind and fair to me.

The last morning dawned, windless and mild; the last breakfast was consumed, on inferior crockery, chiefly with care to eat it decently, and not to gulp. A small pile of traveling luggage, everything long ago planned for and in order, was on the dismantled *k'ang*. From now on action became curiously mechanical. At least one knew what to do!

The hired rickshas were announced. One of Wên-Pin's relatives sat in the kitchen, to be watchman behind a door to which I should not return. My little dog ran out of the open barrier gate to examine the smells of the lane. Farewell with him, thus oblivious, was better so. Then Wên-Pin and Hsü Jung, and I, all three of us, mounted, stooped over in our rickshas until the shafts were lifted; and the pullers began bearing us rapidly along, jolting past the humble sights of the everyday.

The morning was still early; the street criers calling, hawking familiar things to those with other destinies. Men with burdens on carrying poles sidled by. For me it was a ride in a tumbril. The servants had on their best clothes. Their familiar faces, as I glanced at them sidewise while we rode, were rigid with emotion.

Everything turned rapidly past us. Other men were tranquil. We reached the Water Gate of the railway station, where I was to take my place in a train to bear me to Tientsin, and beyond to the sea. Thence a small ship would deliver me to the Japanese port, where finally a larger one would be waiting to take me back to the unreal world of the West.

All was now spinning itself down to a matter of minutes. I inspected the railway carriage, finding that I was to share part of it with a high-ranking Japanese general and his suite. The unaccustomed plush of its upholstery—it was years since I had been on such a boat train—was a repulsively bright Prussian blue; and the jingle of the numerous accessories to the Japanese uniforms also grated on raw nerves.

The general, I discovered, was being given a ceremonious farewell. The broad roofed platform under the high city wall was crowded with the Japanese military of many services, as well as with pigeon-toed Japanese women, in kimonos, white bands bearing black characters fastened obliquely over their shoulders, stating that they had come from the "Sun-Root Country" to "comfort" Japanese troops. The often repeated mechanical bows of everyone present seemed robotlike.

I descended to the platform again. Time kept passing. Now were to come the last farewells of all, those with my servants. They had accompanied me here, for these brief moments, onto territory formerly their own, but now taken over by their enemies. It was rumored that

the Japanese so little liked to see ordinary Chinese come and go in
this place, that if they remained too long they might suddenly be
seized and beaten. All of us knew this; but they had insisted upon
escorting both me and my belongings as far as possible. To have
refused to permit it would have caused a wound, after now many
years, to the very "face" about which they themselves had taught me
so much.

The moment came for me to return to the train. We ceased intermittent exhortations and the repeating of remarks already made. The
stumpy little general and his small court mounted the doorway to
our common carriage; and he stood in the entry, giving last-minute
audiences, with stiff bows from the waist down, all of which were
returned with the slow precision of automata.

We had to concentrate on what was left for us to do! Wên-Pin
stepped forward, to make his manners. "I ask for the well-being of
your family," he said. He became thus Confucian and formal, yet I
knew that he only wished to be able to behave correctly to the last.
His face was flushed and his phrases of politeness stereotyped; but
each of us clung to them at that moment as to a single solidity in a
dissolving world.

I glanced at Hsü Jung—to see that suddenly his face had become
wrinkled and dark red. He was in unashamed and bitter tears.
Breeding at this critical moment did not uphold his less disciplined
nature, but his feelings came from the heart. Thus the three of us
came through our ordeal. We had behaved in the way that men must
at the ends of things; and as all Chinese know from poems throughout
their history, partings are among the fateful and poignant moments
in life. "There is no sorrow like the sorrow of parting!" Then they
turned and disappeared, as I sought my seat.

After a delay I felt the first slow motion of the train; so it was
really over! I was leaving Peking—now beyond its walls. I must have
sat motionless for a long, a very long, while. There was no more any
need to stir. Finally I realized that the train was rattling along, chuffing
resonantly amidst the ordinary fields of familiar North Chinese land-

scape. There, beyond the plush upholstery and the compartment windows, untouched and unhurrying, was the eternal life of the land I was leaving.

Smoke from the engine from time to time spread a whiteness over the panes, obscuring the scene. Then it would slowly evaporate and all would come clear again: mud huts, stunted trees, a duck pond, grave mounds of many shapes and sizes, all so well-known. Yet I was being borne steadily away. Familiar birds, black and like crows but with white patches on their breasts and wings, were flying as they always did over the fields in winter, fanning out to wheel or to alight. Everywhere were blue-robed peasants, stooping or pulling, engaged in one or another of their endless tasks.

Somehow very gradually that sight of quiet work in the impersonal fields stole comfortingly within me as a first and faint consolation. If all were thus simple under the light of day, in its sensible colors of tawny and blue, with its familiar black and white birds, if China labored thus eternally with such deep and unconscious faith in its labor, then—I saw it, for a moment, clear—my own, now past, life bound to this land might elsewhere also not be wholly without another harvest. My loyalty, I knew, would last. So the train rambled on first toward the ugly spreading port of Tientsin and finally to salt air and the sea; and I painfully began in weariness my first steps to descend from lost heights back to the everyday again.

I realized that a significant part of my life was over. Even as the objects in the fields had kept disappearing intermittently in clouds of white smoke, I somehow knew deeply that there was to be no going back. Something had stopped. The next days were stiff with an almost surgical pain; fatigue became mental coagulation. It was not difficult to assume the role of passenger on a small coastal boat, as we passed the islands off the shores of Korea. But to lie, during the day, in my upper bunk, when the cabin I shared with another passenger was vacant: this, with liberty now to allow my mind to turn to me any aspects it would, this was the only thing I desired. It was long before my thoughts began to shape themselves as I have tried to set them out below; long indeed before I should come to be able to write these words of valediction.

Back in the busy West life began anew. Like the fatfleshed cattle in Pharoah's dream, the years that for me also had been seven, passed irrecoverably by. Like all privilege, too, while they had been mine, they had borne within themselves a specious reasoning: why not continue thus forever since mere existence was so agreeable? The leaner years that replaced them bore a different stamp. A fundamental lack of sympathy with existence itself on these other and lesser terms brought with it if not rebellion—for that would have been idle—at least revulsion. Hope deferred may have entailed some confusion of thinking as well. There were moments, not so much desperate as consummately boring, when the way ahead seemed to lead only from the heights where I had once joyfully basked in the Chinese sun, irrevocably downward, into darker stretches. My destiny had been altered.

Then, oddly enough, even as I was almost coming to believe that I should have to accustom myself thus to live permanently, there trembled ahead a gradual awareness of further change. First it had seemed only a slightly greater ability in bearing what I must, in handling the routine of this further, not very attractive, daily life. It seemed to stretch ahead like some unending urban perspective, like dull buildings on a long street, successive and truncated slices, without the benison of foliage. The glories of sun and cloud, of wind and running water, of comforting nearness to the earth, that to me also had been North China, were absent from these scenes.

There occurred what must have been an invisible and very slow shifting of hidden layers, a reclamation going on deep under the surface, far from sight and beyond control. What needed to be discovered was something new again! What could it be, thus beyond my joys and sorrows, beyond the fat and lean of years gone by?

At least there was no excitement and no tension while the depths were shifting. The East had taught me composure. I could also see clearly—as one untempted by a vice reads easily the thoughts of those struggling with it—how little peace of soul existed anywhere about me. Faces were twisted and swollen from the sharp pangs of problems within. Everywhere there were people, thousands of them, so caught in the shifting circumstance of their complex existences that they could not by any chance perceive certain larger issues now visible to me. I had lived one part of my life quite for itself, without illusory goals demanding disproportionate sacrifice; and I had therefore known true freedom.

Because I had remained long in China, further, I apparently also had other awarenesses. I had heard, for instance, the unrepressed wailings of natural grief, over my walls in Peking, in the long nights of neighbors' funerals. I had first shuddered, now long ago, at these and other varieties of sorrow and affliction, put away from the surface in the West, screened or hidden and thus never fully understood; and I had gradually learned to live more comfortably, more honestly, with mortality.

In Asia men thus came more simply out of the soil, and they returned to it also more simply. There was less room for the elaborate misrepresentation of the chief purposes of life that is one of the strange fruits of our present civilization, growing ever more fatally apart from nature. "Only birth and death are great," had said Confucius himself. This now appeared simple and true. "Take large things as small, small things as nonexistent," he had also advised.

Yet my admiration for the Chinese system, which in so many ways had enlarged and helped to free me, was never absolute. I had learned, not from China as it actually was, but from what it had been in its great past; from simple souls, the children of its soil, eager in pleasure and enduring in sorrow—who today were only passive material in the hands of stronger and far less admirable characters. There was thus no call to continue back in the West to "Sinify" myself, to evade responsibility in the pretended interest of some spiritual custodianship, while actually fleeing from reality.

Nor had I ever felt tempted to jettison the values of earlier years, spent in contemplation of worlds other than Chinese, worlds to which I was now by destiny returned. I was of the West, of the one global civilization of our time. I had no thought to struggle against this, and silently took facts as I found them. Unlike those about me, however, I was aware that across the seas I had stumbled across a true discovery; and in happy years there I too had known bliss as from "Another Cave of Heaven."

First I had abounded; and then I had been abased, painfully. Now something further and curious was happening. Through reintegration the losses were turning into gains, turning from lacks to new possessions, new wealth henceforth never to be lost again. As this reclamation proceeded I found that I possessed one valuable technique. Since perseverance over the lean years, after China, had brought these results, willingness to continue patiently in this same course over a whole new front, comprising both worlds, was surely the only attitude to adopt. What was now retrieved, what was further salvaged, became grandly permanent, dependable as land rising out of the sea. One could walk about with a whole and saved body upon it, grateful for its blessings as a mariner after shipwreck.

I do not know that there is more to say beyond this: "More than this the Lord doth not require of thee." To be able to front the unknown problems of tomorrow with maturity is surely all that one can ask of life. The slow heave of the will in action is an act of labor from which no slightest dispensation is ever accorded; daily we must earn each day's existence. Yet properly seen—now as from two worlds away—the beautiful and the less fair, the fat and the lean, are not themselves ultimates. They become in the end only passing unevennesses in the road, which make the incidents of a long journey over hill and down dale. It is the journey that is important; and on the way to its unrevealed goal, ever shimmering somewhere in the mists ahead, one finally leaves all that one has passed lying somewhere behind on the road.